Mental Health in Intellectual Disabilities

A reader
Fourth edition

Geraldine Holt, Steve Hardy and

South London and Maudsley **NHS**
NHS Foundation Trust

*e*stia centre

Mental Health in Intellectual Disabilities:
A reader – Fourth edition

© Geraldine Holt, Steve Hardy and Nick Bouras

Published by:
Pavilion Publishing and Media Ltd
Rayford House
School Road
Hove
BN3 5HX
Tel: 01273 434943
Fax: 01273 227308
Email: info@pavpub.com

Published 2011, 2013

A catalogue record for this book is available from the British Library.

ISBN: 978-1-908066-22-0

Pavilion is the leading training and development provider and publisher in the health, social care and allied fields, providing a range of innovative training solutions underpinned by sound research and professional values. We aim to put our customers first, through excellent customer service and value.

Editors: Geraldine Holt, Steve Hardy and Nick Bouras
Editor: Catherine Ansell-Jones, Pavilion
Cover design: Tony Pitt, Pavilion
Page layout and typesetting: Katherine Jones, Pavilion
Printing: CMP Digital Print Solutions

Contents WITHDRAWN

Mental Health in Intellectual Disabilities: A reader (fourth edition) © Pavilion Publishing (Brighton) Ltd 2011

Introduction

Geraldine Holt, Steve Hardy and Nick Bouras

This reader, like its previous editions in 1995, 1997 and 2005, aims to provide up-to-date information on mental health problems in people with intellectual disabilities and associated issues.

Since the last edition there have been many changes in the field of mental health and services for people with intellectual disabilities. The Mental Capacity Act (2005) came into full operation in 2007 and it is vital that everyone who supports people with intellectual disabilities has an understanding of the act and how it affects everyday practice. The Mental Health Act (1983) was revised in 2007 and in 2008 the Deprivation of Liberty Safeguards were introduced, which all staff working in residential care should be aware of.

In the last six years a wealth of new policies has been introduced to the fields of intellectual disability and mental health. For example, the Care Programme Approach (CPA) is now part of everyday good practice when working with people with intellectual disabilities who have serious mental health problems. Since 2007 the Department of Health has been implementing the Improving Access to Psychological Therapies (IAPT) programme, which should be accessible to people with intellectual disabilities as well as the wider population. There has also been emerging research into the effectiveness of psychosocial interventions for people with intellectual disabilities.

With this in mind, this fourth edition of the reader has been completely revised. For example, chapters have been dedicated to the new legal frameworks in place. The Mental Capacity Act (2005) is covered, offering a practical approach to the assessment of capacity and the implications of the revised Mental Health Act. We have also included chapters on specific mental health problems, which offer greater insight into how to recognise such problems and how they are assessed and treated. Supporting people with personality disorders and those who misuse substances is an emerging issue for services, and chapter 4 addresses these complex issues. The mental health needs of specific groups, such as children, older people, and those with autism, are also addressed.

This edition of the reader also uses the term 'intellectual disability' instead of 'learning disability'. Although the term 'learning disability' is used in the UK, we have decided to use 'intellectual disability' as this is now the term accepted across the world and has a more international relevance.

All the contributors are from multidisciplinary backgrounds and include psychiatrists, psychologists, social workers, family therapists, nurses and trainers. They are all are experts in delivering mental health services to people with intellectual disabilities and have an interest in staff training.

The chapters in this reader provide background knowledge for facilitators using *Mental Health in Learning Disabilities: A training resource*. Nonetheless, participants from the training workshops, as well as professionals who would like a basic knowledge of mental health problems and people with intellectual disabilities, will find much to interest and inform them.

For the majority of the chapters we have interviewed a small group of people with intellectual disabilities and included their thoughts at the beginning of the chapter. We have called this section 'the expert opinion'.

Acknowledgements

We would like to thank Peter Cronin, Liam Peyton and Yolanda Zimock for their support and time. We would also like to thank all the contributors for their work on this reader.

About the editors

Geraldine Holt BSc (Hons), FRCPsych is honorary senior lecturer at the Health Service and Population Research Department, Institute of Psychiatry, King's College London. She is widely published on the mental health of people with learning disabilities and has served on a number of national and international bodies with this focus.

Steve Hardy RNLD, MSc is the education and training lead for the Behavioural and Developmental Psychiatry Clinical Academic Group of South London and Maudsley NHS Foundation Trust. He manages the education and training activities of the Estia Centre. He has worked in mental health services for people with learning disabilities for the past two decades and is widely published in this area.

Nick Bouras MD, PhD, FRCPsych is professor emeritus of psychiatry at the Institute of Psychiatry, King's College London and is currently the director of Maudsley International. He was a consultant psychiatrist at South London and Maudsley NHS Foundation Trust and was the director of the Estia Training and Research and Development Centre from 1982 to 2008. He has been a member of several national and international organisations, including chairman, World Psychiatric Association, Section of the Psychiatry of Mental Retardation, vice president of the European Association of Mental Health in Mental Retardation and vice president of the International Association for the Scientific Study of Intellectual Disability. His research is focused on health service related topics, including assessment and clinical effectiveness of specialist mental health services, evaluation of multi-professional training methods, social and biological determinants of behaviour in psychiatric patients. He has been an editor and member of the editorial board for several journals. He has been published extensively in community psychiatry and mental health aspects of people with intellectual disabilities.

Contributors

Alaa Al-Sheikh MBChB MRCPsych
Consultant psychiatrist in learning disabilities
Lewisham MH-LD
Behavioural and Developmental Psychiatry Clinical Academic Group
South London and Maudsley NHS Foundation Trust
York Clinic, Guy's Hospital, 47 Weston Street, London SE1 3RR

Alaa obtained her medical degree from Baghdad University, Iraq, in 1997. She came to UK in 1999 and started her training in psychiatry in 2001. She trained mostly in southeast London (South London and Maudsley NHS Foundation Trust) and completed her specialist psychiatry of learning disability training in early 2009. She started her consultant career in mental health and learning disability services (SLaM) in Croydon (2009) and then in Lewisham from 2010 to date. She has contributed to a range of publications and is committed to continuing her contribution to the exciting and evolving field of the psychiatry of learning disability.

Nadja Alim, DPsych, MSc, BSc (Hons)
Senior psychologist
South London and Maudsley NHS Foundation Trust, Behavioural and Developmental Psychiatry Clinical Academic Group,
Mental Health in Learning Disability Lewisham Psychology Team,
19–21 Brownhill Road, Catford, London SE6 2HG

Nadja is a senior psychologist in a community learning disabilities team and a visiting lecturer at King's College London and the University of Canterbury Christ Church. Nadja has worked in services for children with pervasive developmental disorders and adults with learning disabilities for the past eight years. She has a special interest in the field of autistic spectrum disorders and therapeutic interventions for people with learning disabilities. Nadja has researched and published on psychodynamic and cognitive behavioural interventions with people with learning disabilities and presented her work nationally and internationally.

Dr Saadia Arshad MBBS MRCPsych
Specialist registrar
Psychiatry of Learning Disability, South London and Maudsley NHS Foundation Trust

Saadia works for people with learning disabilities who have ongoing mental health needs. Her specialist interests include epilepsy and autism. She is currently pursuing a master degree in Epilepsy at Kings College, London. She has published articles in peer reviewed journals.

Jane Barnes

Social work team manager, lecturer, approved mental health professional and best interests assessor
Social Services Department, Lower Ground Floor
Maudsley Hospital, Denmark Hill, London SE5 8AZ

Jane has been a social worker for 30 years and has mainly specialised in mental health and learning disabilities. Between 1996 and 2008 she was senior practitioner at the Mental Impairment Evaluation and Treatment Service, a national specialist inpatient unit for adults with learning disability and complex mental health and behavioural problems run by the South London and Maudsley NHS Foundation Trust. Jane lectures on a number of AMHP courses and has presented at national conferences particularly in relation to the Mental Health Act, the Mental Capacity Act and the Deprivation of Liberty Safeguards. She was a Mental Health Act Commissioner between 2005 and 2008, covering forensic services including Broadmoor Hospital. She has contributed to a number of publications.

Sarah H Bernard MD, MB ChB, FRCPsych, DRCOG

Consultant psychiatrist, mental health of child and adolescent learning disability
The Michael Rutter Centre, The Maudsley Hospital, London SE5 8AZ

Sarah leads a tier 4 national and special service, which assesses and manages children and adolescents with learning disability and mental health or behavioural problems. Her particular areas of interest include high risk/offending behaviour, assessment of capacity and fitness to plead, rare chromosomal disorders, transition, behavioural problems associated with epilepsy. Sarah is actively involved with developing CAMHS for children/adolescents with learning disabilities. She is a member of the examinations sub-committee of the Royal College of Psychiatrists and has an interest in teaching and training.

Dr Simon Bonell

Locum consultant psychiatrist in learning disabilities
Croydon MHLD, Morland Lodge, 4 Morland Road, Croydon CR0 6NA

Simon completed his undergraduate medical studies at King's College London. He trained in psychiatry in east London and on the South London and Maudsley training schemes. He now works as a consultant psychiatrist for people with learning disabilities in Croydon, South London.

Eddie Chaplin

Research and strategy lead
Room E 1.23, Institute of Psychiatry, Box P023, De Crespigny Park, London SE5 8AF

Eddie is the research and strategy lead for the Behavioural and Developmental Psychiatry Clinical Academic Group. He has extensive clinical experience in national learning disability and neurodevelopmetal services and has helped to develop and teaches on a number of academic courses at the Institute of Psychiatry. Eddie is also involved in a variety of research projects involving people with learning disabilities, which include guided self-help, substance abuse and prison pathways.

Dr Karen Dodd

Associate director for specialist therapies (learning disabilities and older people's mental health services)
Surrey and Borders Partnership NHS Foundation Trust, Ramsay House, West Park, Horton Lane, Epsom, Surrey KT19 8PB

Karen is associate director of specialist therapies (learning disabilities) and a consultant clinical psychologist for Surrey and Borders Partnership NHS Foundation Trust. Karen has worked with people with learning disabilities for over 20 years. Her interest in working with people with learning disabilities and sexual and personal relationships has spanned her career, starting with work on sex education during the 1980s, developing and delivering staff training packages on sexuality, developing sexuality and adult protection policies and procedures. She also has a special interest in addressing health inequalities for people with learning disabilities and has developed new materials and published on issues of health, pain recognition and management, end of life issues and organ donation. She is also published in the field of Down's syndrome and dementia. Karen recently co-chaired the joint group between the British Psychological Society and Royal College of Psychiatrists Learning Disability Faculties to write national guidance on the Assessment, Diagnosis, Treatment and Support of People with Learning Disabilities and Dementia (BPS, 2009).

Dr Andrew Flynn

Consultant psychiatrist
Bexley Learning Disability Team, Oxleas NHS Foundation Trust, Stuart House, 45-47 Halfway Street, Sidcup, Kent DA15 8LH

Andrew has a long-standing interest in psychotherapeutic approaches to the management of complex emotional and mood disorders in adults with and without learning disabilities. He has particular interests in

Interpersonal Psychotherapy (IPT), which he teaches at the Anna Freud Centre in London, as well as Mentalization Based Psychotherapy for Borderline Personality Disorder.

Dr Karin Fuchs
Consultant clinical psychologist
Psychological Services in Learning Disabilities (Southwark), Mental Health Learning Disabilities, South London and Maudsley NHS Foundation Trust

Karin is a consultant clinical psychologist based in Southwark, in the mental health and learning disabilities service, South London and Maudsley NHS Foundation Trust. She has a postgraduate diploma in applied systemic theory from the Tavistock Centre. Her clinical work and interests focus on the application of family therapy and systemic staff consultation approaches within learning disability services; developing and providing services for people with challenging behaviour and supporting parents with learning disabilities.

Michael Hearn, PhD, DClinPsych
Clinical psychologist
Lewisham Learning Disability Partnership, 19-21 Brownhill Road, Catford, SE6 2HG

After his undergraduate degree, Michael undertook a PhD at the University of Birmingham researching observational assessment methods for behaviour described as challenging, in adults and children with learning disabilities. He then undertook clinical training at the Institute of Psychiatry, King's College London. Since qualifying in 2007, Michael has worked in community teams for adults with learning disabilities. He currently divides clinical work between talking therapies and behaviour support.

Dr Colin Hemmings
Mental Health of Learning Disabilites,
York Clinic, Guy's Hospital,47 Weston Street, London SE1 3RR

Colin is a consultant psychiatrist and the service line leader of the Mental Health of Learning Disabilities Service Line, South London and Maudsley NHS Foundation Trust. His academic interests include psychosis, mental health services and the relationship between mental illness and challenging behaviours in people with intellectual disabilities.

Dr Jayne Henry
Clinical psychologist

Jane works as a clinical psychologist with offenders with learning disabilities in both medium and low secure services at the Eric Shepherd Forensic Services, HPFT. She is involved in running and delivering the sex offender treatment programme and is involved in a range of individual and group treatment programmes with a particular interest in offenders with personality disorder. She also teaches at the Institute of Psychiatry and University of Hertfordshire on doctorate courses for clinical psychology.

Dr Muthukumar Kannabiran
Consultant psychiatrist
Mental Health in Learning Disability, Kent & Medway NHS Partnerhsip and Social Care Trust

Muthu is a consultant psychiatrist in mental health in learning disability, working with the Kent & Medway NHS and Social Care Partnership Trust. His research interests include mental health of people with learning disabilities and autism, and dementia in people with learning disability.

Lynette Kennedy
Clinical service lead
Estia Centre, 66 Snowsfields, London SE1 3SS

Lynette is the lead for the mental health learning disabilities service at the Estia Centre. She is responsible for the effective daily running of the service, including the operational management of team leaders and professional heads. Lynette studied at Stoke Mandeville Hospital in Buckinghamshire and became qualified as a registered nurse for people with learning disabilities in 1996. She worked for a year in a low secure mental health facility in Leeds, before starting work for the South London and Maudsley NHS Foundation Trust in 1997. Lynette first worked for the mental impairment evaluation and treatment service, before she moving to the mental health learning disabilities service. After five years, Lynette became the team manager, before being appointed her current position of clinical service lead.

Dr Bridget MacDonald

Consultant neurologist
Croydon University Hospital and Atkinson Morley's Neuroscience Centre, 530 London Road, Croydon CR7 7YE

Bridget is a general neurologist with an interest in epilepsy. She trained clinically at Guy's and King's College Hospitals and wrote her doctoral thesis on neuro-epidemiology while at the National Hospital for Neurology and Neurosurgery. She developed an interest in the care of individuals with learning disability in response to the needs of such patients who consulted primarily for epilepsy in general neurology outpatients and who seemed poorly understood. She runs a joint Epilepsy – Learning Disability – Psychiatry Clinic with Max Pickard and Heather Liddiard.

Jane McCarthy MB ChB, MD, MRCGP, FRCPsych

Consultant psychiatrist and clinical director
St Andrew's Nottinghamshire, Sherwood Oaks Business Park, Mansfield, Notts NG18 4GW

Jane is a specialist in the psychiatry of learning disability. She has actively contributed for over 15 years through research, teaching, and as a consultant psychiatrist towards service delivery and development. She has lectured extensively at both undergraduate and postgraduate degree level at University College London, University of Cambridge and St. George's, University of London. Her key research interests include the outcomes of psychiatric disorders in people with learning disabilities across the lifespan including those with autistic spectrum disorders. In the last five years Jane has significantly contributed to research in this area. She is the visiting senior lecturer at the Institute of Psychiatry, King's College London.

Dr Jean O'Hara

Consultant psychiatrist and clinical director
Behavioural and Developmental Psychiatry Clinical Academic Group, South London and the Maudsley NHS Foundation Trust, Estia Centre, Kings College London

Jean has been a consultant in the psychiatry of learning disabilities for 20 years and has extensive experience working with ethnic minority communities in inner city areas. In addition to her clinical and management roles, she has developed and published research and training materials on ethnicity and diversity. This work has been reflected in *Good Practice Guidance* (Royal College of Psychiatrists, 2011) and several books including *Textbook of Cultural Psychiatry* (2007) and *Clinical Topics in Cultural Psychiatry* (2010). She oversees the multidisciplinary and multiagency training programme at the Estia Centre, is an elected fellow of the Royal College of Psychiatrists, an elected member of Council at the Royal Society of Medicine and chairs the London-wide specialist training committee at the London Deanery School of Psychiatry. In 2010, she was appointed as one of the clinical directors in an academic health sciences centre – the only one in the UK to include a mental health NHS trust.

Carol Paton

Chief pharmacist
Oxleas NHS Foundation Trust, Pinewood House, Pinewood Place, Dartford, Kent DA5 7WG

Carol is chief pharmacist at Oxleas NHS Foundation Trust in southeast London, joint head of the Prescribing Observatory for Mental Health (POMH-UK) and an editor of both the Maudsley Prescribing Guidelines, and Psychiatric Intensive Care. She is a past member of the executive committee of the National Association of Psychiatric Intensive Care Units (NAPICU) and has contributed to the development of several NICE guidelines. Carol has a long-standing interest in the quality of medicines use in psychiatry.

Dr Max Pickard

Consultant psychiatrist
Mental health in learning disabilities, MHiLD Building, Morland Lodge
4 Morland Road, Croydon CR0 6NA

Max is a consultant psychiatrist in the mental health of learning disabilities at South London and Mausley NHS Foundation Trust, and member of the Estia Centre. He trained at the South London and Maudsley specialist rotation and has worked in community and inpatient psychiatric services for people with learning disabilities.

Dr Vishwa Radhakrishnan

MHLD department, 47 Weston street, London SE1 3RR

Vishwa is a year six specialty trainee in psychiatry of learning disability. His special interests are autism and ADHD.

Dr Laurence Taggart

Lecturer
Room G230, Institute of Nursing Research, School of Nursing, University of Ulster, Cromore Road, Coleraine, Northern Ireland BT52 1SA

Laurence works as a lecturer in the Institute of Nursing Research at the University of Ulster. He teaches on the BSc (Hons) nursing degree and is the option leader for the specialist practitioner course 'Working with people who challenge' (challenging behaviour or mental health option) for people with learning disabilities. He is dual-qualified, having both a learning disability nurse qualification and a degree in Applied Psychology. In 2003, he was awarded a PhD for research that examined service provision for adults with learning disabilities and psychiatric disorders in Northern Ireland. Laurence's research interests continue to investigate a broad range of topics on people with learning disabilities and psychiatric disorders. He is published in a range of international peer reviewed journals and presented at numerous regional, national and international conferences.

Dr Robert Winterhalder
Consultant psychiatrist
Bassetts Resource Centre, Acorn Way, Starts Hill Road, Farnborough BR6 7WF

Robert works in a community team for learning disabilities in southeast England and manages two specialist teams: a mental health in learning disability team and a learning disability epilepsy service. His main areas of clinical interest in the field of intellectual disability are epilepsy, psychotropic medication, and dementia. He is also interested in the development of specialist clinical teams in order to improve the quality of the service delivery and patient care. Clinical practice within these teams is underpinned by appropriate knowledge and experience in the field of neurodevelopmental medicine. He has an active interest in teaching and training, particularly health professionals at diploma and MSC level, in mental health in learning disabilities.

Peter Woodward RNLD, MSc, PGDipHE, DipA Psychol, DipN
Senior lecturer in learning disabilities
University of Greenwich, Avery Hill, Eltham, London, SE9

Peter has worked with people with learning disabilities since 1993. He qualified as a learning disability nurse working in challenging behaviour, mental health and forensic settings before entering education. He is senior lecturer in learning disabilities at the University of Greenwich and is currently conducting research into mental health in learning disabilities.

Chapter 1

An overview of mental health needs in people with intellectual disabilities

Alaa Al-Sheikh

Introduction

In the last two decades there has been significant interest and growth in the evidence base covering the mental health of people with intellectual disabilities. Mental health problems in adults with intellectual disabilities can be recognised through a psychiatric assessment of the individual and the identification of any vulnerability factors. The reported prevalence rate for mental health and behavioural problems can vary greatly in this population depending on the nature and size of the study. The risk factors that can predispose individuals with intellectual disabilities to mental health problems are numerous and can be biological or psychosocial in origin. This chapter will explore these factors and problems in detail. The chapter will highlight key epidemiological studies that have examined psychiatric disorders and explore specific risk factors in people with intellectual disabilities. The classification of psychiatric disorders in intellectual disabilities will also be discussed.

The expert opinion
'People with intellectual disabilities can have mental health problems like anyone else.'

Terminology

The terms 'mental health problem', 'illness' or 'psychiatric disorder' are used to refer to psychopathology that lasts for a certain period of time and is distressing to the individual.

Mental health problems in people with intellectual disabilities: A general overview

Children and adults with intellectual disabilities experience mental health problems just like the rest of the population, however, the prevention and early detection of such disorders is often delayed for a variety of reasons.

There has been an increase in our understanding of the nature and causes of mental illness in individuals with intellectual disabilities over the last two decades (Bouras & Holt, 2007). The *Valuing People* white paper (DH, 2001) and its progress report *Valuing People Now* (DH, 2009) outlined a new three-year strategy for people with intellectual disabilities. Its principles were: rights, independence, personalisation and inclusion. These principles focused on better personalised services with the health of people with intellectual disabilities as a priority; this included the mental health needs of this population.

The detection of psychiatric disorders in people with intellectual disabilities is difficult and diagnoses are often missed (Bouras & Holt, 2004). As language and communication difficulties are common in people with intellectual disabilities, it is essential that clinicians are flexible and modify their traditional approaches to assessment in order to achieve an accurate assessment of mental health (Al-Sheikh & O'Hara, 2009).

Classification of psychiatric disorder

It is generally accepted that the two main psychiatric classifications – the *International Statistical Classification of Diseases and Related Health Problems* (10th revision) (ICD-10) (WHO, 1992) and *Diagnostic and Statistical Manual of Mental Disorders* (4th edition) (DSM-IV) (APA,

1994) – are limited in the diagnosis of psychiatric problems in people with intellectual disabilities (Al-Sheikh & O'Hara, 2009). In 1996 the World Health Organization (WHO) devised a guide to complement the ICD-10 diagnosis in this population (WHO, 1996) – the *ICD-10 Guide for Mental Retardation*. This modification in the classification system is very useful in clinical practice.

It includes five axes:
Axis I: Severity of retardation and problem behaviours
Axis II: Associated medical conditions
Axis III: Associated psychiatric disorders
Axis IV: Global assessment of psychosocial disability
Axis V: Associated abnormal psychosocial situations

In 2001 the Royal College of Psychiatrists developed *Diagnostic Criteria for Psychiatric Disorders for Use with Adults with Learning Disabilities/ Mental Retardation* (DC-LD) (Royal College of Psychiatrists, 2001) to complement the ICD-10. This is especially helpful for clinicians dealing with individuals with moderate to severe intellectual disabilities.

Epidemiology

It has been established that psychiatric disorders, including behavioural disorders, are more prevalent in adults with intellectual disabilities than in the general population (Deb *et al*, 2001a). However, when behavioural and personality disorders, autism spectrum conditions and attention deficit hyperactivity disorder are excluded, the overall rate is not significantly different from that of the general population (Deb *et al*, 2001b).

The reported prevalence of psychiatric disorders in people with intellectual disabilities varies widely. Some research states that the rate is approximately 10–39% (Deb *et al*, 2001b), whereas a wider range of prevalence from 7–97% was reported in studies carried out in the 1980s and 1990s.

There are few large scale population-based studies examining the cause and triggers of mental health problems in this population. Cooper *et al* (2007a) studied a cohort of 1,023 participants and found the point prevalence of mental ill-health was 40.9% (when they applied clinical diagnostic criteria). This important study identified the factors that are independently associated with mental ill-health, as follows:

► having profound and severe intellectual disabilities

► a higher number of life events or consultations with general practitioners in the preceding 12-month period

► being a smoker or living with a paid carer

► being female.

Epidemiology of specific psychiatric disorders in people with intellectual disabilities

There are two measures of disorder frequency: prevalence and incidence. The prevalence rate of a disorder is the number of individuals with that disorder in a population at a certain point in time or over a period of time; whereas the incidence is the number of new cases of a disorder over a period of time. The prevalence and incidence of specific mental illnesses in people with intellectual disabilities differ from that of the general population. This section looks at certain common mental health problems and psychiatric diagnoses, examining their prevalence by focusing on a recent study by Cooper *et al* (2007a) and a review article by Smiley (2005).

► **Schizophrenia and psychotic disorders**: Few studies have examined psychosis in people with moderate, severe or profound intellectual disabilities, in contrast to the wealth of research in the mild intellectual disabilities population. The generally accepted prevalence of schizophrenia in intellectual disabilities is 3% compared with 1% for the general population.

► **Mood disorders (depression and mania):** The point prevalence of mood disorder was found to be 6.6% (depressive episode 4.1% and bipolar disorder 2.5%), which is higher than that of the general population. Some of the risk factors are shared with the general population, such as low socio-economic status and lack of social support, however, people with intellectual disabilities are further disadvantaged by their limited coping skills and their experiences of discrimination, rejection, stigma and abuse. Other biological risk factors are highlighted in Table 1.1 (on p18), such as thyroid disorder, which is more prevalent in people with Down's syndrome. Therefore, they are more susceptible to low mood compared to the rest of the intellectual disabilities population.

▶ **Anxiety disorder and obsessive compulsive disorder (OCD):** The prevalence rates for generalised anxiety disorder and specific phobias were both estimated at 6%, while OCD and agoraphobia were reported to be 2.5% and 1.5% respectively. Anxiety disorders in people with intellectual disabilities can be associated with certain behavioural phenotypes, such as social anxiety and fragile X syndrome, and generalised anxiety disorder in Williams syndrome. Moreover, OCD symptoms are associated with pervasive developmental disorders and autism.

▶ **Challenging behaviour:** Some clinicians and researchers believe that most challenging behaviour is associated with mental health problems. It is generally accepted that the prevalence rate for challenging behaviour is approximately 10–15% in people with intellectual disabilities. It is more common in males than females and in younger people than the older population with intellectual disabilities. Challenging behaviour is more common in those with more severe intellectual disabilities.

▶ **Dementia:** There has been increasing evidence that people with intellectual disabilities have a higher risk of developing dementia compared to the general population; this is specifically true for people with Down's syndrome who may develop dementia at a much earlier age than is generally seen in the rest of the population (British Psychological Society & Royal College of Psychiatrists, 2009).

▶ **Drug and alcohol misuse:** Substance misuse is generally rare in adults with intellectual disabilities compared to the general population, with a reported rate of approximately 1%. However, clinicians in the field of intellectual disabilities are seeing more people suffering from this problem, especially young adults. In a study by Taggart *et al* (2006) it was found that most people with alcohol problems are within the range of mild intellectual disabilities and those who are living independently.

Risk factors

The risk factors for psychiatric illness in people with intellectual disabilities can fit into the bio-psycho-social model. Identifying these risk factors is generally considered to be an important part of the psychiatric formulation for such complex cases. The individuals with intellectual disabilities and their carers have an important role to play in helping clinicians to identify some of these factors in each case.

Table 1.1: Risk factors for mental health problems in people with intellectual disabilities	
Biological	▶ Genetic conditions (autism, behavioural phenotypes, etc.) ▶ Brain injury ▶ Epilepsy ▶ Sensory impairments (vision/hearing) ▶ Physical illnesses/disabilities ▶ Abnormal thyroid function ▶ Medication/physical treatments
Psychological	▶ Abuse and deprivation ▶ Life events/separations/losses ▶ Poor problem solving/coping strategies ▶ Social/emotional/sexual vulnerabilities ▶ Low self-esteem
Social	▶ Negative attitudes/expectations ▶ Stigma and social exclusion ▶ Poor support/networks ▶ Inappropriate environments/services ▶ Financial/legal disadvantages ▶ Rejection ▶ Lack of job opportunities ▶ Difficulties in making relationships

Biological factors

The biological risk factors include genetics, chromosomal abnormalities, epilepsy, physical disorders and medication.

Psychological factors

People with intellectual disabilities are more prone to psychological stress than the general population, and thus they are vulnerable to mental health problems.

There are numerous psychological risk factors in this population; they are mainly due to impaired intelligence and problem-solving skills, and numerous life events such as bereavement and loss.

▶ **Life events and bereavement:** Mental health problems can follow major life events, such as bereavement. There is good evidence that people with intellectual disabilities are more vulnerable and have increased experience of adverse life events (Hollins, 2002). Hastings *et al* (2004) examined the rate of life events for a large sample of people with intellectual disabilities; the result suggested that life events are associated with affective and neurotic symptoms in this population.

▶ **Abuse:** All forms of abuse, such as physical, sexual, emotional and neglect, are prevalent among people with intellectual disabilities. This can trigger the onset of mental health problems such as depression or post-traumatic stress disorder.

Social and environmental factors

The social restrictions experienced by people with intellectual disabilities may trigger emotional distress and mental illness; these restrictions may include rejection, lack of job opportunities, boredom, and difficulties in making relationships with people other than their families or carers (see Table 1.1).

Specific considerations

Profound intellectual disabilities epidemiology: In Cooper *et al* (2007b) the point prevalence of mental ill-health in this group was estimated at around 52.2% by clinical assessment. The highest two-year incidence rates in mental illness for this population were for mood disorders (6.1%) and the same rate was reported for challenging behaviours. The predictive factors for psychiatric illness were the type of support and the number of life events in the preceding 12-month period.

Gender specific epidemiology in intellectual disabilities: The gender issue has been largely ignored in research of the prevalence of mental health problems in men and women with intellectual disabilities (McCarthy, 2010). According to Cooper *et al* (2007a), women were more likely to show mental ill-health than men in a population study of individuals with intellectual disabilities, however, the overall gender pattern of mental ill-health was not different to that of the general population.

Behavioural phenotype is the repertoire of maladaptive and adaptive behaviours associated with specific genetic conditions that cause intellectual disabilities. Examples include Down's syndrome, fragile X syndrome and Prader Willi syndrome.

Conclusion

Mental health problems in people with intellectual disabilities may have a more complex presentation and management than in the wider population. Studies examining the predictive and risk factors for mental ill-health should be utilised to influence the development of interventions and health and social care policy, to increase sensitivity to the needs of this population (Cooper *et al*, 2007a).

People with intellectual disabilities will benefit from the awareness of paid and unpaid carers of the impact of various risk factors and life events on the potential onset of mental health problems; this in turn can help clinicians in recognising problems earlier. It is essential for services to offer multidisciplinary interventions and provide the holistic support to improve health outcomes for this population.

Summary

- ▶ People with intellectual disabilities have a high prevalence of various mental health problems.

- ▶ The prevalence and incidence of specific mental illnesses in people with intellectual disabilities differ from that of the general population.

- ▶ The risk factors of psychiatric illness in people with intellectual disabilities can be biological, psychological and social.

- ▶ Some of the risk factors are shared with the general population; others are different and specific to the intellectual disabilities population.

References

Al-Sheikh A & O'Hara J (2009) Psychiatric and mental state assessment in learning disabilities. *Advances in Mental Health and Learning Disabilities* **2** (4) 21–28.

American Psychiatric Association (1994) *DSM-IV-TR: Diagnostic and Statistical Manual of Mental Disorders*. Arlington, VA: American Psychiatric Association.

Bouras N & Holt G (2004) Mental health services for adults with learning disabilities. *British Journal of Psychiatry* **18** (4) 291–292.

Bouras N & Holt G (2007) *Psychiatric and Behavioural Disorders in Intellectual and Developmental Disabilities* (2nd edition). Cambridge: Cambridge University Press.

British Psychological Society & Royal College of Psychiatrists (2009) *Dementia and People with Learning Disabilities*. Leicester: British Psychological Society.

Cooper S-A, Smiley E, Morrison J, Williamson A & Allan L (2007a) Mental ill-health in adults with intellectual disabilities: prevalence and associated factors. *British Journal of Psychiatry* **19** (0) 27–35.

Cooper S-A, Smiley E, Finlayson J, Jackson A, Allan L, Williamson A, Mantry D & Morrison J (2007b) The prevalence, incidence, and factors predictive of mental ill-health in adults with profound intellectual disabilities. *Journal of Applied Research in Intellectual Disabilities* **20** 493–501.

Deb S, Thomas M & Bright C (2001a) Mental disorder in adults who have intellectual disability.1: prevalence of functional psychiatric illness among a 16–64 years old community-based population. *Journal of Intellectual Disability Research* **45** 495–505.

Deb S, Thomas M & Bright C (2001b) Mental disorder in adults who have intellectual disability. 2: the rate of behaviour disorders among a 16–64 years old community-based population. *Journal of Intellectual Disability Research* **45** 506–514.

Department of Health (2001) *Valuing People: A new strategy for learning disability for the 21st century*. London: TSO.

Department of Health (2009) *Valuing People Now*. London: TSO.

Hastings RP, Hatton C, Taylor JL & Maddison C (2004) Life events and psychiatric symptoms in adults with intellectual disabilities. *Journal of Intellectual Disability Research* **48** 42–46.

Hollins S (2002) *Depression in People with Intellectual Disabilities* [online]. Available at: http://www.intellectualdisability.info/mental-health/depression-in-people-with-intellectual-disabilities (accessed 24 May 2011).

McCarthy J (2010) Women with intellectual disability and mental health problems: the invisible victims. In: D Kohen (Ed) *Oxford textbook of Women and Mental Health*. Oxford: Oxford University Press.

Royal College of Psychiatrists (2001) *Diagnostic Criteria for Psychiatric Disorders for Use with Adults with Learning Disabilities/Mental Retardation (DC-LD)*. London: Gaskell.

Smiley E (2005) Epidemiology of mental health problems in adults with learning disability: an update. *Advances in Psychiatric Treatment* **11** 214–222.

Taggart L, Mclaughlin D, Quinn B & Milligan V (2006) An exploration of substance misuse in people with intellectual disabilities. *Journal of Intellectual Disability Research* **50** 588–597.

World Health Organization (1992) *The ICD-10 Classification of Mental and Behavioural Disorders: Clinical descriptions and diagnostic guidelines*. Geneva: World Health Organization.

World Health Organization (1996) *ICD-10 Guide for Mental Retardation*. Geneva: World Health Organization.

Chapter 2

Psychosis spectrum disorders

Colin Hemmings

Introduction

This chapter will look at the symptoms, prevalence, presentation, assessment and treatment of psychotic illnesses in people with intellectual disabilities. Two case studies provide examples of psychotic illnesses in people with intellectual disabilities.

What is psychosis?

Psychotic illnesses are among the most severe of mental illnesses. In psychosis a person has lost touch with reality or lost insight. Psychosis can also be described as the experience of various symptoms, such as showing disorganised or bizarre speech and behaviours. The best known and most described psychotic symptoms are delusions and hallucinations. Delusions are false beliefs that are firmly held despite obvious proof or evidence to the contrary. The beliefs are not those ordinarily accepted by other members of the person's culture or subculture. Hallucinations occur when people see, hear, feel, taste or smell things which are not present in reality, yet the person has a compelling sense that these experiences are happening.

People with intellectual disabilities are also thought to be more susceptible to developing short-lived episodes of psychosis, which can be brought on by stressful life events because they often have more limited coping abilities. They also have higher rates of sensory problems such as hearing and visual impairments. Sensory impairments may make people more susceptible to misinterpreting things they see and hear. Psychotic symptoms can occur in a wide range of mental and physical disorders and people with intellectual disabilities can experience all of these. Box 2.1 shows some conditions in which psychotic symptoms can occur.

> ### Box 2.1: Conditions with psychotic symptoms
>
> Dementia
> Delirium eg. due to an infection or alcohol withdrawal
> Drug and alcohol misuse
> Epilepsy
> General medical conditions eg. thyroid hormone excess
> Schizophrenia, schizoaffective and persistent delusional disorders
> Mania
> Severe depression
> Stress

The best known and most studied psychotic disorders in people with intellectual disabilities, as well as in the wider population, are the schizophrenias and associated disorders. The chapter will focus on these.

How common is psychosis in people with intellectual disabilities?

People with intellectual disabilities have higher rates of mental illness compared to the general population and about 3% of people with intellectual disabilities will have schizophrenia-type psychotic symptoms at any one time (Deb *et al*, 2001). This is around three times higher than in the general population. However, this may be an underestimate because psychosis, and schizophrenia in particular, are generally more difficult to detect and diagnose in people with intellectual disabilities.

How does psychosis affect a person with intellectual disabilities?

Psychotic illnesses may be short-lived or longstanding and symptoms may fluctuate even without treatment. The onset of a psychotic episode may be less noticeable in people with intellectual disabilities because they are less likely to have very obvious or clear-cut symptoms. The symptoms of schizophrenia in people with intellectual disabilities can be: a decline in functioning and a deterioration of skills or social withdrawal, rather than obvious hallucinations and delusions (James & Mukhergee, 1996). The reduction in functioning may be temporary but a longstanding psychosis may lead to a prolonged or even permanent reduction in a person's functioning. Due to their reduced opportunity to take part in normal life experiences, the delusions of people with intellectual disabilities, when they occur, may not be complicated. Complex hallucinations, such as hearing voices that give a running commentary of a person's actions, are also less commonly reported.

The *Diagnostic Criteria for Psychiatric Disorders for Use with Adults with Learning Disabilities/Mental Retardation* (DC-LD) (Royal College of Psychiatrists, 2001) noted that early signs of a psychotic illness could be new behaviours (especially those that are odd, bizarre or uncharacteristic), or an increase in frequency or severity of pre-existing challenging behaviours. Certainly, some challenging behaviours can sometimes be improved with antipsychotic medication so it is possible that in a minority of cases mental health problems like psychosis might be driving the behaviour. It has also long been recognised that catatonia is more common in schizophrenia when a person has intellectual disabilities. Catatonia can include disturbances of movement, for example, a person may adopt a motionless posture for long periods. Alternatively, in a catatonic state the person may become constantly overactive and be in a state of continual excitement.

Difficulties in assessment

There are many possible problems in the assessment and diagnosis of schizophrenia and its associated psychoses in people with intellectual disabilities. Psychosis can be missed but also it can be wrongly diagnosed. First, the symptoms of schizophrenia depend on the person being able to articulate their experience, thoughts and beliefs. It is impossible to diagnose schizophrenia with any certainty in people with limited verbal communication. In practice, this means people with intellectual disabilities with an IQ level of about 45. Second, the difficulty of differentiating psychotic symptoms and features related to a person's intellectual disabilities may lead to the problem of psychosis being under-diagnosed. Sometimes it may be suggested that the person's intellectual disability accounts for their odd or unusual behaviours, rather than considering whether or not they may in fact be psychotic symptoms. This error has been termed 'diagnostic overshadowing' (Reiss *et al*, 1982). See the case study for an example of diagnostic overshadowing.

Case study: Diagnostic overshadowing

John is a young man in his 30s who lives with his parents. The family had to move to a very remote house because neighbours had complained about John's loud night-time screaming. John did not talk much, did very few spontaneous activities and showed a general lack of interest. He even needed to be prompted to dress himself and to walk with his parents. John appeared to have severe intellectual disabilities. However, evidence from when he was a teenager suggested that in the past he could do more for himself and had shown much more interest in activities and talking up until his late teenage years.

When being assessed, John seemed to be distracted by possible noises or visions as he turned around and mumbled occasionally. It seemed as if he might have developed a psychotic illness and needed to go to hospital to start treatment. However, the social worker who was asked to see him to support an admission under the Mental Health Act had no experience of working with people with intellectual disabilities. She argued that his problems were due to his intellectual disabilities and would not agree to the admission. Some months later John was seen by a different social worker who had experience in intellectual disabilities and he was admitted to hospital and given antipsychotic medication. John's interest in his environment increased and he stopped screaming at night. His overall functioning improved so that he appeared now to have mild intellectual disabilities.

A tentative diagnosis of schizophrenia in intellectual disabilities may be made on the basis of observations rather than a person's account. For example, behaviour that suggests auditory hallucinations could be a person with intellectual disabilities shouting at people who are not present when this has not been their previous behaviour. Similarly, suspiciousness and social withdrawal that were not previously part of the person's personality and behaviour could also suggest schizophrenia. Non-verbal evidence for possible psychosis is of greater importance in the assessment of people with intellectual disabilities who have limited verbal abilities.

It can also be the case that behaviours that may be appropriate for someone with intellectual disabilities at a certain developmental stage may be wrongly thought of as psychotic behaviours. It can also be difficult to separate hallucinations from self-talk or conversations with imaginary friends. These can all be appropriate for a person's developmental stage if they have intellectual disabilities (Hurley, 1996). People with intellectual disabilities may often recall previous conversations and rehearse them or think out loud. They often do not recognise that this is considered socially odd. Incoherent speech may also be hard to judge in people with intellectual disabilities as it can be difficult to follow the thread of their conversation. It is often difficult to determine whether a person with intellectual disabilities has true delusional beliefs. For example, they may have fantasies that they are famous, such as being a great singer. They then may be wrongly thought to have grandiose delusions. In schizophrenia people often have delusions that they are being controlled (delusions of passivity). However, people with intellectual disabilities may have a real lack of autonomy, or at least a perceived lack of control over their lives and may complain, and this can sometimes be misunderstood as a delusion. People with intellectual disabilities are also often sensitive to how they are perceived by others. This can often be based on real life experiences of being mocked and rejected (Hurley, 1996). They may then be mistakenly thought to show persecutory delusions.

Some symptoms of longstanding schizophrenia have been described as 'negative' symptoms and include social withdrawal, reduced speech, and reduced motivation. These apparent 'negative' symptoms can also be misattributed to a psychotic disorder when they may be due to other factors, such as institutionalisation, over-sedation, lack of environmental stimulation, and severe problems with processing information (James & Mukhergee, 1996).

A guide to whether an odd or unusual belief may be delusional is whether the experiences or beliefs are distressing. A person does not generally tend to fantasise or imagine hearing or seeing things which are frightening or upsetting, or believe things that cause them distress. However, this can only be a rough guide as sometimes genuine psychotic symptoms are not necessarily always upsetting for the person. It has also been suggested that people with intellectual disabilities are more likely to be able to be temporarily persuaded that delusional beliefs are false because of their increased suggestibility. It may be more important to observe them for their readiness to return to these beliefs when not being persuaded against them (Hurley, 1996). Box 2.2 shows some questions to think about during assessment.

Box 2.2: Questions to consider during assessment

▶ Is this experience or behaviour new or very different for the person?

▶ Is this experience or behaviour odd or unusual for the person?

▶ Does this experience or behaviour seem to trouble the person?

▶ What is the usual mood or temperament of the person with intellectual disabilities?

▶ Have there been any other changes in their usual routines?

▶ Is this person in good physical health?

▶ Have they been checked recently by a doctor?

▶ Are there any dangers in these experiences or behaviours, for themselves or for others?

When trying to assess whether a person is psychotic there are some guiding principles to consider. Psychotic symptoms tend to come in clusters, and therefore, one odd or unusual experience on its own may be of less significance for a diagnosis of psychosis than if the person has multiple symptoms. People with intellectual disabilities who have a family history of psychosis are also more likely to develop psychosis than those with no family history. Finally, the basis of health care is accurate diagnosis followed by appropriate treatment. There are circumstances when even though the diagnosis of psychosis is not clear-cut it may still be ethical and in the best interests of the person to have a trial of an antipsychotic medication. The response, or lack of response, to the medication can then be used to help determine (but not prove) whether the tentative diagnosis of psychosis was correct. Quite often clinicians are using information from various sources to try and build up an overall guide to the diagnosis and it may be impossible to give an absolutely conclusive opinion either way.

Autism and psychosis

It can be difficult to differentiate schizophrenia from autism in people with intellectual disabilities. Psychotic episodes can occur in autism but it is not yet clear whether the risk of developing schizophrenia in people with autism is any more frequent than that of developing schizophrenia in the general population. Social withdrawal and lack of empathy can often occur in schizophrenia as well as autism. Unusual preoccupations held rigidly by people with autism may be particularly difficult to differentiate from delusions. Flattened and odd moods, poor non-verbal communication and low amounts of speech are commonly seen in autism as well as schizophrenia. People with autism can be concrete and often preoccupied with their special interests and their view of themselves, and this world can appear so odd to others as to appear delusional. A very detailed history about someone's early life and development is necessary to help establish the right diagnosis.

Epilepsy and psychosis

Epilepsy can also lead to problems with diagnosis, for example differentiating temporal lobe epilepsy from schizophrenia, as psychotic. symptoms such as hallucinations can occur in some types of epileptic seizures. Epilepsy can also cause difficulties in treatment, as antipsychotic medications can make seizures more likely. The phenomenon of 'forced normalisation' in epilepsy can occur whereby a reduction in seizures following the introduction of antiepileptic medication can be associated with an exacerbation of psychosis.

Treatment

The principles of treatment of psychotic disorders in people with intellectual disabilities are essentially similar to those in the general population. Treatment with antipsychotic medications in intellectual disabilities appears broadly similar in efficacy, with no significant increase in side effects. Many doctors have reported that the most effective dosage levels of antipsychotic medications often appear to be lower in people with intellectual disabilities (see Case study: Inzamam). Some antipsychotic medications can make thinking, memory and word finding more difficult, and also make someone more at risk of having an epileptic seizure. There is a consensus that antipsychotic medication prescribing often needs to be instigated and increased more cautiously than in people without intellectual disabilities. People with intellectual disabilities are more likely to have general physical health problems and they tend to be more sensitive to medication. Distinguishing between movement disorders and medication side-effects is more difficult in people with intellectual disabilities as movement disorders are more common, even without antipsychotic medication.

> ## Case study: Inzamam
>
> Inzamam is a young man in his 20s who lives in his own flat near to his mother and younger siblings. His father had left, which had been very traumatic for the whole family. Inzamam is suspicious of others and almost mute. He is withdrawn and unkempt. He lives in squalor with takeaway leftovers all over his flat and flies swarming around. Neighbours often complain about the flies and the smell. Inzamam refuses to see his mother but she leaves food for him on his doorstep. Some people believe Inzamam is withdrawn as he has been so hurt by his life experiences. While this seemed true, from reports of his earlier years Inzamam seems to have undergone a massive change in his demeanour.
>
> Inzamam is admitted into a specialist unit for people with intellectual disabilities and mental health problems. He is given a test (very low) dose of an antipsychotic medication injection and within days there is a dramatic improvement as he starts to speak more, become less suspicious and much more cheerful. Inzamam has a psychotic illness which has gone undiagnosed and untreated for many years.

Although psychosocial strategies may be used in practice for psychosis in people with intellectual disabilities, there is as yet very little published evidence regarding the use of psychosocial (including family) interventions for people with intellectual disabilities. A case series of cognitive behaviour therapy for five patients with psychosis and mild intellectual disabilities has been reported (Haddock *et al*, 2004). Hopefully the use of specific psychosocial interventions for psychosis in intellectual disabilities will become more established.

The course of schizophrenia

Schizophrenia can occur at any age but it is most likely to begin in early adulthood. When it begins in childhood or adolescence it may itself be a cause of intellectual disabilities by severely disrupting learning and normal development. Most clinicians believe that the course of schizophrenia in people with intellectual disabilities will tend to be more severe than in the general population. Doody *et al* (1998) found that people with intellectual disabilities and additional schizophrenia had fewer admissions to psychiatric hospitals than people with schizophrenia alone. However, when they were admitted they needed to be in hospital for longer periods of time, and when discharged they needed more support in the community than people with schizophrenia alone.

Summary

▶ Schizophrenia and associated psychoses are more common in people with intellectual disabilities than in the general population.

▶ They are more difficult to detect and often the symptoms are more subtle or less typical than those in the general population.

▶ Due to the difficulty of assessment, psychosis can either be more easily missed or wrongly diagnosed in people with intellectual disabilities.

▶ Schizophrenia in people with intellectual disabilities may cause more severe problems for the person and be harder to treat than when it occurs in the general population.

▶ The treatment of schizophrenia and associated disorders in people with intellectual disabilities broadly follows that in people who do not have intellectual disabilities.

References

Deb S, Thomas M & Bright C (2001) Mental disorder in adults with intellectual disability: prevalence of functional psychiatric illness among a community-based population aged between 16 and 64 years. *Journal of Intellectual Disability Research* **45** 495–505.

Doody GA, Johnstone EC, Sanderson TL, Cunningham Owens DG & Muir WJ (1998) 'Pfropfschizophrenie' revisited. Schizophrenia in people with mild learning disability. *British Journal of Psychiatry* **173** 145–153.

Haddock G, Lobban F, Hatton C & Carson R (2004) Cognitive behaviour therapy for people with psychosis and mild learning disability: a case series. *Clinical Psychology and Psychotherapy* **11** 282–298.

Hurley AD (1996) The misdiagnosis of hallucinations and delusions in persons with mental retardation: a neurodevelopmental perspective. *Clinical Neuropsychiatry* **1** 122–133.

James DH & Mukhergee T (1996) Schizophrenia and learning disability. *British Journal of Learning Disabilities* **24** 90–94.

Reiss S, Levitan GW & Zyszko J (1982) Emotional disturbance and mental retardation: diagnostic overshadowing. *American Journal of Mental Deficiency* **86** 567–574.

Royal College of Psychiatrists (2001) *Diagnostic Criteria for Psychiatric Disorders for Use with Learning Disabilities/Mental Retardation)*. London: Gaskell Press.

Chapter 3

Mood, anxiety and eating disorders

Vishwa Radhakrishnan and Steve Hardy

Introduction

People with intellectual disabilities are more prone to developing a
mental health problem than people in the general population. They might
have problems with communication, which make it difficult for them to
express themselves, and this could lead to undiagnosed mental health
problems. This can be prevented by timely identification of these disorders
by professionals and carers who are in regular contact with them. This
chapter looks at some of the common symptoms of mood, anxiety and eating
disorders, and information about seeking professional help.

Depression

The symptoms of depression are common. In a national UK study, 2.6% of
the general population were reported to have a diagnosis of depression (ie. a
point prevalence) (ONS, 2000). We all have days when we feel low and less
interested in activities, but when this feeling persists and interferes with
daily activities, depression should be suspected. Stressful life events, such
as the loss of a loved one, chronic physical illness, isolation, being a victim
of abuse and change in accommodation can cause depression in people with
intellectual disabilities. Individuals can experience depression lasting for
several months to several years.

Symptoms of depression include:

▶ feeling sad or irritable

▶ feeling hopeless, helpless or worthless

▶ feelings of guilt

▶ being tearful

▶ loss of appetite

▶ weight loss

▶ feeling tired and low in energy

▶ lacking concentration

▶ low self-esteem

▶ losing interest and not enjoying favourite activities

▶ avoiding interaction with others

▶ expressing thoughts of suicide or self-harm

▶ low sexual desire

▶ disturbed sleep

▶ not attending day centres or other social activities

▶ poor performance at work.

If a person has a combination of the above symptoms it can indicate to carers that they might have depression. Some people with intellectual disabilities might already be functioning at a low level and a worsening in their usual level of engagement in activities might indicate an underlying problem.

If depression is suspected, professional help should be sought from the person's GP. As there are several medical conditions that cause depression-like symptoms (eg. low thyroid hormones in the blood), the GP will initially rule these out through physical examination and blood tests. If no such conditions are identified, they might decide to refer the person to a counsellor or a psychologist (NICE, 2009). If the symptoms are severe or psychotherapy alone is not effective, they might also consider prescribing an antidepressant. If the GP believes that the person would benefit from specialist assessment and monitoring, they will refer them to psychiatrists who are specialists in diagnosing and treating mental health conditions in people with intellectual disabilities. If interventions in the community are not effective, a brief admission to a psychiatric hospital might be considered.

Case study: Joshua

Joshua is a 24-year-old man with moderate intellectual disabilities and Down's syndrome. He lives with his mother and enjoys attending the local day centre. Over the last six months he has become irritable and aggressive towards the staff and other people at the day centre. He avoids others and does not participate in group activities. He was seen by his GP who ruled out physical health problems and later referred him for specialist psychiatric assessment.

During the assessment, it became evident that one of his friends who used to attend the day centre died suddenly in an accident a year ago. Joshua was shocked by this event but has never discussed it with anyone. The key worker who accompanied him to the assessment noticed that he had gradually lost interest in activities after his friend's death. He was referred for psychotherapy focusing on bereavement issues. After a few treatment sessions he started to improve. He did not require an antidepressant medication and was considerably better after five months.

Bipolar affective disorder

Bipolar disorder is when an individual experiences episodes of both depression and mania. The symptoms of depression have already been described.

Some common symptoms of mania include:

▶ elated, euphoric mood

▶ sudden change in mood, becoming irritable or quarrelsome

▶ increased energy, being overactive or restless

▶ disinhibited behaviour

▶ impulsive behaviour

▶ difficulty concentrating

▶ unrealistic ideas about themself

▶ talking rapidly

▶ delusions and hallucinations

▶ reduced need for sleep.

Symptoms of mania are relatively easy to recognise as the person's behaviour becomes overt and more noticeable. Delusions tend be grandiose; in the wider population an example could be of someone believing they have the power to solve world poverty. In people with intellectual disabilities they tend to be relative to the person's ability and experience, an example might be an individual believing they are a support worker.

Case study: Izzy

Izzy is a 33-year-old man with severe intellectual disabilities. He lives in a supported house with 24-hour staff support. Izzy attends classes at his local college and accesses several groups at his local leisure centre. He is described as a quiet person who enjoys the company of people he knows well. He has experienced two episodes of depression in the last few years, which were successfully treated.

Over the last few weeks his behaviour has been notably different. About three weeks ago he was often found laughing, sometimes uncontrollably. He had difficulty in getting to sleep and appeared to have endless energy. He was no longer his usual reserved self at the leisure centre. He had been going up to strangers, grabbing their arms, and laughing. Over the last week his behaviour has become more irritable. He has been running in and out of his housemates' bedrooms, screaming for no apparent reason, and is not sleeping at all.

An appointment was made for Izzy to see his psychiatrist. After an assessment and the staff recording behaviour, sleep, activity etc. he was diagnosed with bipolar disorder. He was prescribed a mood stabilising medication and the behaviour support team helped the support staff develop strategies to help calm Izzy when he became agitated.

Anxiety disorders

Anxiety is experienced by most of us when we face a stressful situation but it can become a problem if it affects the person's life. People with intellectual disabilities might experience higher rates of certain anxiety conditions, such as phobias (Deb *et al*, 2001). There are different types of anxiety disorders, which include generalised anxiety, phobias, obsessive-compulsive disorder and panic disorder. The presentation of these conditions can vary depending on the person and their circumstances.

Some common symptoms of anxiety include:

▶ being inappropriately fearful

▶ a dry mouth

▶ feeling sick

▶ sweating

▶ trembling

▶ shortness of breath

▶ feeling faint

▶ an increased heart rate.

Generalised anxiety

This is where an individual experiences lots of the common symptoms of anxiety frequently. The anxiety may be about common everyday situations or there may be no identifiable cause. Sometimes it is referred to as 'free floating anxiety'.

Phobias

Phobias are when an individual focuses their anxiety on a very specific trigger, which causes extreme fear. The fear is out of proportion with the objective risk of the situation and is generally regarded as irrational. Common phobias include heights, insects, animals and situations where escaping might be difficult, such as a crowded area.

Obsessive-compulsive disorder (OCD)

OCD is when a person experiences repeated unwanted intrusive thoughts (ie. obsession), which cause intense feelings of anxiety. An example might be a person continually thinking that their hands are dirty. The anxiety is relieved by the person engaging in repetitive behaviours, such as hand washing. The obsession and resulting behaviours are likely to have a significant negative impact on the person's life.

Panic disorder

Panic disorders are when a person experiences episodes of intense anxiety and believe that something bad is going to happen. The feelings can be so severe that the individual believes they are about to die. The person may then get into a cycle of having intense anxiety about the thought of having another panic attack.

Although reassurance can be helpful, many people suffering from anxiety may need professional help to deal with the problem. The treatment begins with a physical health check by a GP who will rule out certain medical conditions that can be similar to anxiety (eg. high thyroid hormone in the blood), which may be followed by a referral to psychologists. They might also prescribe antidepressants or sedatives and refer for specialist input if indicated. Psychological treatments usually involve one-to-one sessions with a therapist who will explore ways of combating anxiety through techniques such as relaxation and breathing exercises. Having supportive carers and/or relatives will enable the person to make a quick recovery.

Case study: Sarah

Sarah is a 45-year-old female with mild intellectual disabilities. She loves cooking and enjoys making cakes for her fellow residents at the care home. She recently became more withdrawn and complained of a rapid heartbeat, feeling faint and restlessness. Her carer was concerned about these symptoms and took her to the GP. Following investigations to make sure she did not have a physical health issue, the GP referred her for psychotherapy. During the therapy sessions, she revealed her anxiety about attending a catering course, which was due to start in two months. Arrangements were made for her to informally visit the college and meet the staff on a few occasions before starting the course. She used the breathing exercises learnt during psychotherapy and sometimes used a mild sedative prescribed by her GP when she became very anxious. She was eventually able to complete the college course and secure a job at a local restaurant.

Eating disorders

Eating is a significant part of everyone's life. It is not only vital for survival, but helps us to define our identities through our likes and dislikes. It is influenced by our culture, plays a large role in socialising and affects the way we see our body. Problems with eating are influenced by a wide range of factors including stress, loneliness, low self-esteem, abuse and mood disorders. People may use their control of food and eating to cope with these factors.

When thinking about problems with eating it is important to have a clear idea of what is considered to be a healthy weight. The most common method to assess an individual's weight is a scale called the body mass index (BMI).

A BMI score is calculated using a formula which involves the person's height and weight. Box 3.1 shows the BMI scale.

Box 3.1: BMI scale

BMI below	18.5 = underweight
BMI between	18.5–24.9 = normal weight
BMI between	25–29.9 = overweight
BMI over	30 = obesity

Despite increasing focus on the nutrition of adults with intellectual disabilities there has been less interest in diagnosable eating disorders (Royal College of Psychiatrists, 2001). The main types of eating disorders are classified in the *Diagnostic Criteria for Psychiatric Disorders for Use with Adults with Learning Disabilities* (DC-LD) (Royal College of Psychiatrists, 2001). Gravestock (2000) reviewed the literature and found prevalence rates of eating disorders in those with intellectual disabilities to be 3–42% in adults living in institutions and 1–19% in the community. The most commonly known eating disorders follow.

Anorexia nervosa

This is where an individual deliberately restricts the amount of food and drink they consume, and may exercise excessively to significantly lose weight or maintain a low weight. Individuals may self-induce vomiting or use laxatives to quickly remove food from the body before calories can be absorbed. Commonly, the person will have a distorted image of their body. There are many physical effects of anorexia nervosa, including; feeling dizzy, loss of sexual interest, constipation, stomach pains, and poor circulation. There are also psychological effects including denying that the problem exists, mood swings and relationship difficulties.

Bulimia nervosa

This involves repeated episodes of binge eating, which are typically followed by behaviour to remove the food from the body (ie. vomiting, using laxatives) or behaviour to counterbalance the calorie intake (ie. excessive exercise). Bulimia may not be as noticeable as anorexia as weight loss can be slow and often fluctuates. Bulimia can affect an individual physically; this includes tiredness, poor skin condition, frequent changes in weight and symptoms associated with frequent vomiting. Psychological and behavioural changes include disappearing after meals (ie. to vomit, use laxatives), reduced socialising, excessive amounts of food in the person's residence, or hidden food.

Binge eating disorder

This is where the individual repeatedly consumes large amounts of food (binge) but unlike bulimia they do not purge (ie. vomit or take laxatives). This is likely to result in obesity and the health risks associated with it.

Pica

Pica is the eating of substances or objects that have no nutritional value and would generally be considered inedible eg. dirt, clothing, tissues. In reviewing the literature, Gravestock (2000) found that pica in people with intellectual disabilities was associated with having severe to profound intellectual disabilities, autism, being male, self-injurious behaviour and difficulty socialising. Pica is often considered as a 'challenging behaviour' and assessment/interventions tend to be based on positive behaviour support (see Chapter 13).

Other eating disorders include regurgitation; bringing swallowed food back into the mouth and food rumination. Food faddiness is where an individual continually fails to eat a balanced diet, which may be due to refusal of food and/or extreme fussiness.

Case study: Jackie

Jackie is a 22-year-old woman with mild intellectual disabilities living in a supported house. For several years she has been eating sporadically and her weight has fluctuated. She has a volatile relationship with her family and has recently stopped attending college. She was recently supported to see her GP as the staff team noted her weight was lower than normal. The GP recorded Jackie's BMI at 17 and for her height and weight the GP considered this to be low and referred her to the specialist mental health team.

During the assessment it was found that Jackie has a distorted image of her body, seeing herself as fat, and has been exercising excessively over recent months. She also reported experiencing low mood. She agreed to enter into individual therapy with a psychologist and work with a dietician and her support staff on a diet plan. The psychiatrist prescribed antidepressants to lift her mood. It was agreed that if Jackie's BMI went below 15 she would be encouraged to go into hospital for a period of assessment and treatment.

Conclusion

Mood, anxiety and eating disorders affect people with intellectual disabilities, but can sometimes be difficult to identify. It is essential that those who support people with intellectual disabilities recognise the signs and changes associated with these mental health problems so that individuals can access the appropriate assessment and range of treatments.

Summary

▶ People with intellectual disabilities are at an increased risk of developing mood and anxiety disorders.

▶ The literature relating to eating disorders in people with intellectual disabilities is limited and requires additional research to develop an evidence base for good practice.

▶ Those who support people with intellectual disabilities play a significant role in the recognition, assessment and treatment of mood, anxiety and eating disorders.

References

Deb S, Thomas M & Bright C (2001) Mental disorder in adults with intellectual disability. 1: prevalence of functional psychiatric illness among 16–64 years old community based population. *Journal of Intellectual Disability Research* **45** 495–505.

Gravestock S (2000) Eating disorders in adults with intellectual disability. *Journal of Intellectual Disability Research* **44** (6) 625–637.

NICE (2009) *Treating Depression in Adults*. London: NICE.

Office for National Statistics (2000) *Psychiatric Morbidity Among Adults Living in Private Households*. London: ONS.

Royal College of Psychiatrists (2001) *Diagnostic Criteria for Psychiatric Disorders for Use with Adults with Learning Disabilities*. London: Gaskell.

Chapter 4

Personality disorders and substance misuse

Andrew Flynn and Laurence Taggart

Introduction

Mainstream mental health services have developed expertise in supporting people with personality disorders and/or substance misuse difficulties over many years. These are relatively new concepts in services for people with intellectual disabilities and this is reflected in the lack of research and practice guidance. However, this chapter attempts to draw on the available evidence and offer some insight into these complex and challenging areas.

Personality disorders

Case study: Claire

Claire is a 22-year-old woman with mild intellectual disabilities. She has been referred to the local intellectual disabilities team by her GP who has only known her for a short time but already has a number of concerns. Claire recently moved into a residential project for women with vulnerability and emotional issues from a residential home out of the area. Her previous placement lasted six months following her discharge from a mental health unit. At the placement Claire had become very attached to a male member of staff. Over time she developed jealous rages when the staff member paid attention to other residents and when he moved on to work at another residential home, she self-harmed. Although this was Claire's first admission to a mental health unit, she has regularly attended A&E departments over the years. Sometimes she has been admitted for physical complaints, but other

(continued)

> ## Case study: Claire (continued)
>
> admissions have followed minor overdoses or were due to superficial injuries to her wrists, which were self-inflicted with razor blades or broken glass.
>
> Claire was taken into foster care when she was eight. Her mother had intellectual disabilities and her father had problems with alcohol. Throughout her childhood and adolescence Claire suffered with emotional difficulties and challenging behaviours. This meant that sustained placements with various foster families were hard to achieve. Intense, and ultimately destructive, attachments to both male and female carers and support staff occurred periodically and would necessitate Claire moving on, usually in the aftermath of an emotional crisis.
>
> Initially surly and uncommunicative in the clinic, Claire eventually admitted problems with 'mood swings'. The social worker who came to clinic with her described Claire as a very 'up and down' character, who could go through periods of deep despondency and energetic enthusiasm. When Claire loses her temper with people she often goes 'overboard' to make up afterwards. She falls out with people easily and has had a hard time keeping (but not apparently making) friends. Disagreements tend to happen because Claire misinterprets what people say and can take things very personally and be very literal.

The concept of personality disorder

Claire represents an important group of individuals who are said to suffer with personality disorder. Although a number of different personality disorders are currently recognised (see Table 4.1), what binds them together is their appearance early in life and their persistence into adulthood, well beyond the period where they might otherwise be attributed to issues of simple emotional maturation or 'adolescent turmoil'. The features of personality disorder persist not only over time but across situations, affecting many different aspects of life from home to leisure to work. Personality disorders are usually thought of in terms of underlying 'traits' – the relatively stable psychological building blocks of personality (themselves reflecting subtle neurological structures) that interact with environment to govern our emotions and behaviours. Personality disorder as distinct from 'normal personality' is the maladaptive dominance of these internal factors so that they seem to work against rather than with external circumstances, including, of course, the personalities of others. For this reason they are often talked about as disorders of relationships.

In contrast to the general population there is comparatively little research on personality disorder in people in intellectual disabilities and less still on its treatment and long-term outcome. However, a number of studies (eg. Flynn *et al*, 2002) confirm that personality disorders are a common issue for intellectual disability services.

Table 4.1: The principal categories of personality disorder with their basic descriptors (APA, 1994)

Schizoid	solitary
Paranoid	suspicious
Borderline	erratic, moody, impulsive
Antisocial	aggressive, irresponsible
Histrionic	shallow, capricious, melodramatic
Narcissistic	egocentric, arrogant
Anxious	shy, timid
Obsessive-compulsive	rigid, moralistic
Dependent	self-sacrificing

Personality disorder and mental illness

Personality disorders are usually thought of as being distinct from traditional mental illnesses, although the boundaries between them are often hard to define. However, it can be helpful to think of their connections in the following ways.

1. Having a personality disorder may make someone **vulnerable** to mental illness. For example, by alienating the person from sources of social support at times of stress or because the person may expose themselves to potentially traumatic events.

2. A personality disorder may make a mental illness **harder to recognise**. The problem of diagnostic overshadowing can apply here. It is easy to miss (or dismiss) a depressive episode in the context of a lifelong tendency to emotional instability or chaotic relationships.

3. A personality disorder may make a mental illness **harder to treat**. This could be because of special aspects of their underlying 'neurobiology' as

well as the problems helping such individuals access and make effective use of medical and psychological therapies.

4. Some personality disorders may be **attenuated** or **modified** forms of mental illness. Some studies indicate that many patients with borderline personality disorder (see below) may have features of bipolar disorder or post-traumatic stress disorder and the personality disorder is in fact an 'atypical' presentation of those illnesses and not just a vulnerability factor. This is a controversial area but emphasises how essential (not to mention challenging) accurate diagnostic assessment can be.

Borderline personality disorder

Claire closely fits the pattern of behavioural features that constitute borderline personality disorder (see Box 4.2), which is probably the most important of the various types of personality disorder presenting to community mental health services. People with borderline personality disorder are especially vulnerable to a wide range of emotional disturbances and risky behaviours, ranging from self-harm to substance misuse to sexual vulnerability. Treating the disorder is also difficult due to the individual's problems with forming relationships, which extends from caregivers to health professionals, and the resistant nature of the disorder, which does not respond to the usual range of interventions on offer in intellectual disabilities (and mainstream) services.

Also, of particular interest are the reactions of others (including professionals) to the challenges of people with the disorder, reactions that range from negativity and rejection to unhelpful over-involvement, which may inflame some aspects the disorder. The chapter will later explore how these reactions can be recognised and consider the key role they play in care and treatment.

What causes borderline personality disorder?

Borderline personality disorder in the general population has a strong relationship with abuse and neglect in early life – a finding that has found some support in research with people with intellectual disabilities (Flynn *et al,* 2002). Childhood abuse has a wide variety of mental health outcomes, both in early life and into adulthood, ranging from general difficulties with relationships to clinical depression, substance misuse and borderline personality disorder. Despite this, there are people using services where no such catastrophic failures in early upbringing are found. Here it is presumed that other factors (for example, genetic) confer vulnerability to the effects of minor or even minimal disruptions in early care-giving relationships. Modern conceptions of borderline personality disorder (eg. Linehan, 1993) are therefore increasingly bio-social in outlook, acknowledging an interaction between biological vulnerability and family environment to produce the disorder.

Box 4.1: The principal features of borderline personality disorder

Affective instability: Rapid and intense mood changes, sometimes for little or no obvious reason, frequently involving anger (which may be severe), irritability, depression and anxiety.

Impulsivity: Acting to satisfy some immediate emotional or physical need without planning or considering the negative consequences.

Interpersonal sensitivity: A low threshold for thinking that others might be rejecting or abandoning. This can cause very high levels of anxiety and disturbed behaviour as a result.

Intense emotional attachments: Becoming rapidly and intensely involved with others, often insisting on exclusivity. Such relationships are typically unstable and potentially destructive.

Black-and-white thinking: Things may seem all good or all bad with little sense of a middle ground. Often applies to views of other people and may sometimes dramatically switch between the two.

Changeable views and preferences: Ranging from finding it hard to stick to planned courses of action, to experiments with aspects of personal appearance. Often interpreted as an expression of an unstable sense of self.

Self-harm and threats of suicide: With complex, and frequently mixed, motivations, this often occurs in the context of an interpersonal crisis and may be seen as 'manipulative'. Cutting behaviour is sometimes a coping strategy to relieve unpleasant mood states.

Recent research suggests that underlying borderline personality disorder arises because of a wider failure to understand the actions and emotions of people (including oneself) in terms of underlying beliefs, desires, wishes and expectations, an ability known as 'mentalisation' (Bateman & Fonagy, 2006), which is a psychological capacity that incorporates empathy. Developing throughout childhood, mentalisation is crucial to successful relationships and the self-regulation of emotion. Mentalisation now forms the theoretical basis for a novel form of psychotherapy – mentalisation-based therapy.

Supporting people with borderline personality disorder

Although he did not specify their diagnosis, the most famous account of the experience of working with people with borderline personality disorder was written almost 60 years ago by psychiatrist and psychoanalyst Tom Main in *The Ailment* (Main, 1989). Main wrote about the staff support group on a psychiatric ward that he had established to investigate the patterns of interactions among staff, and between staff and the challenging people under their care. He described a demanding and conflict-ridden environment as the ward team grappled with challenging behaviour, demands for medication, and the competing demands of the various doctors who admitted to the ward. Although this was an inpatient setting, it contained lessons that apply to other care environments.

In particular, Main described 'splitting' – a complex process in which a person's inner emotional disturbance influences those around them, playing itself out not only through their own behaviour but through that of others. An 'intra-psychic' disturbance becomes an interpersonal one and under certain conditions – such as on an inpatient unit or in a residential service – it becomes a group disturbance. He noted, too, that the splits among the staff did not happen in flawless rock but along subtle fault lines that pre-dated the individual's arrival, almost as though a wedge was being pushed into cracks that already existed. But his point ran deeper: the forces driving the process were opaque – we might say 'unconscious' – to both the person and the care team. It may well be that a psychic crowbar was being inserted, though neither side, at the time, realised how or why it was happening, or knew what to do about it. Main was clear, though, that the dynamics the group uncovered contributed to the disturbance of the individuals and that the group, by providing a way to manage these conflicts, could minimise their impact.

While staff groups like Main's are not always practical, it is still possible to derive some principles for general good practice from them. Box 4.2 outlines some of these.

Box 4.2: Good working practices for supporting people with borderline personality disorder

▶ Understanding the complex nature of the condition

▶ Committing to working **as a team** and in **collaboration with the person**

▶ Pragmatic approach and taking the 'long view' about progress and recovery

▶ Positive professional relationships

▶ Adopting internal **team supervision** and **reflective practice**

▶ **Acceptance of risk** so that it is neither neglected nor over-responded to

▶ Balancing **limit-setting** with **flexibility**

There are also more specific psychological treatments in development for borderline personality disorder with a growing interest in their modification for people with intellectual disabilities (eg. Baillie *et al*, 2010), though there are issues over how widely available these will eventually become. Medication has an important, though limited, role in some individuals but is best reserved for the treatment of co-occurring mental illness when this can be identified. The interested reader can refer to the NICE guideline for borderline personality disorder (NICE, 2009), which outlines the current status of these treatments as well as gaps in the evidence. Significantly, however, the guideline places its emphasis on the principles of good practice that have already been considered.

In the absence of anything aside from 'good practice', what are Claire's prospects for recovery? The encouraging news is that borderline personality disorder may have a better prognosis than was at one time presumed, at least in the general adult population. Another recent study suggests that up to two-thirds of those with borderline personality disorder no longer meet diagnostic criteria after six years of follow-up (Zanarini *et al*, 2003). A strategy of 'not making things worse' while awaiting a natural recovery has something to be said for it.

Conclusion on personality disorders and intellectual disability

It is useful to conclude on this chapter by reflecting on how much of this is really new. Staff in intellectual disability services are used to being pragmatic and working with people whose behaviour has been challenging individuals over long periods of time and can readily understand the emotional pressures. In fact, some may even recognise aspects of mentalisation in the functional analysis of challenging behaviour where behaviours (often emotionally upsetting to witness) become reframed as failed attempts at communication; as expressions of frustration, boredom, overstimulation or pain. People with borderline personality disorder, even those without intellectual disabilities, struggle to communicate too. Though for them what is missing lies with the complex language of the emotions. It may well be that experienced staff in intellectual disability services instinctively know more than they might think about borderline personality disorder.

Substance misuse

There has been growing interest in alcohol and illicit drug misuse in people with intellectual disabilities, with a number of recent studies offering insight into the needs of this population. This information has helped to develop more focused interventions.

Prevalence and risk factors

Prevalence rates of alcohol misuse and illicit drug use in people with intellectual disabilities is lower compared to their non-disabled peers. However, these figures may be an underestimate as many people with intellectual disabilities who are at risk of abusing such substances do not use intellectual disability services. McGillicuddy (2006) argues that the potential for people with intellectual disabilities to misuse both alcohol and illicit drugs is greater than for their non-disabled peers. Taggart *et al* (2008) identified a range of risk factors that illustrate that people with intellectual disabilities may be more likely to abuse such substances.

Identified risk factors for substance misuse

▶ Having borderline to mild intellectual disabilities

▶ Being young and male

▶ Having a specific genetic condition

▶ Adolescents with conduct disorders, attention deficit hyperactivity disorders and antisocial personality disorders

▶ Coming from an ethnic minority group

▶ Co-existence of a mental health problem

▶ Low self-esteem

▶ Disempowerment

▶ Inadequate self-control/regulatory behaviour

▶ Impulsivity

▶ Cognitive limitations (illiteracy, short attention span, memory deficits, poor problem-solving skills, tendencies to distort abstract cognitive concepts, over-compliant dispositions)

▶ Frustration

▶ Living in the community with low levels of supervision

▶ Poverty

▶ Parental alcohol-related neuropsychiatric disorders

▶ Presence of negative role models with punitive child management practices

▶ Family dysfunction

▶ Negative life events (eg. neglect, abuse, bereavement)

▶ Unemployment

▶ Limited educational and recreational opportunities

▶ Excessive amounts of free time

▶ Deviant peer group pressure

▶ Limited relationships/friends

▶ Lack of meaning in life

▶ Lack of routine

▶ Loneliness

▶ Desire for social acceptance/method for 'fitting in'

Taggart *et al* (2007) conducted one-to-one interviews with 10 people with intellectual disabilities who abused alcohol and/or used illicit drugs, and also over-used prescribed medications. The reason voiced by these individuals as to why they used such substances was to get away from 'psychological trauma' that they had experienced (ie. bereavements, physical, psychological and sexual abuse, and deterioration of their mental health). Another core reason cited by these individuals was to avoid the unemployment, loneliness, lack of companionship/relationships, and the isolation as they lived in their community. Many individuals spoke about using such substances as a way of 'fitting in' to their local communities.

Assessment and treatment

Assessment and treatment of people with intellectual disabilities who abuse alcohol and illicit drugs can be complex as some can be 'unwilling' about engaging fully in a range of assessments and interventions. Huxley and Copello (2007) highlighted that this 'unco-operativeness' should not be interpreted as poor motivation, but partly due to a lack of understanding, communication difficulties, illiteracy, short attention span, memory deficits, low self-esteem, and inadequate self-control/regulatory behaviour. These individuals have also been found to have poorer understanding regarding alcohol units and the impact of such substances. Any successful treatment package therefore must be adapted to reflect the learning style of the individual.

Degenhardt (2000) has indicated that 'abstinence' might be a more appropriate treatment goal than 'controlled drinking'. Controlled drinking involves understanding the norms about units of alcohol, when and where to drink, and what not to drink, and gives the individual responsibility for managing their own consumption, whereas abstinence requires the individual to abstain totally from alcohol. Nevertheless, other interventions have been developed and adapted for this population. Taggart *et al* (2008) provide a summary of these interventions.

Interventions for people with intellectual disabilities who misuse alcohol and illicit drugs

Interventions include:

▶ detoxification, ensuring the person's safety

▶ individual education (ie. anger management, relaxation training, challenging negative statements)

▶ modifications of Alcoholics Anonymous (AA) and the 12-Step Programme

▶ use of group therapy (ie. art, music and drama therapy) to promote feelings of acceptance, belonging and peer support

▶ use of social skills training (ie. develop coping and refusal skills, self-monitoring skills, promote interpersonal communication, facilitate expression of emotions, respond appropriately to criticism, engage in realistic role plays)

▶ behavioural and cognitive approaches (ie. assertiveness skills, distinguishing between positive and negative role models in substance abuse situations)

▶ motivational interviewing – a counselling approach which uses a question and answer method of interviewing, which aims to increase the person's motivation to change their substance misuse behaviour

▶ relapse prevention programmes focusing on self-regulation of thinking and feeling, accepting past relapses, identifying the causes of relapse and learning to prevent and interrupt relapses

▶ mainstream addiction and intellectual disability staff education on preventative programmes, identification of risk factors, promoting early recognition/screening and prompt referral

▶ promotion of social support including family, friends, neighbours, social support groups, education, recreational opportunities and employment.

Conclusion on substance misuse in intellectual disability

This section has offered a brief review on the issues concerning people with intellectual disabilities who misuse alcohol and/or illicit drugs. Prevalence rates and risk factors have been explored and suggestions have been given regarding how to understand why a person with intellectual disabilities may abuse such substances and also the range of interventions available.

Summary

▶ Personality disorders can affect an individual over a long period of time and affect many areas of their life, such as work, home and relationships.

▶ There is little research on personality disorders in people with intellectual disabilities.

▶ People with personality disorders often present services with complex and challenging situations.

▶ The reported prevalence of substance misuse in people with intellectual disabilities is lower than the general population and tends to affect those with milder intellectual disabilities. It is likely that alcohol and substance misuse occurs in a number of people with intellectual disabilities unknown to services.

▶ It is likely that treatment programmes for substance misuse will need to be adapted for people with intellectual disabilities, reflecting the needs of the person, specifically their comprehension and communication.

References

American Psychiatric Association (1994) *Diagnostic and Statistical Manual of Mental Disorders (DSM-IV)* (4th edition). Arlington, VA: APA.

Baillie A, Slater S, Millington R, Webb H, Keating G, Akroyd S, Ford C, Brady C, Swash J & Twist E (2010) What it takes to set up a DBT service for adults with a learning disability: The lessons so far. *Clinical Psychology and People with Learning Disabilities* **8** 12–20.

Bateman A & Fonagy P (2006) *Mentalization-Based Treatment for Borderline Personality Disorder: A practical guide*. Oxford: OUP.

Degenhardt L (2000) Interventions for people with alcohol use disorders and a intellectual disability: a review of the literature. *Journal of Intellectual and Developmental Disability* **25** (2) 135–46.

Flynn A, Matthews H & Hollins S (2002) Validity of the diagnosis of personality disorder in adults with learning disability and severe behavioural problems: preliminary study. *British Journal of Psychiatry* **180** 543–546.

Huxley A & Copello A (2007) An overview of psychological interventions for addictive behaviours. In: E Day (Ed) *Clinical Topics in Addiction*. London: Gaskell.

Linehan MM (1993) *Cognitive Behavioral Treatment of Borderline Personality Disorder*. New York: The Guilford Press.

McGillicuddy NB (2006) A review of substance use research among those with mental retardation. *Mental Retardation and Developmental Disabilities Research Review* **12** 41–7.

Main T (1989) The ailment. In: *The Ailment and Other Psychoanalytic Essays*. London: Free Association Books.

National Institute for Health and Clinical Excellence (2009) *Borderline Personality Disorder: Treatment and management. Clinical Guideline 78*. London: NICE.

Taggart L, Huxley A & Baker G (2008) Alcohol and illicit drug misuse in people with learning disabilities: Implications for research and service development. *Advances in Mental Health and Learning Disabilities* **2** (1) 11–21.

Taggart L, McLaughlin D, Quinn B & McFarlane C (2007) Listening to people with intellectual disabilities who abuse substances. *Journal of Health and Social Health Care* **15** (4) 360–368.

Zanarini MC, Frankenburg FRR, Hennen J & Silk KR (2003) The longitudinal course of borderline psychopathology: six-year prospective follow-up of the phenomenology of borderline personality disorder. *American Journal of Psychiatry* **160** 274–283.

Chapter 5

Assessment of mental health problems

Simon Bonell

Introduction

The recognition and assessment of mental health problems in people with intellectual disabilities can be challenging and complex. Carers and support staff play an important role in the assessment process. These roles include the recognition of possible mental health problems, the provision of support in seeking help, supporting the service user through the assessment process, and sharing information to support a full assessment. This chapter introduces the reader to some of the issues and challenges that may be faced.

The expert opinion

'Professionals need to respect you when you go to see them. They should ask the person with intellectual disabilities how they feel and not the staff.'

Recognising mental health problems

People with intellectual disabilities are at particular risk of developing mental health problems. Recent research suggests that mental health problems and challenging behaviour occur in 40% of people with intellectual disabilities (Cooper *et al*, 2007). (See Chapter 1 for a discussion on the reasons for this increased vulnerability.)

Mental health problems present with changes in feelings, thoughts and behaviours (see vignette 1). These changes can be grouped into internal experiences that are described by the person (symptoms) and external changes that can be seen by others (signs).

> ### Vignette 1
>
> For the last few weeks Jackie has been feeling sad and has not been interested in her usual activities (feelings). She says that she believes she is worthless and would be better off dead (thoughts). She has not been eating much and has been spending most of her time in bed (behaviours).

People with reasonable verbal abilities are likely to be able to self-report symptoms. People with mild intellectual disabilities tend to describe similar symptoms to the general population (Marston *et al*, 1997). However, even those with mild intellectual disabilities might find it difficult to describe internal experiences if they have a mental illness.

People with more severe intellectual disabilities and lower verbal abilities may have difficulty in recognising symptoms of mental illness and communicating them to others. People with autism also have particular difficulties in recognising and describing their mood and internal experiences. This may lead to delays in accessing appropriate help and is challenging for professionals who are completing a full assessment.

Given these difficulties, it is important that carers are aware of and alert to possible signs of mental illness. These are described in chapters 2, 3 and 4 (see Box 5.1 for examples).

> ### Box 5.1: Signs that carers should be aware of that may suggest a person has a mental illness
>
> ▶ Deterioration in self-care
> ▶ Withdrawal from social contact and activities
> ▶ Loss of interest in usual activities
> ▶ Changed sleep and appetite
> ▶ Restlessness
> ▶ Over/under-activity
> ▶ Confusion
> ▶ Inappropriate laughter
> ▶ Screaming
> ▶ Reduced communication
> ▶ Aggression
> ▶ Self-injurious behaviour

People with intellectual disabilities may have longstanding behavioural difficulties. These are often related to communication difficulties and associated frustrations. Challenging behaviour can often be disregarded as an aspect of the person's normal disposition and can lead to 'diagnostic overshadowing'. This phrase is used when emotional problems or disturbed behaviour are incorrectly seen to be due to the person's intellectual disabilities rather than a physical or mental illness (see vignette 2). This can lead to individuals being denied the treatment and help that they need. An assessment for possible underlying biological, psychological or social factors may identify ways in which the person's quality of life can be significantly improved.

Vignette 2

Jimmy is a 19-year-old man who lives with his parents. He has recently started at a new college and is studying numeracy and computing. His parents started noticing changes in his behaviour six months ago. He stopped looking after himself as well as he had done in the past, spent more time alone in his room and became less talkative. They felt that this behaviour was related to his level of intellectual disability and because he had started at a new college. For the last four weeks he has been refusing to go to college and rarely talks to his parents. He seems irritable and has complained about people talking outside his window. His parents are very concerned and take him to see his GP. A mental health assessment is then organised as the GP suspects that he has a psychotic illness.

A worsening in longstanding behaviour difficulties can signify a new physical or mental health problem. Certain behaviours, such as aggression or self-injury, are more likely to lead to a mental health assessment than less dramatic behaviours. Withdrawal from social contact or becoming less talkative might not be seen as significant. Carers need to be alert to these changes in behaviour.

Seeking help

Support staff and carers have a valuable role in recognising possible features of mental illness and supporting the person to seek help. In the UK this is through a GP in the first instance. The GP will be able to assess the person for any possible physical illness that may account for the changes in their behaviour or mental state. Physical illnesses occur more frequently in people with intellectual disabilities and are often not recognised or treated. This is because they are less likely to seek help and may have difficulties in describing their symptoms. Physical health problems can present in ways that mimic mental health problems. Special care is needed in ruling out sensory impairments that might also be having an impact on the person.

If the GP suspects that a mental illness is present they will refer the person, when appropriate, to a specialist intellectual disability team for a full mental health assessment. This will usually be carried out by a psychiatrist, a psychologist or a nurse.

Structured assessment tools have been developed to help in the recognition of mental health problems in people with intellectual disabilities. One of the most widely used screening tools is the *Psychiatric Assessment Schedule for Adults with Developmental Disabilities* (PAS-ADD) *Checklist* (Moss *et al*, 1998). This is a 25-item checklist that can be completed by carers and support staff to help them decide if further assessment is required. It should be noted that it is not a diagnostic tool.

Aims of the mental health assessment

A mental health assessment has three main aims: to obtain a holistic understanding of the person's difficulties; to group clusters of symptoms and signs together to reach a diagnosis; and to initiate a treatment plan. In order to obtain a holistic understanding of the individual, information will be required from the individual and those who know and support them. The information required is summarised in Table 5.2.

Diagnostic labels are based on recognised classificatory systems, which include the World Health Organization's *International Classification of Diseases* (ICD-10) (WHO, 1992), and the American Psychiatric Association's *Diagnostic and Statistical Manual* (DSM-IV) (APA, 1994). A diagnosis describes a group of signs and symptoms that are recognised to occur together. They give professionals a shorthand way of communicating a person's needs, help to guide treatment and give some information regarding prognosis. They also enable services to be planned and aid research (Cooper *et al*, 2003). A shortcoming of standard classification systems is that they rely heavily on experiences described by the individual and this can lead to difficulties for people whose communication is limited. Specialist classificatory systems have been developed for people with intellectual disabilities that recognise these difficulties (Royal College of Psychiatrists, 2001).

The use of diagnostic labels in psychiatry has been an important area of discussion for many years. There are positive and negative aspects to receiving a diagnosis of a mental health problem (see Table 5.1). A diagnosis is only useful if it leads to positive changes in the person's life through treatment or changes in the provision of care. Unfortunately, while society continues to have negative perceptions of mental illnesses, stigma and prejudice will continue to be attached to diagnostic labels.

Table 5.1: Positive and negative views of psychiatric diagnosis

Positives	Negatives
Help to highlight the needs of the person	Can lead to stigmatisation and prejudice
Guide appropriate treatment	People do not see past the diagnostic label
Can help give the person meaning and understanding of their experiences	Some people may treat the person differently
May help the person meet people with similar problems	People are given labels needlessly
Allows a shorthand method to communicate the person's needs	Labels tend to stick
Enables effective research	May limit the person's opportunities
Enables organisations to plan services	

The ultimate goal of the assessment is to understand the person's current difficulties and find ways of addressing them. Mental health problems are often thought about as having three factors: a physical or biological component, a psychological component, and a social or environmental component. Treatment and care plans are developed to intervene in all three areas, taking into account the person's developmental, cultural and spiritual background.

The assessment will also identify factors that make the person vulnerable to developing a mental illness, factors that might have triggered the development of the mental illness and those that might contribute to prolonging it. The identification of these factors will help to guide the treatment plan. Protective factors should also be explored during the assessment, such as areas of particular strength or positive relationships. Developing or strengthening protective factors can then be included in the treatment plan.

Information required during the assessment

Thought will need to be given as to who is best placed to support the service user during the assessment. The person should be given the opportunity to choose who they feel should be there and should be given an opportunity to see the clinician on their own. In general, it is most helpful if the person can be supported by someone who has known them for a reasonable length of time and has a good knowledge of the presenting concerns. Table 5.2 summarises the information that will be sought during the assessment.

Table 5.2: Summary of information required for a mental health assessment

Current	Historical
Presenting problems	Family history
Physical health problems	Early development
Medication	Personal history
Recent life events	Previous medical and psychiatric history
Relationships	
Daily living skills/functioning/level of support	Personality
Housing	
Daytime activities	
Use of drugs and alcohol	

The current problems that have led to the person being referred are explored in detail. The time of onset, severity and frequency of behaviours are enquired about. This detail can be challenging for people with intellectual disabilities who may find it difficult to recall the sequence and timing of events. Anchor events such as birthdays or holidays may help with their recall but information from carers is often essential. Life events that have potentially triggered the problems are also an important piece of information.

It can be seen that a great deal of information is required during a mental health assessment. The assessor must consider the communication and cognitive needs of the person throughout and adapt their communication to be appropriate to the person's abilities. This might include speaking more slowly and allowing more time for responses; using short sentences or questions with simple words; using communication aids when available; being aware that yes/no questions might always be answered 'yes' as the person thinks that this is the answer that is looked for. If the person has a document outlining their communication needs (for example, a communication passport), it should be shared with the professional completing the assessment.

Further assessment

In certain situations, further information is required to complete the assessment. This might include further physical investigations such as blood tests to investigate for physical illnesses, a scan of the person's brain or a measure of the electrical activity in the brain to check for conditions such as epilepsy (electroencephalogram or EEG).

It is often also necessary for other members of the multidisciplinary team to complete further assessments. For example, this might include a communication assessment by a speech and language therapist or an assessment of daily living skills by an occupational therapist. This will help to identify and address all of the person's needs.

Further assessment may be required if the person presents with challenging behaviour that is not attributable to mental or physical illness. This may require a detailed analysis of the function of the behaviour, usually completed by a psychologist or a behaviour specialist (see Chapter 13 on challenging behaviour). In certain circumstances carers may also be asked to complete standardised assessment questionnaires. One example where these are routinely used is in the evaluation of people for dementia. These may help to quantify some of the person's difficulties and help the clinician reach a diagnosis.

Conclusion

The assessment of mental health problems in people with intellectual disabilities is complex. Early detection by carers and support staff is essential to ensure that people get help when they need it. Carers play an important role during the assessment process, both in supporting the person through a difficult and anxiety-provoking experience and in providing essential information to clinicians. When this works in a co-ordinated, person-centred way, it is possible to achieve a comprehensive, holistic assessment. This leads to an intervention plan with the ultimate aim of improving the quality of life of the individual.

Summary

▶ Mental health problems are common in people with intellectual disabilities.

▶ Carers play a valuable role in detecting possible signs of mental health problems and should have an awareness of the signs that might suggest a person has developed a mental illness.

▶ Mental health assessment is complex and carers need to support the person with intellectual disabilities through the process.

▶ Carers often play an important role in providing professionals with information relevant to the mental health assessment.

References

American Psychiatric Association (1994) *Diagnostic and Statistical Manual IV.* Arlington, VA: American Psychiatric Publishing.

Cooper SA, Melville C & Einfeld S (2003) Psychiatric diagnosis, intellectual disabilities and diagnostic criteria for psychiatric disorders for use with adults with learning disabilities/mental retardation (DC-LD). *Journal of Intellectual Disability Research* **47** (1) 3–15.

Cooper SA, Smiley E, Morrison J, Williamson A & Allan L (2007) Mental ill-health in adults with intellectual disabilities: prevalence and associated factors *The British Journal of Psychiatry* **190** 27–35.

Marston GM, Perry DW & Roy A (1997) Manifestations of depression in people with intellectual disability. *Journal of Intellectual Disability Research* **41** (6) 476–480.

Moss SC, Prosser H, Costello H, Simpson N, Patel P, Rowe S, Turner S & Hatton C (1998) Reliability and validity of the PAS-ADD Checklist for detecting psychiatric disorders in adults with intellectual disability. *Journal of Intellectual Disability Research* **42** 173–183.

Royal College of Psychiatrists (2001) *DC-LD: Diagnostic Criteria for Psychiatric Disorders for Use with Adults with Learning Disabilities.* London: Gaskell.

World Health Organization (1992) *The ICD-10 Classification of Mental and Behavioural Disorders: Clinical descriptions and diagnostic guidelines.* Geneva: World Health Organization.

Chapter 6

Biological interventions

Rob Winterhalder and Carol Paton

Introduction

This chapter covers the use of medications commonly prescribed to people with intellectual disabilities and psychiatric or behavioural disorders. It covers their indications for use, side effects and how to overcome them. The information given in this chapter is geared to help those who care for people with intellectual disabilities to understand the basics about medication so that they can support people better and to help them recognise when a problem may be medication-related, and when to contact the GP or psychiatrist.

The expert opinion

'If the doctor gives me medication I want to know what it's for, the side effects and how long I should take it. Being given leaflets would help me.'

Classes

The medications most commonly prescribed by psychiatrists in intellectual disabilities fall into the following classes.

1. Medicines used to treat psychotic symptoms such as hearing voices, being paranoid or having strange ideas or very muddled thoughts. This group of medicines is called **antipsychotics** (also sometimes called neuroleptics or major tranquillisers), and include haloperidol, risperidone and olanzapine. These medicines are also sometimes used to manage behaviour disturbances such as aggression.

2. Medicines used to treat depression. These are called **antidepressants** and include fluoxetine and sertraline.

3. Medicines used to stabilise mood. These are called **mood stabilisers** and include lithium, valproate, carbamazepine and lamotrigine.

4. Medicines used to treat anxiety are sometimes referred to as **anxiolytics**. Examples include diazepam, lorazepam, pregabalin and buspirone.

5. Medicines used to treat insomnia (sleep inducing) are sometimes called **hypnotics**. Examples include zopiclone and melatonin.

6. Medicines used to improve memory (**cognitive enhancers**), such as donepezil and rivastigmine.

7. Medicines used to reduce the hyperactivity that is part of attention deficit hyperactivity disorder (ADHD). Examples include methylphenidate and atomoxetine.

Names

People with intellectual disabilities and their carers usually know the brand names of drugs eg. Prozac or Risperdal. This is the name given by the company that manufactures the medication. These names are designed to be pronounced and remembered more easily. The name used by the doctor is the generic name. For the examples above, the generic names are fluoxetine (Prozac) and risperidone (Risperdal). The generic name is written on the prescription and this allows the pharmacist to supply the medicine in the cheapest way to the NHS and to substitute another brand if the first is not available.

In this chapter, the generic names of medications have been used.

Classes of medication

Antipsychotics
Older (also called typical, traditional or first generation) antipsychotics include:

▶ haloperidol (Serenace)

▶ chlorpromazine (Largactil)

▶ trifluoperazine (Stelazine)

▶ flupentixol (Depixol injection).

Newer (also called atypical or second generation) antipsychotics include:

▶ aripiprazole (Abilify)

▶ olanzapine (Zyprexa)

▶ risperidone (Risperdal)

▶ quetiapine (Seroquel).

Uses

In general, the main use of these medicines is in the treatment of psychoses, hence they are grouped together and called antipsychotics.

Antipsychotics are used in the treatment of disorders such as schizophrenia and mania (elevated mood). For a first episode of schizophrenia it is . recommended that the antipsychotic is prescribed for two years after the individual has recovered, to reduce the risk of relapse. The majority of people who stop taking antipsychotics soon after recovery will become unwell again. Individuals who have relapsed may need to take antipsychotics on a long-term basis.

Antipsychotics are also used in the emergency control of severe behaviour disturbances to produce calm and minimise the risk of harm to self or others. These medicines can sometimes be used in the short-term control of anxiety. Finally, they are sometimes used to treat certain symptoms that may develop in people who are suffering with dementia for example, agitation, hyperactivity, delusions, hallucinations and aggressive behaviour. People with dementia are particularly vulnerable to developing serious side effects from antipsychotic medicines (see below).

Antipsychotics are not addictive, that is, people do not develop a craving for them.

Side effects

Antipsychotics have unwanted side effects that must be weighed against their benefits. Not everyone will develop all the possible side effects associated with a particular drug. Indeed, some may not develop any. The following side effects may be associated with antipsychotics as a group.

Sometimes, soon after starting the medication, stiffness may develop or a tremor or dribbling of saliva. These symptoms are similar to those experienced by people who have Parkinson's disease and are therefore called 'Parkinsonian symptoms'. The newer antipsychotics are less likely to cause these effects than the older ones. Anticholinergic medicines (sometimes called anti-Parkinsonian or anti-muscarinic), such as procyclidine (Kemadrin) or orphenadrine (Dispal), are used to treat Parkinsonian side effects if they are problematic. Anticholinergic medications have their own side effects, such as dry mouth, constipation, urine retention and blurred vision.

Another side effect of antipsychotics, which may be noticeable soon after starting the medication, is restlessness and fidgety movement. This restlessness especially affects the legs and has been described as an inability to sit still. It is known as akathisia.

Abnormal face and body movements may occur soon after starting antipsychotics; the jaw may clench, the tongue protrude, or, rarely, the head and body may become rigidly bent backwards and the eyes rolled upwards. This is called an acute dystonic reaction. The treatment is to give an anticholinergic drug immediately. If the person has difficulty swallowing, they may need an intramuscular injection of a drug like procyclidine. This usually needs to be done in casualty.

The newer antipsychotics such as olanzapine (Zyprexa) and quetiapine (Seroquel) are less likely to cause these side effects. It is therefore important to review medication and try to change to a different antipsychotic medication if there are problems with movement-related side effects.

Those who have been taking antipsychotics in the longer-term may develop tardive dyskinesia, that is, abnormal face and body movements characterised by chewing and sucking movements, grimacing, and slow turning movements of the head and limbs. These side effects are a social handicap and may improve after stopping the medication. It is important that the lowest dose of antipsychotic that keeps the person well is used, and that treatment is regularly reviewed and stopped if necessary.

Many antipsychotic medicines can also cause the amount of prolactin (a hormone) to rise in the body. Effects of this are most noticeable in women as periods can stop and breast milk can be produced. If you think this may be happening to someone you provide care for, tell the doctor. Raised levels of prolactin may also cause sexual problems. Antipsychotics such as quetiapine, aripiprazole and olanzapine rarely cause these problems.

Mental Health in Intellectual Disabilities: A reader (fourth edition) © Pavilion Publishing (Brighton) Ltd 2011

Some antipsychotic medicines can lower blood pressure (especially chlorpromazine). This may lead to feeling dizzy when standing up and people may fall and hurt themselves. The elderly are particularly likely to suffer from this problem. Fortunately, the dizziness usually wears off after a few weeks. Antipsychotic medicines may also cause abnormal heart rhythms that lead to palpitations and fainting etc. The doctor may do an ECG (electrocardiogram) to check that the heart is healthy if they are worried about these side effects.

Some people who are treated with antipsychotic medicines may put on excessive amounts of weight because the medication increases appetite. Weight gain can lead to diabetes and to increased cholesterol levels. It is important that everyone who takes antipsychotics long-term has a physical health check once a year that includes body mass index (a measure of body weight in relation to height), blood pressure, and a check for diabetes and high cholesterol. If someone who takes antipsychotic medicines seems to be very thirsty, passes water often, is more tired than normal, or seems to be confused, tell the doctor.

Many people with intellectual disabilities suffer with epilepsy. Antipsychotic medication tends to make epilepsy worse and the antiepileptic medication may have to be increased to compensate for this.

All antipsychotics can also cause side effects that are specific to that medicine. For example, chlorpromazine can cause skin photosensitivity and pigmentation, which means that the individual is more likely to burn in the sun. Thus, the person taking chlorpromazine must apply sunscreen before going in the sun. Olanzapine can cause swollen legs (this is rare) and risperidone can cause a runny nose.

In older people with dementia, antipsychotic medicines increase the risk of stroke. It is particularly important that treatment is reviewed regularly in this group to make sure that the benefits still outweigh the risks (see the following section below on challenging behaviour).

Depot injections
In addition to the usual route of taking medication orally, some of these medications may be given by injection into the buttock every two, three or four weeks (none of the other classes of psychotropic medication, eg. antidepressants come in a depot form). They are formulated to be absorbed slowly from this site. This method is good for those who are not reliable

with taking oral medication. However, this is not the method to use if the dose needs to be altered frequently.

Examples of depot medication are flupentixol (Depixol), zuclopentixol (Clopixol), haloperidol (Haldol) and risperidone (Risperdal Consta). Risperidone is the only atypical antipsychotic currently available in a depot form. Risperidal Consta must be given every two weeks but the frequency of administration of the other depots is more flexible.

Antidepressants

Types:

▶ tricyclic antidepressants eg. amitriptyline (Tryptizol)

▶ selective serotonin reuptake inhibitor antidepressants (SSRIs) eg. sertraline (Lustral) and fluoxetine (Prozac)

▶ monoamine oxidase inhibitors (MAOIs) eg. phenelzine (Nardil)

▶ newer antidepressants eg. venlafaxine (Efexor), mirtazapine (Zispin) and reboxetine (Edronax).

Uses

Antidepressants are used for the treatment of major depressive disorders. They start to lift mood as soon as they are started but it may take a week or two for the size of this effect to be significant enough for you to notice. After someone has recovered from a first episode of depression they should continue to take the antidepressant for at least six months to have the best chance of staying well. People who have had several episodes of severe depression may benefit from taking antidepressants for much longer. Antidepressant medicines should be gradually withdrawn at the end of treatment.

Antidepressants can also be used in the treatment of anxiety, phobias or panic attacks. Some SSRI antidepressants are also used to treat obsessive compulsive disorder (OCD) and bulimia nervosa.

Side effects
Tricyclic (TCA) antidepressants

These older antidepressants tend to be sedating. This can be helpful in some people with depression, particularly if they are also anxious and agitated. The antidepressant can produce a calming effect and help the person sleep. This calming effect is usually seen before the antidepressant effect.

Common side effects include dry mouth, constipation, blurred vision and sweating. These medications can also increase appetite, which may be an advantage in those who have lost weight due to depression. Like some of the antipsychotics, tricyclic antidepressants can lower blood pressure and cause dizziness, especially when the person stands up too quickly. People who are already unsteady on their feet, such as the elderly or those with physical disabilities, are particularly susceptible to falls because of this dizziness. These antidepressants may also worsen heart problems and cause palpitations. In addition, they lower the epilepsy threshold and can increase the number of fits a person has.

Selective serotonin reuptake inhibitor (SSRI) antidepressants
SSRIs are similarly effective to TCAs. The advantage of these newer antidepressants is that they are less likely to cause dry mouth, blurred . vision and constipation, and less likely to affect the heart and blood pressure. They are also safer in overdose. Instead of being sedating, they may cause restlessness. When they are first started they may cause an upset stomach and nausea. These side effects usually wear off but some people may find that SSRIs cause them to lose their appetite, leading to weight loss. Less usually, people taking these medicines may actually be sick. With both the TCAs and SSRIs, most of the side effects become less noticeable after awhile. SSRIs (and TCAs) may also cause sexual side effects.

Newer antidepressants
Several new antidepressants have become available in the last few years. They are all equally effective but have different side effects. Venlafaxine can cause nausea and can raise blood pressure when given in higher doses. Mirtazapine can cause sedation and weight gain. Reboxetine can cause insomnia and agomelatin can (rarely) cause problems with the liver, and regular blood tests are required.

Mood stabilising medications
Include:

▶ lithium (Priadel, Camcolit etc.)

▶ carbamazepine (Tegretol)

▶ valproate (Epilim, Depakote)

▶ lamotrigine (Lamictal)

Lithium

People who suffer from bipolar (manic depression) may benefit from taking medicine to stabilise their mood. People may need antidepressants to lift their depressed mood, but their mood may suddenly swing the other way and became manic, and this may need to be treated with an antipsychotic. To prevent these swings in mood, which are so disruptive, a mood stabiliser may be prescribed. Mood stabilisers may reduce the number of episodes of low or high mood, decrease the severity of the episodes, or make the episodes shorter. Sometimes, in people with depression, their illness is resistant to other forms of treatment and lithium may be added to antidepressants to lift this depression. Lithium is also used to lower the mood of those with hypomania.

Monitoring

Lithium is taken on a long-term basis to prevent relapses. It is an effective medication but has potentially serious side effects. Before starting treatment with lithium, blood tests need to be done to make sure that the kidneys and thyroid are working properly. Once treatment with lithium has started, the blood level of the drug should be stabilised somewhere between 0.4–1 mmol/l depending on the person being treated and the symptoms they have. Thereafter, blood tests need to be done every three months to check that the amount of lithium in the blood is right, and every six months to check that the kidneys and thyroid are still working properly. If the level of lithium in the blood is too high, kidney damage may occur.

Some medicines interact with lithium and cause the level of lithium in the blood to become too high. One important example is ibuprofen. You should never give ibuprofen to someone who takes lithium, unless the doctor has prescribed it to be given regularly for a long-term condition. The National Patient Safety Agency has produced an information pack about lithium that gives further details about blood tests and medicines that should be avoided. Make sure that you have a copy of this pack if you look after someone who takes lithium (NPSA, 2009).

Apart from lithium and some anticonvulsants that are used as mood stablisers, it is not routine practice to check blood levels of other drugs such as antidepressants and antipsychotics etc. Due to the need to closely monitor lithium with blood tests, people who are not compliant with blood tests are not usually prescribed lithium. If a mood stabiliser is required, drugs such as carbamazepine and sodium valproate may be considered.

Side effects

The side effects which are immediately noticeable include nausea, loose bowels, tiredness, fine tremor, feeling thirsty and passing a lot of urine. Some of these side effects may get better with time, but feeling thirsty and passing a lot of urine generally do not. Some people on lithium develop hypothyroidism (their thyroid gland is underactive) and need to be treated with thyroxine.

Toxicity

Toxicity occurs when the blood level of lithium is too high (above 1.5 mmol/l). This may occur if the person taking lithium becomes dehydrated – due to diarrhoea and vomiting, for example – or if they are unable to drink a normal amount. It can also happen when other medicines (such as ibuprofen) are taken without altering the dose of lithium. Signs and symptoms of toxicity include appetite loss, vomiting, diarrhoea, coarse tremor, slurred speech, unsteadiness, sleepiness and seizures. Lithium toxicity is serious and can lead to long-term health problems. Lithium toxicity is life threatening.

Carbamazepine

Carbamazepine is generally used for the treatment of epilepsy, but can also be used to stabilise mood. Although lithium is more effective, carbamazepine has the advantage of not having adverse effects on the kidneys or thyroid. Sometimes, if lithium is not effective at controlling mood fluctuations, carbamazepine is added. Carbamazepine is also sometimes used to control challenging behaviour such as aggression or acting very impulsively.

Sodium valproate (Epilim, Depakote)

Valproate is used to treat many different types of epilepsy and is also used to stabilise mood. It is more effective in treating and preventing mania (high mood) than depression (low mood). Valproate is most effective in stabilising mood when it is taken with lithium.

Lamotrigine

Lamotrigine is also mainly used to treat epilepsy but can be helpful in treating low mood in people with bipolar disorder. Lamotrigine can cause skin rashes, some of which are very serious. If someone you care for develops a rash while taking lamotrigine, tell their doctor straightaway.

Hypnotics and anxiolytics

Benzodiazepines

Examples include:

▶ diazepam (Valium)

▶ nitrazepam (Mogadon)

▶ lorazepam (Ativan)

▶ temazepam (Restoril).

Uses

Benzodiazepines have both hypnotic (sleep inducing) and anxiolytic (anxiety reducing) properties. They can be very useful for a few days, but are addictive and people can experience unpleasant withdrawal symptoms when they are stopped. It is important that the underlying causes of these problems are identified and treated rather than relying on the long-term use of medicines.

Lorazepam can also be used for the control of acutely disturbed behaviour as it is rapidly sedative when given by injection. Other benzodiazepines can be given by mouth if the individual will accept them. Some benzodiazepines like clonazepam (Rivotril) and diazepam (Stesolid) are used to control epilepsy. Benzodiazepines are also used to manage withdrawal symptoms from other drugs, such as alcohol.

Side effects

Benzodiazepines differ in the length of time their effects last after they have been taken. For example, temazepam is effective for about eight hours and is therefore useful to help people sleep, whereas diazepam stays in the blood for several days and is used to reduce anxiety. A common side effect of these medicines is drowsiness, which leads to poor concentration and decreases the ability to learn. This side effect may be dangerous in situations where it is important to be able to react quickly, for example when crossing the road.

After a few weeks, tolerance to benzodiazepines may develop ie. the same dose no longer has the desired effect and more has to be taken to get the same effect. Stopping the medication can make anxiety worse and cause restlessness, decreased sleep, sweats, confusion, headaches and craving for the medication. Weaning an addicted person from hypnotics can be a slow and difficult process.

Taking too much of a benzodiazepine may cause unsteadiness, drowsiness and slurred speech.

Non-benzodiazepines
Examples include:

▶ zopiclone (Zimovane)

▶ buspirone (Buspar)

▶ pregabalin

▶ melatonin (Circadin)

Zopiclone is used for the short-term treatment of insomnia. It is addictive and side effects may include a bitter or metallic taste, nausea and vomiting, dry mouth and irritability.

Buspirone is used for the short-term treatment of anxiety. It is not addictive. Side effects may include nausea, dizziness, headache and nervousness.

Pregabalin is used for the treatment of anxiety and also for certain types of epilepsy and pain. Side effects may include weight gain, blurred vision and sedation.

Melatonin is used to treat insomnia. It is not addictive. Melatonin is generally considered to be well tolerated, although it is important to note that side effects have not been systematically evaluated.

Cognitive enhancers
These medicines are used to improve memory in people with dementia. Examples include:

▶ donepezil (Aricept)

▶ rivastigmine (Exelon)

Uses
Cognitive enhancers are given to individuals with dementia, especially those with Alzheimer's disease. They help with memory and behavioural problems, and loss of skills.

Side effects
May include nausea, diarrhoea, difficulty sleeping, and tremors and jerks.

Attention deficit hyperactivity disorder – specific medication

Examples include:

► methylphenidate (Ritalin)

► atomoxetine (Strattera).

Uses
These medicines are used specifically for people with attention deficit hyperactivity disorder and can reduce impulsivity and hyperactivity, and increase levels of concentration. Methylphenidate is a psycho-stimulant and is similar to amphetamine ('speed') and can be abused. Atomoxetine is not a psycho-stimulant.

Side effects
Methylphenidate may include nausea, not wanting to eat, and a fast heart beat. Atomoxetine may include dry mouth, constipation, dizziness on standing up and a fast heart beat.

Choice of medication
Which medication is prescribed depends on the problem being treated, any prominent symptoms and compliance issues. Medicines differ in the range of problems that they treat, and in their sedative properties and general side effects.

How medications work

The brain contains hundreds of millions of nerve fibres. These nerve fibres communicate with each other, not by touching, but by sending chemical messengers from one nerve fibre to the next. Different chemical messengers have different jobs. For example, if too much dopamine (a chemical messenger) is sent from one nerve fibre to the next, psychotic symptoms such as hallucinations may occur. If there is too little serotonin (another chemical messenger) depression may result. There are dozens of chemical messengers in the brain and each group of medication targets a different one or different combination.

Figure 6.1: How nerve fibres communicate

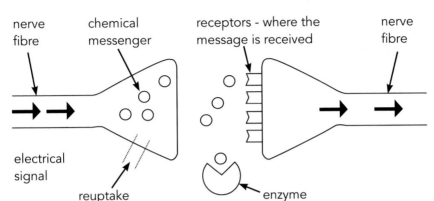

In each illness there is a different problem with under or over-activity of these communication channels. The aim of medication is to correct this underlying problem. For example, antipsychotic drugs work by reducing the activity of dopamine and antidepressants work by increasing the activity of serotonin, noradrenaline or both. Unfortunately, these actions by medication on chemical messengers are also responsible for some side effects.

As no two medications have exactly the same effect on nerve fibres, people may respond well to one medication but not to another that is very similar. Choosing the right medication from a group is often a process of trial and error as it cannot be predicted which one a person will respond to best.

Use of medication in challenging behaviour

When psychological and social interventions have failed to help reduce severe challenging behaviour, it may be necessary to use psychotropic medication. There are three ways in which psychotropic medication may help:

▶ in a non-specific manner, by reducing agitation and producing calmness

▶ in a specific way by targeting abnormally functioning chemical messenger systems in the brain which are thought to contribute to the challenging behaviour

▶ medication may also work by treating an underlying mental illness which has not been recognised as contributing to the challenging behaviour.

Some behaviours – such as over-activity, aggression and ritualistic behaviour without an apparent purpose, which are sometimes seen in people with intellectual disabilities, and particularly those who also have autism – may respond to antipsychotic medication. Antipsychotics may reduce agitation, aggression and other challenging behaviours; antidepressants have been used to treat self-injurious behaviour, ritualistic behaviours etc. and mood stabilisers may be used for aggression or self-injurious behaviour. It is less clear how long psychotropic medication should be prescribed for in the case of challenging behaviour that is not due to mental illness. Regardless, it is good practice to periodically review the need for ongoing psychotropic medication.

Finally, antipsychotic medication has frequently been used to treat behavioural symptoms associated with dementia. Recent evidence has shown that people with dementia are at an increased risk of stroke if they are prescribed antipsychotic medication. Therefore, antipsychotic medication should only be prescribed if there is clear evidence of significant clinical benefits and other non-pharmacological approaches have been unsuccessful.

National Standards for Administration of Medication in Care Homes

Whether a care home is large or small and whether the staff have a nursing qualification or not, there is a duty of care placed on the employer and carers that requires medication to be safely handled so that the people cared for are supported to take it safely (DH, 2000). For a care home member of staff to administer medication, it must have a printed label containing the following information: the person's name, date of dispensing, the name and strength of medication, and the dose and frequency of administration. An information leaflet must be supplied with each medication (including those supplied in monitored dosage systems) and these should be made available to the person taking the medication (where appropriate). Sources of information that have been developed specifically for people who have intellectual disabilities can be found in the further reading list at the end of the chapter.

The use of complimentary/alternative treatments, as with other treatments, should only be undertaken with the expressed agreement of the individual, or person who is authorised to speak on the person's behalf. Advice should always be sought from the pharmacist about any potential interactions between the non-prescription medication and the person's regular medication.

It is the responsibility of the registered manager to ensure that staff access training that meets basic requirements. Where care home staff are required to administer medication by an invasive route, for example administration of rectal diazepam, additional training is necessary. This training should incorporate an assessment of competence regarding consent to treatment on an individual basis.

Individuals should be supported and facilitated to take control of and . manage their own health care, including support to manage their own medical conditions where feasible. The registered manager and staff should encourage and support individuals to retain, administer and control their own medication within a risk management framework, and comply with the home's policy and procedure for the receipt, recording, storage, handling, administration and disposal of medication.

In residential care homes all medication, including controlled drugs (except those for self-administration), should be administered by designated and appropriately trained staff. The training for care staff must include:

▶ basic knowledge of how medications are used and how to recognise and deal with problems in use

▶ the principles behind all aspects of the home's policy on handling medication and records.

The role of carers is summarised in Box 6.1.

> ## Box 6.1: Role of carers
>
> 1. Make sure you know:
>   - ▶ what the medication is expected to do
>   - ▶ what the side effects might be
>   - ▶ how long it needs to be taken for.
> 2. Ensure/support the person to take the medication as prescribed
> 3. Tell the doctor if the person seems to be having side effects
> 4. Keep a list of all the medication the person is receiving
> 5. Take it with you each time the person sees a doctor (GP, psychiatrist etc.), or if you buy any medication from a pharmacy
> 6. If you have any questions at all about any of the medication the person is taking, ask the doctor or pharmacist

Conclusion

It is important to remember that medication should be used as part of a management programme. For instance, a person who has a depressive illness may have their mood lifted with an antidepressant, but for the person to make a full recovery any stresses which precipitated the depression should be resolved. Attention to psychological and environmental factors may also help prevent a relapse.

The medications discussed in this chapter are a selection of common medications used by psychiatrists, but by no means all of them. Neither are all the examples of medication, given in order to illustrate points, the best medication of their class. Other doctors may prescribe another medication of that class because they are more familiar with its potency and side effects, or because that medication best meets the needs of a particular person.

If a carer has concerns regarding medication, they should discuss this with their supervisor or line manager. If appropriate, these concerns should then be shared with the prescribing doctor or pharmacist.

Summary

▶ Medicines can play an important role in treating psychiatric or behavioural disorders in people with intellectual disabilities, but they must be part of a broader management plan.

▶ Often, doctors and nurses have to balance improvements in mental functioning and behaviour against side-effects, and ultimately have to judge responses to medicine in terms of overall quality of life.

▶ People who do not respond to one type of medicine may respond to a different medicine. Where side effects are a problem, there is often another medicine that can be tried instead.

▶ Carers need to be aware of what each medicine is expected to do and what the side effects might be. This is because carers often play a key role in helping the doctor or nurse decide whether a medicine has helped and whether side effects are causing a problem.

References

Department of Health (2000) *Care Homes for Adults (18–65). National Minimum Standards. Care Homes Regulation (2nd edition). Care Standards Act*. London: TSO.

National Patients Safety Agency (2009) *Safer Lithium Therapy*. London: NPSA.

Useful websites

National Institute for Mental Health in England
http://www.nimhe.org.uk/

North Mersey Community NHS Trust
http://www.northmersey.nhs.uk/informed/index.htm

National Care Standards Commission for England
www.carestandards.gov.uk

Information guides

▶ **Ask about medicines** – My medicine at: http://www.askaboutmedicines.org/Assets/16796/my_medicines_sheet.pdf
This is a free, template information sheet with pictures and easy language that can be used to explain what a medicine is for and how it should be taken.

▶ **Easy Health.org** at: http://www.easyhealth.org.uk/
This website brings together health related information from a wide range of sources. Some is aimed at health professionals, but most is aimed at patients. All of the information is very easy to understand and much of it is available in pictorial form or as podcasts. All information is free.

▶ **The Elfrida Society** at: http://www.elfrida.com/publications.html
The Elfrida Society publishes materials by people with intellectual disabilities, for people with intellectual disabilities and for people who work with them. There is a set of leaflets that cover commonly used psychotropic medicines, as well as a wide range of health related information. Some items need to be purchased.

▶ **Royal College of Psychiatrists** – Your guide to taking medicine for behaviour problems at: http://www.rcpsych.ac.uk/pdf/erg07.pdf
This free and easy read booklet about the use of medicines to manage behavioural problems in people with intellectual disabilities.

▶ **University of Birmingham** – LD medication guidelines at: http://www.ld-medication.bham.ac.uk/medical.shtml
This site provides free, easy to read leaflets covering most of the medicines used to treat mental health problems or challenging behaviours in people with intellectual disabilities. Podcasts are also available.

▶ **University of Bristol** – Norah Fry Research Centre at: http://www.bristol.ac.uk/norahfry/easy-information/
This site provides general information to help people with intellectual disabilities make choices about their medicines.

Information for carers

▶ *Handbook on Medication for Carers of People with Learning Disabilities* by Miriam Wilcher
Contains information about medicines for carers of people with intellectual disabilities.

▶ Clear Thoughts at: http://www.clearthoughts.info/
Website dedicated to the mental health needs of people with learning disabilities. It has separate pages for people with intellectual disabilities, carers and professionals.

Information for clinical staff

▶ *The Frith Prescribing Guidelines for Adults with Intellectual Disability* at: http://www.ukppg.org.uk/frith-guidelines-2008.pdf

Information about the contents of the Frith prescribing guidelines; the most up-to-date source of information for clinical staff about prescribing for people with intellectual disabilities. Needs to be purchased.

▶ *Using Medication to Manage Behaviour Problems among Adults with a Learning Disability* at: http://www.ld-medication.bham.ac.uk/1qrg.pdf

An evidence-based guide to using medication to manage behavioural problems among adults with an intellectual disability.

Chapter 7

Psycho-social interventions

Nadja Alim

Introduction

People with intellectual disabilities and mental health problems often require a high level of support. The bio-psycho-social model of mental health attempts to understand individuals by taking into account biological (eg. physical health), psychological (eg. emotional well-being) and social (eg. their interpersonal competence) factors (Krantz *et al,* 1985). This health promotion model suggests that biological, psychological and social factors have a direct impact on a person's mental well-being. Where a person presents with mental health difficulties, treatments may take a bio-psycho-social stance. This chapter aims to provide an outline of psychological and social interventions as exemplified through two case examples to help those who support people with intellectual disabilities understand what types of treatments are available and facilitate referrals to services.

> ### The expert opinion
> 'Psychologists and counsellors can help you. You can talk about your problems, and that can help make you feel better.'

The well-being of individuals is influenced by social parameters, and vice versa. Bronfenbrenner's (1979) theory of 'development in context' suggests that individuals function under the influence of four levels: the micro-level (ie. systems the individual has direct experiences of eg. home, work, family, day centre); the meso level (ie. the links between different micro-levels eg. parents and siblings, family); the exo level (systems that influence the person, their micro and meso levels eg. the day centre management, the country's transport system); and the macro level (ie. larger scale systems that determine the prevailing ideology and social structure guiding the person and the different levels eg. societal views of disability, the current rate of unemployment). As we develop, so does our influence and control over these levels (ie. what holiday to go on with the family, earning money, influencing politics through voting etc). As individuals mature and grow from childhood to adulthood, they start to acknowledge their increasing autonomy and independence. This developmental process contributes to maintaining psychological health.

At times, people with intellectual disabilities can experience a lack of control over their environment. It was hoped that the closures of large inpatient settings and integration into the community would lead to people with intellectual disabilities having more choice and control. However, the Department of Health still continues to encourage today's intellectual disability services and professionals to keep in mind principles of rights, independence, personalisation and inclusion (DH, 2009). It may be somewhat due to the disempowerment and lack of choice and control for people with intellectual disabilities that a greater need for mental health services and interventions is experienced and that people with intellectual disabilities remain one of the most ignored populations in terms of receiving psychological and mental health services (eg. Dodd & McGinnity, 2003). This further perpetuates mental ill health and highlights the need for research and practice supporting bio-psycho-social interventions for this client group.

Dagnan (2007) suggests that psychosocial interventions may occur on four levels.

1. **Individual interventions** aimed at supporting the person directly, for example, through the help of a psychologist or therapist. Therapeutic interventions of this kind aim to address underlying factors associated with mental ill health (Butler *et al*, 2006), reduce symptom-distress (Tarrier, 2005) or increase social or vocational skills (Kopelowicz *et al*, 2006).

2. **Interventions in the immediate social context of the person** aim to, for instance, support carers to understand and address the impact of their attitudes and expressed negative emotions in order to prevent relapse and reduce symptom presentation (Pharaoah *et al*, 2006).

3. **Interventions aimed at the wider social context of the person** may include a focus on housing, leisure activities and employment (eg. McGurk & Mueser, 2006).

4. **Service structures influencing the delivery of services** further play a role in supporting individuals' mental health. For instance, literature highlights assertive outreach and early intervention services as examples for the delivery of care within a psychosocial model (Marshall & Rathbone, 2006).

Case study: Rami

Rami is a 35-year-old man. He grew up in the UK but his family is originally from Morocco. Rami has two siblings – one older sister and a younger brother called Youssri. Both Rami and Youssri have moderate intellectual disabilities. Rami has difficulties with motor co-ordination and presents with a malformation of one of his feet. His ability to walk is impaired and he does not like his feet to be touched or his toenails being cut, which leads to him regularly suffering with ingrown toenails. Rami communicates using single words and struggles to understand people unless they use pictures or symbols. Rami has a place at the local college, but he has not attended for several months. Rami's big interest is collecting leaflets. He has a big collection of leaflets, which he enjoys stacking in an orderly fashion and can spend hours in his room sorting his leaflet collection.

Youssri still lives at home with his elderly parents who are devout Muslims. Youssri has, over the past few years, experienced several bouts of ill health which have led him to be in pain, as well as having sleep problems. During this time, Rami became aggressive towards the family, becoming very upset and physically attacking the people around him. This led to Youssri having to go to hospital at one point. Following this incident, Rami moved away from home into his own flat where he started to be supported by a team of staff. His behaviour escalated following his move and he has been very aggressive towards staff as well as throwing furniture in the house and breaking things. Rami now receives 2:1 support but visits his family every Friday, when they visit a local mosque for Friday prayer. Rami still becomes upset when around his family but is always accompanied by a staff member when he visits them. His father has told a member of staff that Rami is usually calmer when they attend the mosque, where staff do not accompany him.

Rami's father believes that Rami's difficulties improve 'with the help of prayer'. Other than attending the mosque, Rami does not go out much as staff worry about Rami's lack of balance, particularly when walking on uneven surfaces. They feel that Rami becomes upset when he stumbles, which triggers a behaviour outburst. Staff have also recently become worried that the collection of leaflets is becoming too big and would like to support Rami to address this issue.

Understanding Rami from a bio-psycho-social perspective

The staff team took Rami to his GP after they noticed an injury on one of his toes following stumbling and falling. The GP referred Rami to a chiropodist as he felt that Rami's ingrown toenails were causing him pain and that he might require special shoes to give his malformed foot extra support. He also referred Rami to the local community team for adults with intellectual disabilities for an assessment by a nurse, a psychologist and an occupational therapist.

The psychologist and the occupational therapist assessed Rami jointly. The psychologist suggested that Rami may present with features of autism as he appears to struggle with social communication and changes in routines and environments. It was said that Rami experiences a need for sameness and reacts in a volatile manner when there are changes, such as his brother being unwell, moving to a new house and having new people to support him. This then leads to Rami creating 'safe environments' such as those that he has control over, eg. his room and leaflet collection. Moreover, Rami's foot pain and lack of balance were thought to raise his anxieties further.

The occupational therapist proposed that Rami lacks meaningful activities, structure and interaction, which exacerbate his presentation. The occupational therapist suggested that Rami may benefit from a clearer structure to his day and engaging in activities with his staff team that he finds stimulating. It was suggested that Rami's cultural and religious background may be important to him and that he manages well within the mosque environment because it is the only place that has remained the same and is hence predictable. Speaking to his father, the occupational therapist found out that Rami knows how to say some of the Muslim prayers, which he rehearses every time he attends the mosque, making this environment predictable and less anxiety-provoking.

The assessment by the nurse suggested that Rami may be in pain with his toes a lot of the time. In fact, Rami has to take his shoes off at the mosque and the nurse felt that Rami appeared to be in pain less, concluding that walking with bare feet may be less painful.

Figure 7.1: Rami's formulation

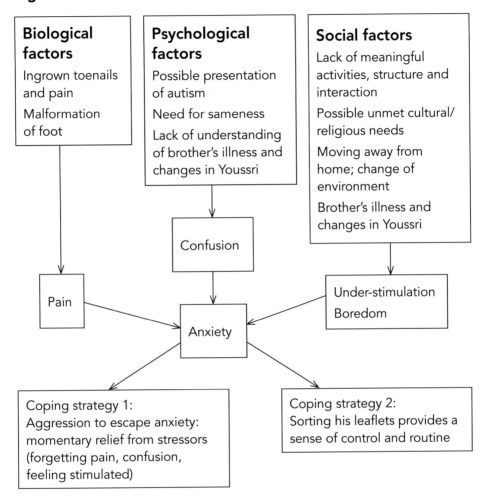

As illustrated in Figure 7.1, different bio-psycho-social factors may lead Rami to experience pain, confusion about his environment and under-stimulation/ boredom. When Rami starts to feel overwhelmed by these stressors his anxiety may increase to a degree that does not feel manageable. Rami may then react aggressively in some situations as his aggression will provide momentary relief from stressors (**maladaptive coping strategy**). In other words, when Rami reacts aggressively, various stressors are likely to be removed. For instance, if Rami reacts aggressively because he feels overwhelmed and unable to understand the changes in his brother (eg. his brother crying etc.), then it is likely that Youssri will be removed from Rami's environment to ensure that he is safe. This will provide momentary relief from Youssri's crying and Rami will feel a little less confused. He has also learned that when he becomes aggressive in this situation, the stressor (here: Youssri) is likely to be taken away. Rami may be able to cope with his anxiety by means of putting in place a routine activity which provides a sense of predictability and control: sorting his leaflets. When at home, he may be able to take himself to his room and engage in this activity, which counteracts under-stimulation and boredom and lifts his confusion over his environment (**adaptive coping strategy**). Unfortunately, and despite the adaptive nature of this strategy, staff have become concerned over Rami's leaflet collection as it is getting so big. However, interrupting this activity carries the risk of increasing Rami's anxiety, which may lead to further maladaptive behaviours. Also, one may consider Rami running the risk of isolating himself more and more with this activity if he is unable to regulate his anxieties in other ways.

Interventions relating to Rami's case

An intervention tailored to Rami's needs may require both **preventative** and **reactive** strategies.

Rami and his family and carers may be encouraged to seek out the bio-psycho-social origins of Rami's anxiety, which lead to him reacting in maladaptive ways. They already understand that, from a biological perspective, Rami may be experiencing pain due to his ingrown toenails and the malformation of his foot. Rami's carers may need to work together with the chiropodist to help find ways to encourage Rami to allow staff to cut his toenails. With the help of the community intellectual disability nurse, the chiropodist has recommended the use of accessible information to help Rami understand why cutting his nails will be good for him. They also suggested that Rami has a bath prior to cutting his toenails so his nails are softer and easier to cut. It was also recommended that they prepare Rami for the nail cutting by outlining this activity clearly on his weekly timetable. With regards to Rami's foot malformation, he has been provided with new shoes which help him to walk more safely. Nevertheless, the staff were advised to risk assess new environments before Rami visits them and ensure that Rami does not go places where there are uneven surfaces.

Rami's assessment by a psychologist and an occupational therapist concluded that he presents with autism, which explains his need for sameness and routine, and his psychological presentation. The psychologist conducted a functional analysis of Rami's behaviours and made recommendations that his environment needed to be as predictable as possible (**individual intervention**). Staff found new activities which allowed Rami to create routines, increase his interactions and encourage engagement with staff and others. For instance, they put together an activity book – a folder which displayed a different picture of an activity per page. Once the activity is completed, Rami turns over the page to start the next activity. The book included activities such as household chores and interactive and independent games. Also, Rami now has a visual timetable that he goes through with staff in the morning. This way, Rami can appreciate his environment as being more predictable.

From a 'social' perspective, Rami's carers feel more confident that they are now offering Rami more meaningful activities and a sense of structure. Rami has also started to attend college again where his tutors have taken care to allow him to take part in a programme that best suits his needs. While he used to be asked to attend a beach volleyball class, it is now . acknowledged that this will raise Rami's anxieties as he is so unsteady on his feet. The college tutors also took part in a training session with the psychologist to help them understand Rami better so that they are able to support his needs (**intervention aimed at the immediate social context**). Rami now attends a baking class where he really enjoys following a recipe. Staff asked Rami whether he would like more opportunities to say his prayers at home. They invited a member of the mosque to visit one evening per week and help Rami rehearse his prayers at home. Rami's father arranged for him to be involved in helping out at the mosque with Rami spending one afternoon per week sorting out the recycling. Rami enjoys this activity and it uses his paper-organising skills in a meaningful way (**intervention aimed at the wider social context**).

There are still incidences when Rami becomes anxious and upset, although his aggressive outbursts have become less and less since the above interventions were put in place. Therefore, a reactive intervention has been developed. Rami's carers have been advised to assist Rami asking for help when he cannot cope. They have noticed that Rami's body language changes when he is becoming upset. They have given Rami a card with the symbol for 'Help', which he carries in his pocket. Staff support Rami to say 'Help' and show the card when his body language indicates that he is likely to become upset. Rami has now started using his card independently, thus preventing himself becoming upset and aggressive. Staff have also made good links with the community intellectual disabilities team. The team runs a drop-in session for the carers of people with challenging behaviour and his staff visit regularly to help them think about good ways to manage Rami's behaviours (**service structures influencing the delivery of services**).

Understanding Rami's case from a bio-psycho-social perspective has helped to inform his family, staff and professionals how best to support Rami and reduce maladaptive strategies to cope with his anxieties. He now presents with less challenging behaviours and has found constructive and positive ways of coping with his environment and disabilities.

Case study: Daisy

Daisy is a 54-year-old white British woman with mild intellectual disabilities and mental health problems. Daisy shares a home with two male residents, Sanji and Pete, who also have mental health problems. During the day, the residents are supported by two members of staff and at night one staff member sleeps at the house. Daisy attends an art class and a drop-in centre and sometimes enjoys shopping and doing her make-up. Daisy and Sanji have been a couple for some time now. Although they enjoy spending time together and go on holidays, their relationship is strained when Sanji's mental health breaks down. Sanji becomes very worried about 'being watched' and imagines that he is under surveillance by state security, who he suspects monitor him via television, by tapping his telephone and getting information from people around him. He will accuse Daisy of spying on him and sharing this information with others. He will then lock himself in his room and refuse to speak with her, sometimes for weeks.

Daisy suffers with depression and self-harm. She is also very overweight and tends to buy sweets and crisps in bulk, binge eating when she feels 'low'. Daisy often experiences days where she feels very lethargic and tired but struggles to sleep. She also thinks a lot about her past during these times and says that she will 'dwell on' traumatic events, thinking about them over and over in her head. When Daisy feels overwhelmed by these thoughts and difficult feelings she often cuts her upper arms and inner thighs with a sharp object. Daisy regularly goes to see a psychiatrist who helps her manage her depression with medication.

Daisy comes from a large family and is the second youngest child of nine. Her mother suffered with symptoms of depression and alcohol dependency. Daisy's parents had a difficult relationship and Daisy vividly recalls episodes of domestic violence at home. When she was 12 years old, she fainted at school and was rushed off to hospital. It was noted that she was malnourished and had been neglected. Daisy and some of her siblings were moved in with a foster family at the time. Daisy's foster mother was very

(continued)

Mental Health in Intellectual Disabilities: A reader (fourth edition) © Pavilion Publishing (Brighton) Ltd 2011

Case study: Daisy (continued)

nice, but after some time Daisy started to feel uncomfortable as the foster father was touching her in 'private places'. Daisy was unsure whether the foster father's behaviour was wrong, so only hesitantly mentioned this to her teacher at school who had asked her about her foster family. Social services became involved and Daisy was moved to a children's home. When Daisy was 17 she ran away from the children's home and was homeless for several years. During this time Daisy was begging and looking through rubbish bins to find food and drink. When Daisy was 24 she attempted suicide by cutting her wrists, but was found and taken to hospital. She then spent some time on a psychiatric ward before moving to a residential home in the community. Daisy got on well with the other residents and staff there and was said to 'blossom'. She started working in a cafe and the medication the psychiatrist had put her on was reduced. The residential home closed down and Daisy moved to another area and came to live in her current house when she was 36. She did not return to work as she could not find a job in the new area.

Understanding Daisy from a bio-psycho-social perspective

After her last appointment, the psychiatrist referred Daisy to a psychologist and contacted her social work team to ask for a review of her case. The psychiatrist was particularly worried as Daisy started to say that she was feeling like 'ending it all', saying that she did not feel valued by Sanji and generally lacked energy to 'pull herself up'. She had also put on more weight and her self-harm had increased, with her now inflicting deeper cuts and at one point having to be rushed to hospital to receive stitches. The psychiatrist agreed with Daisy that he would increase her medication and showed her and a member of staff how to clean her wounds properly. She advised Daisy when to go to hospital with her injuries and urged her to seek help from staff before she felt the need to cut herself.

The psychologist met with Daisy and found out more about what was going on for her. She said that she usually felt better when Sanji was well and that they encourage each other to do things together. During times of 'gloom', Daisy said she remembers difficult experiences from her past, for example, how her dad hit her mum, how her foster father sexually harassed her, and difficult nights sleeping on the streets when she was homeless. She then feels 'tired out', tearful and lacks energy. She is also unable to sleep properly at night, which leads to more 'dwelling'. During these times Daisy recently started contemplating suicide and says that she feels hopeless. Daisy explained that the cutting makes her feel better when she feels so low. She said that feeling pain 'shakes her out of the gloom' by replacing the 'empty feeling in her stomach'. Also, she explained that eating makes her feel better when she feels that nothing is ever going to change.

A social worker from the intellectual disabilities team organised a review and invited Daisy, the staff from the home, the psychologist and the psychiatrist to attend. The social worker was interested in Daisy's daytime activities. He was told that Daisy does very little and even when she attends her art class or the drop-in centre, she is often not very motivated to engage in activities. Daisy said that she was bored by the activities offered to her and unmotivated to engage. She couldn't think what else she might like to do. The social worker also expressed concern over Daisy's vulnerabilities in her relationship with Sanji. He asked Daisy whether she felt in any way obliged or pressured to remain in the relationship and Daisy said that this was not the case. She explained that Sanji and she had experienced tough but also very good times together and that the relationship was important to her. The staff said at the meeting that they worried about Daisy self-harming at night and having to go to hospital, when there is only one member of staff on duty who is not able to accompany her. The social worker also wondered whether the time in Daisy's life when she had a job was a happier time; Daisy said that she liked having a job and earning money as it gave her a sense of purpose and routine.

It may be suggested that past experiences and trauma have evoked Daisy's difficulties and led to biological, psychological and social problems. Psychological theory suggests that as we go through life, we will develop and be guided by schemas/rules about the world and life depending on our experiences (eg. Lindsay, 1999). In Daisy's case, it is likely that her experience of domestic violence between her parents led to her seeing the world as being unsafe and other people as being intrusive and aggressive. This way of seeing the world possibly led her to only mention the abuse by her foster father hesitantly and led to her tolerance of Sanji's behaviour. Moreover, this fosters the development of mental health problems and maladaptive coping, leading to an interplay between bio-psycho-social difficulties. These difficulties further underpin and maintain Daisy's thoughts/feelings/behaviours/physiological reactions. She may be attending the drop-in centre, feel bored, hopeless and sad and think to herself that

Figure 7.2: Daisy's formulation

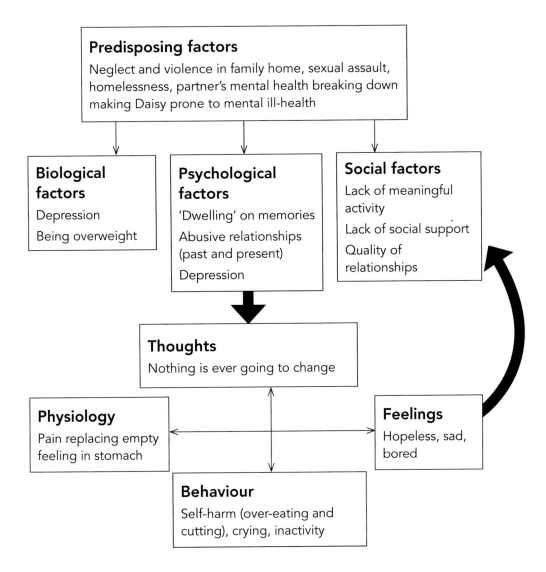

nothing is ever going to change. A negative cycle of thoughts might lead to Daisy noting an empty feeling in her stomach and dwelling on the past, and present difficulties may make this feeling worse. In order to distract herself and feel physiologically different, Daisy may then engage in the cutting and overeating behaviour. This **maladaptive coping strategy** inadvertently leads to maintenance of the bio-psycho-social factors underpinning Daisy's mental health problem.

Interventions relating to Daisy's case

Following multidisciplinary discussions it was agreed that Daisy would receive support from her staff team, the psychiatrist, social worker and psychologist. The psychiatrist continued to support Daisy with medication, regularly liaising with the psychologist who started seeing Daisy for weekly therapy sessions and regularly monitored her mood, affect and coping behaviours. The psychiatrist also supported Daisy to learn about cleaning her wounds, which supported Daisy to be more mindful of injuring herself and maintaining a level of self-care (**individual intervention**).

The psychologist offered a course of therapy to Daisy (**individual intervention**). They decided to work together using a cognitive behavioural framework to help Daisy reduce the occurrence of the maladaptive coping mechanisms and allow her to find more **adaptive ways of coping**. The above formulation is partially derived from the cognitive behaviour therapy (CBT) model (Beck, 1995), which suggests that the interplay between thoughts, feelings, physiological reactions and behaviours maintains psychological difficulties. Psychologists have shown that by altering one of the elements of this maintenance cycle, other elements can also be alleviated. In Daisy's case, the psychologist and Daisy agreed that they would try to reduce her self-harming behaviour ie. the cutting and over eating. They found that Daisy is most likely to react in this way if she thinks about the past and has an empty/unwell feeling in her stomach. Daisy started to use thought-distraction exercises with the help of her staff team to stop dwelling on the past, which helped to reduce the cutting and episodes of overeating. Also, through their confidential relationship, Daisy felt safe with the psychologist. She started talking about her past traumatic experiences, which supported her to reflect on these in a safe environment. Daisy and her psychologist used a box with a lid in the therapy room, which Daisy would 'pour' all her bad memories into and which would be closed and kept safe in the room. This helped Daisy to leave her memories behind.

Daisy's social worker supported her to reduce the social impacts on her mental health. He supported Daisy to find a job in a local shop, which she took pride in and which provided a meaningful structure for her week, as well as financial reward (**intervention aimed at the wider social context of the person**). Daisy also really enjoyed chatting with the customers who were coming to the shop and staff noted her speaking in an animated manner about her experiences when she returned home in the evening. It had became apparent that Sanji's mental health problems made Daisy more vulnerable to experiencing low mood and 'dwelling on her thoughts'. With the support of staff, Sanji and Daisy were able to agree a way in which they could protect themselves from the impact of the other's mental health problems. They agreed that they would have certain 'safe topics of conversation' for when Sanji was not well to prevent Sanji from accusing Daisy of spying on him (**intervention aimed at the immediate social context of the person**). For a while, the social worker also paid for an additional member of staff at night to support Daisy if she had to go to hospital because of cutting. However, this resource was eventually removed as Daisy was coping with her negative thoughts, which led to reducing the cutting much more effectively. Daisy's psychologist also made contact with a generic adult mental health assertive outreach team within Daisy's borough of residence to see whether they could provide further support to Daisy and her staff team. As Daisy's intellectual disabilities are mild, she was accepted for a period of assertive outreach support and was assigned a community psychiatric nurse who specialises in working with people who self-harm (**service structures influencing the delivery of services**).

Conclusion

This chapter aimed to highlight the importance of bio-psycho-social interventions for people with intellectual disabilities and how these can be supported within the four ecological levels highlighted by Dagnan (2007). It also shows that staff and carers play a vital role in supporting people with intellectual disabilities to benefit from bio-psycho-social interventions that promote mental health. This support from staff will further foster people with intellectual disabilities to experience a level of control over the different aspects of their lives, in turn improving their mental health.

Staff and carers are encouraged to support service users to be referred to community intellectual disability teams when they notice changes in the person's behaviour, emotional reactions, physiological presentations and ways of thinking that are not immediately triggered by recent events. It will further be beneficial to support service users to ask for bio-psycho-social formulations of their cases and engage in interventions in accordance with this model.

Summary

▶ Biological, psychological and social factors have a direct impact on someone's mental well being.

▶ A bio-psycho-social approach to working with people with intellectual disabilities promotes mental health.

▶ To sustain the holistic approach to mental heath issues it is important that there is good communication between the person with intellectual disabilities, staff, families and professionals.

References

Beck JS (1995) *Cognitive Therapy: Basics and beyond.* New York: The Guildford Press.

Bronfenbrenner U (1979) *The Ecology of Human Development: Experiments by nature and design.* Cambridge: Massachusetts: Harvard University Press.

Butler AC, Forman EM & Beck AT (2006) The empirical status of cognitive-behavioral therapy: a review of meta-analyses. *Clinical Psychology Review* **26** 17–31.

Dagnan D (2007) Psychosocial interventions for people with intellectual disabilities and mental ill-health. *Current Opinion in Psychiatry* **20** 456–460.

Department of Health (2009) *Valuing People Now: A new three year strategy for people with learning disabilities.* London: DH.

Dodd P & McGinnity M (2003) Psychotherapy and learning disability. *Irish Journal of Psychiatric Medicine* **20** (2) 38–40.

Kopelowicz A, Lieberman RP & Zarate R (2006) Recent advances in social skills training for schizophrenia. *Schizophrenia Bulletin* **32** 12–23.

Krantz DS, Grunberg NE & Baum A (1985) Health psychology. *Annual Review of Psychology* **36** 346–383.

Lindsay WR (1999) Cognitive therapy. *The Psychologist* **12** 238–241.

Marshall M & Rathbone J (2006) Early intervention for psychosis. *Cochrane Database of Systemic Reviews* **4** CD004718.

McGurk SR & Mueser KT (2006) Cognitive and clinical predictors of work outcomes in clients with schizophrenia receiving supported employment services: 4-year follow-up. *Administration and Policy in Mental Health* **33** 598–606.

Pharaoah F, Mari J, Rathbone J & Wong W (2006) Family interventions for schizophrenia. *Cochrane Database of Systemic Reviews* **4** CD000088.

Tarrier N (2005) Cognitive behaviour therapy for schizophrenia: a review of development, evidence and implementation. *Psychotherapy and Psychosomatics* **75** 136–144.

Chapter 8

Policy and mental health care for people with intellectual disabilities

Eddie Chaplin and Lynette Kennedy

Introduction

This chapter describes the history and development of mental health services for people with intellectual disabilities and the recent key policy developments that have influenced mental health care, in particular the Care Programme Approach (CPA). Case studies are used to look at appropriate health care routes and where the CPA is indicated for people with intellectual disabilities and complex mental health needs.

Inequality and inclusion

Government guidance and policy following deinstitutionalisation over the last 30 years has tried to reflect the move towards community care and independent living; including how people access mental health services, how these services are run, and the expectations required of them. However, the reality is that health care is not only more difficult to access for people with intellectual disabilities (Michaels, 2008) but for those who do access it the experience is often unsatisfactory and can, in extremes, be abusive and lead to death. For further information on institutional failings, see *Death by Indifference* (Mencap, 2007), *Closing the Gap* (Disability Rights Commission, 2006) (which examined general failings in primary care) and recent public inquiries into Cornwall and Merton, and Sutton, that reported a history of abuse and failing services (Commission for Healthcare Audit and Inspection, 2006; 2007a). In terms of mental health there are broad variations in the quality of inpatient services for this group, which has led the Healthcare Commission, the UK regulator for intellectual disability services, to call for 'sweeping and sustained' changes to services accessed by people with intellectual disabilities (Commission for Healthcare Audit and Inspection, 2007b).

Mental health services

The first point of access for people with mental health issues is usually their GP at a primary care level. At this stage assessment is carried out and treatments prescribed. The GP will usually manage cases such as mild depression, anxiety or low level symptoms that may not be so serious as to warrant a formal diagnosis but are serious enough to effect the individual's day-to-day functioning and quality of life. Primary care also will focus on mental health promotion, self-management and early intervention. Where the person needs additional input and/or expertise they will be referred to secondary care services. These services are made up of both community teams offering assessment and intervention and high support teams who will generally try and prevent the need for admission. Within this tier of services are inpatient wards for those acutely ill and suffering from severe and enduring mental health problems. For people with intellectual disabilities the preferred option – from Valuing People – is to access general mental health services like anyone else seeking mental health care and that the staff teams are attuned to and aware of their needs (DH, 2001). For some, there is a need for specialist mental health services if it has become clear that general mental health wards are inappropriate. This is usually at a clinical level, and problems include complexity of presentation, the need for more detailed or specialist assessment, and issues of vulnerability (Chaplin *et al,* 2009). Perhaps the earliest example of these services was the mental health in intellectual disabilities service in south-east London, which opened in 1983. The service is comprised of outpatient clinics and a small specialised inpatient assessment and treatment unit based at the Bethlem Royal Hospital. Specialist services today range from traditional models that manage an individual's mental and physical health in one team to specialist mental health services for people that can operate either dependant or independent of general adult mental health teams. This may include virtual services where expertise is added to complement existing mental health services or as stand-alone services which can also provide inreach.

Key policy, guidance and legislation

A number of policy initiatives have been put forward to address the inequality in the delivery of and access to mental health services. These include the National Service Framework for Mental Health (NSF) (DH, 1999b), which sought to end geographical disparity (the 'postcode lottery') by introducing care standards that were to be met across services. In

2004, the Green Light Toolkit was introduced (Foundation for People with Learning Disabilities, 2004). This was in the spirit of the NSF and aimed at ensuring equality for people with intellectual disabilities by setting standards and seeing if local services matched up to these. The toolkit is scored through self-assessment using a traffic light system; red means that the service has not achieved the standard, amber that it has met part of it; and green means it has met the standard. From the original 39 standards, services are currently being assessed on 12 key requirements of the framework. These requirements are:

1. Local partnerships with primary care service

2. Local partnerships with people with intellectual disabilities

3. Local partnerships with carers of people with intellectual disabilities

4. Agreed criteria and boundaries between services

5. Transition protocols

6. Police and criminal justice services

7. CPA – Sharing information and accessing care plans

8. CPA – Person-centred and whole life

9. Culturally specific services

10. Workforce planning

11. Representative workforce

12. Mental health promotion

As well as policy and guidance, there have also been legislative changes to improve safeguards eg.

1. *The Mansell Reports* (1992; 2007) address the needs of people with challenging behaviour and/or mental health problems in relation to service development and advise how commissioners should respond to this group. See also *Commissioning Specialist Adult Learning Disability Health Services: Good practice guidance* (DH, 2007); *Commissioning Person-centred, Cost-effective, Local Support for People with Learning Disabilities* (Emerson & Robertson, 2008).

2. Offenders with intellectual disabilities and those at risk of offending. This group is mentioned in *Valuing People Now* (DH, 2009) although more specific guidance has come from *The Bradley Report* (2009). Among its 80 plus recommendations it has called for earlier screening in police stations and prisons so that vulnerable people can be identified earlier

to get the support they require; earlier diversion; and a decrease in the assessment and transfer time between the criminal justice system and health placements.

3. Mental Health Act (2007). Changes have included the introduction of advocacy amendments to the provisions for displacing and appointing nearest relatives and the introduction of new community treatment orders for certain patients.

4. Mental Capacity Act (2005) in England and Wales, which offers guidance and frameworks in which to make decisions in the person's best interests where they lack capacity to make a decision. Among the aims of the act is:

   ▶ to allow adults to make as many decisions as they can for themselves

   ▶ to enable adults to make advance decisions about whether they would like future medical treatment

   ▶ to allow adults to appoint, in advance of losing mental capacity, another person to make decisions about personal welfare or property on their behalf at a future date

   ▶ to ensure an independent mental capacity advocate to support someone about serious medical treatment, or about hospital, care home or residential accommodation.

5. For those requiring multi-agency input for mental health care, the Care Programme Approach (CPA) brings together the individuals needed to deliver a person's mental health care package and manages risk to self and others where it exists. The implementation of the CPA is the responsibility of a care co-ordinator and those assigned to deliver the agreed care package.

Box 8.1: What is the Care Programme Approach (CPA)?

The CPA has been part of mental health services since April 1991; but unlike medication or counselling it is not something you take or something that is done to you. Being 'on' or 'off' CPA should not stop you receiving a particular service that you need. CPA is simply a term for describing the process of how mental health services assess your needs, plan ways to meet them and check that they are being met.

From *Refocusing the Care Programme Approach* (DH, 2008)

History of the CPA

The Care Programme Approach was introduced in England in 1991 (DH, 1990). It required health and social services to put in place specified arrangements for the care and treatment of mentally ill people in the community. The CPA was introduced following a number of high profile serious incidents involving people with mental health problems. The subsequent inquiries highlighted failures across services and organisations to communicate and work together.

Since its introduction the CPA has undergone a number of changes. Shortly after the CPA was introduced there was a tragic incident involving a mental health patient called Christopher Clunis and a member of the public. This caused a rethink of how the CPA was implemented. The resulting report highlighted a familiar story and stated: *'We do not single out just one person, service or agency for particular blame'* and *'in our view the problem was cumulative; it was one failure or missed opportunity after another'* (Ritchie *et al*, 1994). The blame was shared between psychiatrists, social workers, the police, community psychiatric nurses, the Crown Prosecution Service, the Probation Service, hostel staff, and private sector care workers. The report described a range of violent acts over four years. The last one was a week before and involved weapons where a man was injured with a screwdriver and later that day a group of adults and children were chased by Clunis with a screwdriver. The absence of joined-up working between agencies meant each incident was treated in isolation, so a strategy was never put in place to address the issues. The report recommended the introduction of a supervision register which would examine risk as part of the CPA process. It had four parts: name; nature of risk; key worker and relevant professional; *Introduction of Supervision Registers for Mentally Ill People from 1 April 1996* (NHS Executive, 1994). A year later *Building Bridges* (DH, 1995) was published and defined the four main elements of the CPA:

▶ assessment

▶ a care plan

▶ care co-ordination

▶ review.

In 1999 *Modernising the CPA* (DH, 1999a) was published, which saw the integration of the CPA and care management for those in specialist mental health services. It also introduced two levels of the CPA: standard and enhanced, and the term 'key worker' changed to 'care co-ordinator'. The supervision register – regarded by many as duplication and something that was more likely to be used in people from ethnic minorities – was abolished along with the requirement to review care plans every six months, with the expectation that review and evaluation would be ongoing and the requirement that following each review the date of the next meeting would be set. Another change was the requirement of a regular audit of the CPA process. The aim of this was to provide a greater responsiveness to change through risk assessments, with crisis and contingency plans.

Refocusing the Care Programme Approach

In 2008 *Refocusing the Care Programme Approach* (DH, 2008) was published. Among the changes introduced in the report was the abolition of two levels of the CPA. From 2008 the CPA was only for those defined as 'complex' or 'high risk' and those whose care was being provided across agencies. The review provided more information for those using services.

New Horizons (DH, 2010) saw an end to the National Service Framework and announced the arrival of the recovery model as standard across mental health services. This puts more emphasis on the role of the CPA care co-ordinator to ensure that the process is recovery-focused and user-centred. The recovery approach is for everyone who needs ongoing mental health care and support where a number of agencies are involved. Recovery principles go past managing symptoms and illness; they also help the person define their goals, with hope as a key concept. It provides a view of the person and looks at a journey based on expectations and attitudes of the person. To that end it has its ups and downs where the journey breaks down. Effective recovery requires a robust support system from all of those around the person where they enjoy and take advantage of society and their environment so that they are included and feel valued.

Do people with intellectual disabilities need to be on the CPA?

Some people who work with, or advocate for, people with intellectual disabilities argue that there are already frameworks in place that look at the needs of individuals and argue that the CPA conflicts with these, and in particular individual choice. The difference is that the CPA is statutory, with its main priority being risk to self and others, so that the individual and those around them are protected. The issue of choice for this group needs to be placed in context and ensure that it is both realistic and appropriate in terms of the risk management plan.

The Care Programme Approach in practice

In practice the CPA is a dynamic process requiring the regular assessment and review of clients, usually after six months. It reviews clinical presentation and measures the effectiveness of the interventions outlined in the care plan. If there are concerns about clients then the CPA may be called at any time.

The CPA is designed to ensure that a person's needs are assessed and met by health and social services. As part of the CPA the person receives a written care plan. This outlines what is expected from clinicians and professionals and outlines the help and support that the person will receive. The CPA is confidential to those involved, but to help with the assessment the person is also asked if they would be happy for their family or carer to be contacted to be part of the process. The carer, where involved, will also get a plan which is reviewed yearly. This is specific to their needs in supporting the person. The care plan is updated at the regular review meetings which are organised and facilitated by the care co-ordinator (this can be a nurse, social worker, doctor, psychologist, occupational therapist, or at times and with agreement, a service in the community that is involved with the individual). Reviews take place as required and will be set according to the person's needs. Within the care plan are contingency and crisis plans. This is not only for those involved in the person's care, but for the person so that they are aware of the plan and what additional support is available in times of crisis. Some examples of how CPA is decided can be found in the appendix of this chapter.

Assessing health and social care needs

The CPA team is brought together by the care co-ordinator and meets to discuss and assess the person's health and social care needs. The aim is to agree a plan of care, including the support and services that will be provided and what to do and who to contact in times of crisis. The team can also discuss wider health issues such as the person's health action plan, if appropriate. The CPA needs to be accessible so that information is understood and the person's voice can be heard. To help with this people should be encouraged to bring their carer, advocate or a friend along for support. All care plans should be accessible to the individual ie. using appropriate media. This might include symbols, audio, appropriate fonts, or plain English. There is no set format so each organisation should have its own guidance. In some circumstances people who are normally able to speak up for themself may be unable to express themselves. An example of this is when someone becomes unwell and may lose touch with reality. In these circumstances there are 'advance directives' or 'statements'. The advanced statement is made by the person and witnessed, when they are well. The advanced statement outlines the person's wishes as to how they want to be treated when they are unable to advocate for themselves eg. types of medication preferred, not to have ECT etc. Although the CPA aims to put the person at the centre of the process there will be times when they are not in agreement with the outcome. If the person is unhappy with the outcome they should be informed about where they may get further support eg. an advocate. In the appendix of this chapter there are two examples of people who need to be on CPA and two that do not, to illustrate mental health care pathways. The CPA should be integral to the recovery process and personalisation agenda with the person at the centre of the process. In 2004, NIHME published the 10 shared capabilities to guide good practice. They were developed in consultation with service users and carers together with practitioners to show what person-centred practice and services looked like and came up with the following list of capabilities:

1. Working in partnership

2. Practising ethically

3. Respecting diversity

4. Promoting recovery

5. Challenging inequality

6. Identifying people's needs and strengths

7. Providing user-centred care

8. Making a difference

9. Promoting safety and positive risk taking

10. Personal development and life-long learning

(NIHME, 2004)

Conclusion

Currently, there is inequality in the delivery of mental health care for people with intellectual disabilities, although there have been attempts to address this through policy guidance and legislation. In the last 20 years there has been the addition of specialist services for people with intellectual disabilities and mental health problems, and more recently standards through the Green Light Toolkit on what people should expect from mental health services. Another issue has been the need for joined-up services and multi-agency working; the CPA came about as a result of a number of high profile incidents where this had been deficient. The CPA was to provide a care co-ordinator with the responsibility to construct and deliver a care plan across agencies. Since its inception the CPA has become more person-centred with the adoption of the recovery model. For people with intellectual disabilities accessing mental health care across agencies is the same as for others, albeit with additional support to make the process accessible.

Summary

▶ Since the introduction of Valuing People in 2001, there has been a plethora of guidance relating to people with intellectual disabilities in a number of policy areas, including mental health, service development and for those who offend.

▶ In terms of mental health to ensure equal access and entry to services for people with intellectual disabilities, there has been the introduction of the Green Light Toolkit, based upon the National Services Framework for Mental Health.

▶ In terms of managing mental health for people requiring multi-agency input, there is the Care Programme Approach, which brings together an individual's treatment and risk management programme.

▶ The CPA is now being implemented in line with recovery principles with the procedure becoming more accessible across mental health services as awareness grows to the needs of people with intellectual disabilities.

Appendix

Below are four cases that illustrate various care experiences and indicate when the CPA is necessary.

Case 1: Stacey

Stacey is 21-years-old and is attending Thord College to do a computer course. She is known to intellectual disabilities services and her community nurse has observed that Stacey has not 'been herself' recently. When the nurse asks Stacey how she is, she says she is 'feeling sad'. After talking for some time the nurse finds out that Stacey has been feeling like this for a while, although she cannot say how long. She is also missing college but is unable to give a reason for either how she feels or why she is missing college. Stacey's mother is able to add to the picture and reports that her daughter has been off her food and is finding it difficult to sleep. The nurse recommends that Stacey should see her GP who starts her on antidepressants and refers her to the local psychiatrist. By the time her appointment comes Stacey is feeling not so bad and her mother has noticed an improvement. The psychiatrist makes a diagnosis of clinical depression and confirms the GP is doing the right thing with regards to treatment, and that Stacey may also benefit from counselling at the health centre.

Should Stacey be under the CPA?

Although Stacey has had a number of people involved in her care; the GP and resources within the health centre can successfully treat her depression. The early treatment and good response indicate that a good prognosis (outcome) is likely for her. There are also factors present that offer stability, such as her mother and her college course.

Case 2: Leroy

Leroy is a 30-year-old man with a history of challenging behaviour. This is characterised by bouts of self-injury and lashing out at staff when they remind him to attend to his personal hygiene. More recently the house manger has noticed an increase in aggression towards staff, both in intensity and in frequency with the behaviour now appearing random with no noticeable antecedents. The staff are increasingly scared and call upon the local mental health care team to prescribe medication to stop these behaviours. After making an assessment the team feel that medication is not indicated as there is no mental illness, but there is a need to get at the root of why Leroy's behaviour has changed. They recommend that he is referred to the local psychology and behavioural support team to look at alternative ways of managing his aggression. Following further assessment it is clear that the increase in aggression has coincided with a number of changes in staff and routine, which has impacted on the consistency of the staff approach towards Leroy. Following a new programme aimed at providing a structure and limits, Leroy's behaviour improves. In spite of the evidence, some of the staff are still worried.

Should Leroy be under the CPA?

Although Leroy's behaviour has become a challenge to those living with and supporting him, he is not suffering from any mental illness. The presence of a psychologist in this case does not indicate this. In this case it is appropriate that Leroy is monitored by this community team and offered extra support during this time.

Case 3: Michael

Michael is a 25-year-old man who is about to be discharged from hospital. His admission began when he was brought in by police after being found naked walking down the high street. On admission Michael was mute for several days and when he did speak he expressed that he was being controlled by Pokemon. He is put on medication for psychosis and after a couple of weeks there is a noticeable improvement in his mental state. One problem is that Michael keeps going up to people gesturing to fight them and adopting strange postures. This has made him vulnerable to attack. To help this psychology, the occupational therapist and nurses from the ward have devised a programme to keep Michael safe and try and find out more about his behaviour to see if it is linked to his mental health or other factors.

Should Michael be under the CPA?

Michael is leaving hospital with a number of questions that still need to be addressed around his vulnerability and the function of his unusual behaviours and whether they are occurring in the context of a mental health problem. Given that he is new to medication, this will also need to be monitored along with any changes in his mental state or functioning, which will need to be completed across a number of agencies. Therefore, it is likely that Michael will be monitored by CPA.

Case 4: Olivia

Olivia is already on CPA. At her review the team are concerned that she is deteriorating. Olivia has bipolar disorder and recently become increasingly erratic, being unable to make decisions. Staff are also worried she might be giving her money away and be vulnerable to sexual predators as her behaviour has become more sexualised and suggestive. On hearing these concerns Olivia disagrees and tells the meeting that she is above them and knows best how to handle her life. Olivia is subject to a community treatment order, which means that she can be recalled to the hospital, where she was earlier in the year. The team are reluctant to do this, as knowing Olivia, these episodes can be relatively short-lived with support and adjustments to her medication. Taking Olivia's wishes into account and with her agreement to comply, the care co-ordinator arranges for her community care package to be intensified by bringing in the 24-hour high support service, ensuring compliance with medication and for Olivia to agree to be accompanied when out. This would be reviewed weekly by the nurse, residential home staff and psychiatrist, who would feed back to others involved in her care. Failure to comply would result in re-admission.

Should Olivia be under the CPA?
Olivia is already on CPA but her example shows how risk can be managed with agreement from the individual and temporary increase in resources to try and prevent unnecessary readmission to hospital.

References

Bradley Lord (2009) *Lord Bradley's Review of People with Mental Health Problems or Learning Disabilities in the Criminal Justice System.* London: Department of Health.

Chaplin E, O'Hara J, Holt G & Bouras N (2009) Mental health services for people with intellectual disability: challenges to care delivery. *British Journal of Learning Disabilities* **37** 157–164.

Commission for Healthcare Audit and Inspection (2006) *Investigation into the Provision of Services for People with Learning Disabilities at Cornwall Partnership NHS Trust.* London: Commission of Healthcare Audit and Inspection.

Commission for Healthcare Audit and Inspection (2007a) *Investigation into the Service for People with Learning Disabilities Provided by Sutton and Merton Primary Care Trust.* London: Commission of Healthcare Audit and Inspection.

Commission for Healthcare Audit and Inspection (2007b) *A Life Like No Other*. London: Commission of Healthcare Audit and Inspection.

Department of Constitutional Affairs (2005) *Mental Capacity Act*. London: TSO.

Department of Health (1990) *Caring for People: The Care Programme Approach for people with a mental illness referred to specialist mental health services*. Joint Health/Social Services Circular. C(90)23/LASSL(90)11. London: DH.

Department of Health (1995) *Building Bridges: A guide to arrangements for interagency working for the care and protection of seriously mentally ill people*. London: TSO.

Department of Health (1999a) *Effective Care Co-ordination in Mental Health Services: Modernising the Care Programme Approach*. London: Department of Health.

Department of Health (1999b) *A National Service Framework for Mental Health: Modern Standards and Service Models*. London: DH.

Department of Health (2001) *Valuing People: A new strategy for learning disability for the 21st century*. London: DH.

Department of Health (2007) *Commissioning Specialist Adult Learning Disability Health Services: Good practice guidance*. London: DH.

Department of Health (2008) *Refocusing the Care Programme Approach: Policy and positive practice guidance*. London: Department of Health.

Department of Health (2009) *Valuing People Now: A new three-year strategy for people with learning disabilities*. London: Department of Health.

Department of Health (2010) *New Horizons: A shared vision for mental health*. London: Department of Health.

Disability Rights Commission (2006) *Equal Treatment: Closing the gap*. Stratford-upon-Avon: Disability Rights Commission.

Emerson E & Robertson J (2008) *Commissioning Person-Centred, Cost Effective, Local Support for People with Learning Disabilities.* Lancaster, UK: Lancaster University Social Care Institute for Excellence.

Foundation for People with Learning Disabilities, Valuing People Support Team and National Institute for Mental Health (2004) *Green Light: How good are your mental health services for people with intellectual disabilities?* London: Mental Health Foundation.

Mansell JL (1992) *Services for People with Learning Disability and Challenging Behaviour or Mental Health Needs.* London: HMSO.

Mansell JL (2007) *Mansell Report 2: Services for People with Learning Disabilities and Challenging Behaviour or Mental Health Needs: Report of a project group (rev. ed.).* London: Department of Health.

Mencap (2007) *Death by Indifference.* London: MENCAP.

Michaels J (2008) *Healthcare for All: Report of the independent inquiry into access to healthcare for people with learning disabilities.* London: Department of Health.

National Health Service Management Executive (1994) *Introduction of Supervision Registers for Mentally Ill People from 1 April 1996. HSG (94) 5.* London: HMSO.

National Institute for Mental Health (2004) *10 Essential Shared Capabilities: A framework for the whole mental health workforce.* London: National Institute for Mental Health.

Ritchie JH (1994) *The Report of the Inquiry into the Care and Treatment of Christopher Clunis.* London: The Stationery Office.

Chapter 9

Neuropsychiatric disorders and epilepsy

Max Pickard and Bridget MacDonald

Introduction

People with intellectual disabilities are at increased risk of various psychiatric conditions (as detailed in other chapters) as well as epilepsy. The relationship between psychiatric and neurological disorders is complex and not always clear cut. This chapter will consider epilepsy, its relationship to psychiatric problems, and other neuropsychiatric conditions as they present in people with intellectual disabilities.

> **The expert opinion**
>
> 'It must be really frightening having seizures. People need medication to help them and support from their family and friends.'

Epilepsy

Epilepsy is a tendency towards recurrent episodes of altered movements, cognitions or behaviour caused by abnormal electrical discharges in the brain. It is common, affecting 1 in 50 people with intellectual disabilities over a lifetime, while 1 in 200 of the general population has active epilepsy. Epilepsy is even more common in people with intellectual disabilities and may be the cause of intellectual disabilities in certain syndromes. Additionally, people with intellectual disabilities may have more variable and frequent seizures, and seizures that are more resistant to treatment (Cardoza & Kerr, 2010).

Seizure types

Seizures can be divided into generalised (affecting all the brain) or focal/localised (affecting only part of the brain). For a more complete discussion on the classification of seizures, see the International League Against Epilepsy (ILAE) (1981), although the classification is currently being reviewed by the ILAE. Youtube.com has some good educational videos, which can help you to recognise seizures.

Generalised seizure types

Primary generalised tonic clonic seizure: Without warning, the person extends their body and limbs. Sometimes there is a cry at onset as air is pushed out of the chest, incontinence as the abdominal wall contracts, or blood from the mouth as the jaw clamps shut. There are then tense synchronous jerks which can start as fairly large fastbeats but diminish in size and speed. 98% of these seizures will be over within two minutes. The person will often be very sleepy for a further 30 minutes and will have no recall for the event.

Cortical myoclonus seizure: Appear as very brief startles – like when someone makes you 'jump out of your skin'. Sometimes, there is apparent discontinuity of consciousness.

Typical absences seizure: The person goes blank for 20–30 seconds, remaining in the same posture as at onset. There are no added features of chewing, postures or gestures, which would make such an episode a complex partial seizure.

Tonic seizures: Brief tightening of axial muscles (under 10 seconds) often causing rigid falls 'like a tree' and injury. These may occur in bouts.

Atonic seizures: Abrupt, brief loss of muscle tone often causing falls and facial injury as the person falls in a limp heap on the floor.

Focal onset or localisation related seizures

Simple partial seizures: There is no impairment of consciousness.

Complex partial seizures: With impaired consciousness (from mild to profound) secondarily generalised seizure – the seizure spreads from one bit of the brain, which may produce an aura and then affects the whole brain, becoming indistinguishable from a primary generalised tonic clonic seizure (as above).

In some people there may be multiple areas of the brain that trigger seizures.

The after-effects

After a seizure (which is termed 'post ictal') people can feel very grumpy, hungover and have a headache. They may desperately need to sleep. Some people experience post ictal symptoms to a greater degree than others. Even in the same person, one seizure may have a worse aftermath than another. Other phenomena which can be seen are post ictal aggression and rage, fugue states (where the person may not communicate and be fully functioning, but continues with day-to-day tasks), and non-convulsive status epilepticus (partial seizures that last for longer than 30 minutes). These vary in length from minutes to days

Investigating seizures

Epilepsy can, to a degree, be investigated with neuroimaging (such as CT or MRI scanning of the brain) or EEG (electroencephalogram) recording. It should be noted that people with intellectual disabilities, particularly those who also have autism, may well find investigations frightening and even intolerable. Carers and hospital staff can try to put the person at ease by showing pictures of the process, providing careful explanation before the procedure, limiting time in busy waiting areas, and keeping noise and sensory stimulation to an appropriate level (as much as possible) during the procedure. On occasion, a one-off dose of a sedative may be helpful for brain scanning, but not EEG (as it will alter the reading).

However, the diagnosis of epilepsy and related conditions such as NEAD (see below) vitally hinges on good quality history, ideally from observers who witness the seizures. Medical investigations, as above, are no substitute for this. The importance of good quality recording cannot be over emphasised – it is this information that is the cornerstone of diagnosis and treatment, and accurate descriptions of the seizures are essential. See Table 9.1.

Table 9.1: Important points for recording seizures/attacks
1. What was the environment like? Was the person under any stress?
2. Did the person describe or display any symptoms prior to the attack? Were they confused/irritable/depressed/elated? Did they feel like they were going to have a seizure? Was there an aura?
3. What motor/physical activity occurred? In what order? In what parts of the body? For how long?
4. Was the person responsive to voice or communication? How long were they unresponsive for?
5. Did the person fall? Did they injure themself?
6. How did the person feel or behave after the seizure? (Drowsiness is common) For how long?

In addition, frequency of seizures should be recorded as this will provide a guide to how severe the problem is and the response to treatment.

Epilepsy: psychiatric issues

It is, as yet, not entirely clear if and how epilepsy impacts on mental health in people with intellectual disabilities. Some studies suggest epilepsy is linked with increased day-to-day impairment (Smith & Matson, 2010; McGrowther *et al,* 2006) with no link with psychiatric illness (Mathews *et al,* 2008; Deb, 1997) or even that epilepsy (or seizures) may provide a modest protection against mental illness (Ring *et al,* 2007; Cooper *et al,* 2007). However (and confusingly), among people with epilepsy, intellectual disability has been found to be the major risk factor in developing a psychiatric disorder (Mastuura *et al,* 2003; 2005). The situation is even less clear for other neurological difficulties.

Nevertheless, the presence of epilepsy does clearly present with several challenges from a psychiatric point of view, as summarised in Table 9.2.

Considering the latter point, the psychiatric symptoms associated with seizure activity are collectively termed peri-ictal and cover a wide variety of symptoms. In people with intellectual disabilities, these complex and vague symptoms may be hard to describe. They may be communicated in

Mental Health in Intellectual Disabilities: A reader (fourth edition) © Pavilion Publishing (Brighton) Ltd 2011

Table 9.2: Important interactions between epilepsy and mental health

1. Anticonvulsant medication can raise or lower levels of psychiatric medication.

2. Psychiatric medication can raise or lower levels of anticonvulsant medication.

3. Many psychiatric medications (particularly antipsychotic medications) can lower seizure threshold, possibly making seizures more likely or more severe (BNF, 2010).

4. Anticonvulsant medication may have psychiatric (as well as other) side effects, including impaired cognitive performance (akin to drunkenness), mood disturbance, clumsiness, behavioural disturbance, and psychosis. This can occur intermittently (usually after taking tablets) – a phenomenon known as peak dose toxicity (BNF, 2010).

5. Seizures can cause psychiatric symptoms either during, prior to, or after, the actual seizure.

terms of feeling odd or peculiar, and disturbances of mood or behaviour may be noticed by carers or friends. Sometimes, hallucinations or other frank psychotic symptoms can be present.

Confusion is a clinical term that indicates disorientation (not knowing where you are, or what time it is) and possible lower level of consciousness. This is often present before or after a seizure.

It is worth noting that these psychiatric symptoms can be present before and after a seizure. Most seizures involve a loss of consciousness, so these symptoms will not be present during the actual seizure itself.

Non-epileptic attack disorder (NEAD)

Non-epileptic attack disorder (NEAD) involves an apparent seizure – like state without the pathological brain state that occurs in epilepsy. It was previously known as 'pseudo seizures'.
The definitive way to diagnose NEAD is to capture an attack while monitoring brain activity with an EEG. This is usually done by video

telemetry: videoing the person while they have an EEG recording done. Video telemetry requires an inpatient admission and normally takes a few days. Hopefully, an attack will occur during this period.

While video telemetry provides strong evidence, NEADs often show some classical features – the attacks often differ from classical epileptic seizures, and there is not total loss of consciousness. If there is a fall, or shaking, it will occur in a relatively safe manner. Shaking may be one sided or isolated. It may stop on command and the person may be able to communicate to a variable degree.

The risk factors for NEAD in the intellectual disabilities population are not clear, although intellectual disabilities may be a factor in itself. A history of trauma or bereavement is often present in the general adult population with NEAD and it is reasonable to suspect a similar association in the learning disablities population. For a review, see Reuber and Elger (2003).

It is important not to view NEAD as 'malingering' or 'attention seeking'. Current thinking views NEAD as a dissociative disorder – an unconscious process that the person has no control over. In psychoanalytic terms, dissociation is a primitive defence mechanism where the conscious brain can 'switch off' from various parts of routine function under duress.

As a non-epileptic attack can often occur when a person is feeling neglected or stressed, it is only natural to be tempted into labelling it as a conscious 'attention-seeking' process, and thus get angry with the person. This is unhelpful as it just reinforces the cycle. At present, treatment modes of NEAD in people with intellectual disabilities is unclear – although specialised cognitive behaviour therapy techniques have been used for NEAD in people without intellectual disabilities.

Dysexecutive syndrome

Dysexecutive syndrome is caused by specific problems, such as damage to, or developmental problems of the frontal lobes of the brain. Hence, it is sometimes referred to as 'frontal lobe syndrome'. It is not, as such, treatable. It gives rise to specific symptoms that can mimic psychiatric illness as well as being distressing to the person and challenging to services.

Table 9.3: Symptoms of dysexecutive syndrome

1. Rapidly changing mood from moment to moment (hence, it can be confused with bipolar affective disorder, which involves mood disturbance that persists over many days or weeks)

2. High degree of impulsivity and/or recklessness (possibly including aggression and irritability)

3. Very poor forward planning

4. Highly distractible

5. Disinhibited

6. Perseveration (getting 'stuck' on same topic or task)

7. Memory problems (short-term and working memory)

8. Short attention span (poor concentration)

There is some overlap between frontal lobe problems and attention deficit disorder, which is unsurprising as particular areas of the frontal lobe are implicated in attention deficit disorder.

Other common neuropsychiatric disorders

Vertigo

Vertigo is defined as a sensation of movement in relation to the world in the absence of such movement (or movement of the world in relation to the subject in its absence). It is a nasty feeling producing nausea, a feeling of falling, sweating, and anxiety. In the author's experience, in people with intellectual disability it is commonly due to peak dose drug toxicity or benign paroxysmal positional vertigo (BPPV).

In BPPV during head movement each ear is telling the brain that it is doing a movement incompatible with the other ear. The brain fails to compute this bizarre information and the person feels dizzy briefly (<20seconds) on abrupt head movements eg. turning over in bed, bending over, crossing the road. This can happen many times a day. Afterwards the person feels washed out and light-headed as well as worried about what is going on. It may occur spontaneously but a minor head injury – easily sustained during a seizure – is a common cause (Davies & Luxon, 1995). Treatment is with vestibular sedatives such as prochlorperizine or betaserc and referral for Crawthorne Cooksey exercises.

In people with intellectual disabilities, vertigo symptoms may be quite difficult to describe and may even manifest as challenging behaviour. However, careful observation and communication techniques may help – particularly noting how BPPV can occur with sudden head movements. Vertigo symptoms might even serve as a self-stimulatory function if they can be elicited on head movement.

Hyperventilation

In theory, we all breathe exactly as much as we need. However, in response to anxiety or habit, some people breathe too fast. This makes the blood alkaline and causes shifts in extra cellular calcium – an ion important for nerve conduction. This can occur abruptly in the very fast breathing of a panic attack but also more slowly and less noticeably when the breath rate is slightly above normal (>15 breaths per minute) for protracted periods. Classically, one feels light-headed, has a dry mouth, tingling around the mouth, palpitations, jelly legs and can faint and feel tired all the time. In practice, people do not usually have all the symptoms. Getting the person to breathe very fast for two minutes and comparing the symptoms produced to those experienced day-to-day may help some people, if they have good insight and can reflect on the sensations this brings about. Management includes a short-term measure – breathing in and out of a paper bag – and in the longer-term, physiotherapy to aid the breathing pattern and dealing with triggers and management of anxiety (Gardner, 1996).

Migraine

Migraine affects one in five women and slightly fewer men. People with epilepsy experience more migraines than the rest of the population and this may be post ictal (after a seizure). Migraine with an aura (symptoms occurring before the full blown headache) is less common. The most frequent aura is of bright flashes of light migrating across the visual field lasting 20 minutes. However, all sorts of odd phenomena are experienced – vertigo, loss of, or double vision, hallucinations and distortions, or altered strength or feeling down one side. These complex migraines are well described elsewhere (Sacks, 1992). Migraine should be treated by avoiding precipitants such as seizures, anxiety, and sleep deprivation. Acute attacks can be managed with painkillers and anti-nausea agents but if these are needed more than three days a week, or the migraines are particularly severe, prophylactic agents should be considered.

Sleep disorders (sleep apnoea)

Sleep can be disturbed as a result of psychiatric conditions (such as anxiety and depression) and physical symptoms, particularly pain. Some specific conditions can also cause sleep disturbance – the most common (adult) one being sleep apnoea. This generally happens in overweight people with short necks and small jaws as they block their upper airway as they drop off and their muscles relax. It is associated with loud, irregular grunting/snoring as the person wakes up briefly and then falls back to sleep. It is common in people on anti-epilepsy tablets and those with vagal nerve stimulators. People on such medication can get very sleepy and cannot stop themselves from falling asleep during the day. Their thinking may be profoundly impaired by fatigue and they may appear to lose consciousness abruptly as they go into brief 'catnaps' even while standing or sitting. The treatments include weight loss, specialised apparatus worn at night (positive pressure ventilation),. which can be very poorly tolerated, and even learning to play the didgeridoo! However, more unusual sleep problems can occur, including night terrors or sleep paralysis, nocturnal hallucinations and REM sleep disorders. The interpretation of intermittent behavioural disturbance at night may require an overnight stay at hospital and video telemetry (as described above).

Space occupying legions

Rarely, various illnesses can cause what is termed a 'space occupying legion within the skull'. The most dramatic cause is a brain tumour although there are others. Symptoms can vary widely according to the location of the tumour, but they are almost always slowly progressive, in that they appear over some weeks or months (or even years), and get worse. It is impossible to do justice to the diagnosis and treatment of space occupying legions in this chapter, but it is worth noting that they are an occasional cause of neuropsychiatric symptoms and should be considered if the symptoms are unusual in nature or pattern. Neuroimaging (such as a CT or MRI scan) is an effective way of investigating for space occupying legions.

Conclusion

People with intellectual disabilities are at an increased risk of a wide range of neurological, psychiatric and neuropsychiatric problems, and it can be difficult to disentangle them. Aside from the inherent complexity of these issues, people with intellectual disabilities may have communication difficulties, which can be particularly problematic for describing the sometimes vague and elusive symptoms that accompany neuropsychiatric conditions.

It is therefore extremely helpful for carers to be alert and vigilant, and make sure detailed, descriptive accounts of behaviour, emotional states, symptoms, and environmental triggers are made. These are invaluable and in many cases are the main diagnostic tool for clinicians.

Given the high prevalence of these co-morbid conditions, it is always worth considering neuropsychiatric conditions when managing psychiatric and behavioural problems in intellectual disabilities. While they may not be common, missing them will likely result in an inaccurate and ineffective (and possibly harmful) approach to management.

Summary

▶ Epilepsy and neuropsychiatric conditions are more common in people with intellectual disabilities.

▶ Epilepsy may cause a wide range of psychiatric symptoms, which are often intermittent.

▶ Drug management of epilepsy and psychiatric illness together may lead to complex interactions and side effect problems.

▶ Detailed, accurate, and descriptive records of seizures and related problems (by observers) are the cornerstone of managing these conditions.

References

British National Formulary (2010) *British National Formulary* **61**. London: BMJ Group.

Cardoza B & Kerr M (2010) Disorders of the nervous system and neurodevelopment. In: J O'Hara, J McCarthy & N Bouras (Eds). *Intellectual Disability and Ill Health*. Cambridge: Cambridge University Press.

Commission on Classification and Terminology of the International League Against Epilepsy (1981) Proposal for revised clinical and electroencephalographic classification of epileptic seizures. *Epilepsia* **22** 489–501.

Cooper SA, Smiley E, Morrison J, Allan L, Williamson A, Finlayson J, Jackson A & Mantry D (2007) Psychosis and adults with intellectual disabilities. Prevalence, incidence, and related factors. *Social Psychiatry and Psychiatric Epidemiology* **42** (7) 530–536.

Davies RA & Luxon LM (1995) Dizziness following head injury: a neuro-otological study. *Journal of Neurology* **242** (4) 222–230.

Deb S (1997) Mental disorders in adults with mental retardation and epilepsy. *Comprehensive Psychiatry* **38** (3) 179–184.

Gardner WN (1996) The pathophysiology of hyperventilation disorders. *Chest* **109** 516–534.

Mathews T, Weston N, Baxter H, Felce D & Kerr M (2008) A general-practice based prevalence study of epilepsy among adults with intellectual disabilities and of its association with psychiatric disorder, behaviour disturbance and carer stress. *Journal of Intellectual Disability Research* **52** (2)163–173.

Matsuura M, Oana Y, Kato M, Kawana A, Kan R, Kubota H, Nakano T & Hara T & Horikawa N (2003) A multicentre strudy on the prevalence of psychiatric disorders among new referrals for epilepsy in Japan. *Epilepsia* **44** (1) 107–114.

Matsuura M, Adachi N, Muramatsu R, Kato M, Onuma T, Okubo Y, Oana Y & Hara T (2005) Intellectual disability and psychotic disorders of adult epilepsy. *Epilepsia* **46** (1) 11–14.

McGrowther CW, Bhaumik S, Thorp CF, Hauck A, Branford D & Watson JM (2006) Epilepsy in adults with intellectual disabilities: prevalence, associations and service implications. *Seizure* **15** (6) 376–386.

Reuber M & Elger CE (2003) Psychogenic non-epileptic seizures : review and update: *Epilepsy and Behaviour* **4** (3) 205–216.

Ring H, Zia A, Lindeman S & Himlok K (2007) Interactions between seizure frequency, psychopathology, and severity of intellectual disability in a population with epilepsy and a intellectual disability. *Epilepsy and Behaviour* **11** (1) 92–97.

Sacks O (1992) *Migraine*. London: Vintage Books.

Smith KR & Matson JL (2010) Psychopathology: differences among adults with intellectually disabilities, cormorbid autism spectrum problems and epilepsy. *Research in Developmental Disabilities* **31** (3) 743–749.

Chapter 10

Staff support and training

Peter Woodward and Steve Hardy

Introduction

This chapter discusses some of the issues involved in providing effective support and training for staff who work with people with intellectual disabilities who may have additional mental health problems.

> **The expert opinion**
>
> 'Staff need training on mental health, like how to tell if something is wrong, and about medication.'

Supporting the staff team

The majority of people with intellectual disabilities live with their families or independently, but a significant number, especially those with complex needs such as mental health problems, may live in accommodation with paid staff. As staff are central to the delivery of services, they should be considered as one of the most important assets, particularly as staff salaries constitute a significant part of service expenditure. As such, the quality of staff performance should be a prime concern in light of scarce resources (Rose *et al*, 2005).

Staff performance can be affected by a range of factors and this includes the stress that individuals experience and the support available. There is little evidence directly related to stress experienced by staff working with people with intellectual disabilities who have mental health problems, but there is a wealth of research when it relates to behaviour that is described as challenging. Some research has found that there is an association between staff stress and challenging behaviour (eg. Hatton *et al,* 1995; Rose, 1999). However, Hatton *et al* (1999) suggest that it is not the challenging behaviour itself that causes the stress, rather it is the organisational culture and the environment in which staff work.

Recognising stress

Menaghan and Merves (1984) define stress as a 'discrepancy between environmental demands and individual capabilities'. A limited amount of stress can be beneficial to individuals. In fact, some may thrive on it. Stress may 'keep people on their toes' and help improve performance. But, on the other hand, unwanted or too much stress can have a negative impact on the individual's performance at work, their health and their personal life. Stress can manifest in many different ways, affecting an individual physically (eg. high blood pressure), emotionally (eg. irritability) and behaviourally (eg. alcohol abuse). It is important that stress is recognised and that there are appropriate reactive strategies to situations (ie. debriefing, incident reflection). Each organisation needs to have a proactive approach to stress management, which involves a range of strategies that support the individual and the staff team, which improve work performance and ultimately improve the care and support that people with intellectual disabilities receive.

Some examples of proactive strategies include:

▶ **A clear and common purpose:** It is vital that the whole team shares a common goal and philosophy, and have a consensus on how this will be achieved.

▶ **Supervision:** Each staff member should have access to regular supervision. Supervision should be a collaborative process that supports the staff member to identify clear and achievable goals, to give positive feedback, and when there are concerns over performance, that it is reflected upon and a clear plan to improve performance is developed.

▶ **Team meetings:** Regular team meetings are important as they offer the opportunity for individuals to express their thoughts and feelings and to have some influence on how a service is managed and develops.

▶ **Open and honest culture:** All staff should feel empowered to make improvements and feel able to raise concerns within their service without fear of reprisal and know that their concerns will be effectively managed.

▶ **Risk assessment and management:** Taking risks is a part of everyday life and it is important that people with intellectual disabilities are supported to take risks. However, there should be a robust process in place in which risks are identified, where staff can contribute to the assessment process and contribute to effective risk management plans. If staff are fully involved in this process they are more likely to feel safe in implementing care plans that improve the quality of life of the people they support.

Developing a competent staff team

The skills and knowledge of staff working with people with intellectual disabilities has been highlighted as a significant issue (DH, 2001). There are further concerns regarding the knowledge base of staff working with people with intellectual disabilities who also have mental health problems (Woodward & Halls, 2009).

People with intellectual disabilities are just as, or more likely to suffer from mental health problems. However, due to difficulties in the assessment, implementation and evaluation of interventions, it is essential that frontline staff have the necessary skills for this. This can be addressed by ensuring that staff who support people with intellectual disabilities have supplementary training to ensure that the additional needs of this group are met.

Since 2001, there has been a number of government initiatives to introduce new qualifications for staff who work with people with learning disabilities, in an attempt to address skills deficits. These have included the Learning Disability Awards Framework (LDAF) and the Learning Disabilities Qualification (LDQ), both of which have now been superseded. 2011 saw the introduction of a whole new qualifying framework for health and social care staff with the Qualifications and Credit Framework (QCF). Within this framework, staff can now undertake a learning disability award, certificate, or pathway within the full health and social care diploma. There are also options for taking specialist units which reflect individuals' roles, for example, in mental health or specific communication needs. Workers who are new to the industry have to meet the eight Common Induction Standards (refreshed by Skills for Care in 2010) that ensure they have undergone a thorough 12-week induction process, can demonstrate providing safe and high quality care, and prepare them for entry into future training and qualifications. The Standards can be contextualised for the worker's role and for learning disability settings.

Ensuring that staff are enrolled on the induction award provides a significant burden on service providers who are required to send staff on training. In addition to this there is a need for staff to attend mandatory training, which can eat into services' training budgets. For example, residential services are often required to fulfil health and safety obligations such as fire safety, moving and handling, first aid or food hygiene. This draws funds away from mental health training.

There is no policy or guidance that states how much education intellectual disabilities staff require in mental health. Skills for Care Common Induction Standards acknowledge that sometimes staff may be required to undertake tasks beyond the scope of induction training. It suggests that when staff are required to perform tasks that are beyond the remit of induction standards, appropriate training must be provided before the tasks can be undertaken. The Care Homes Regulations of 2001 require that at all times suitably qualified, competent and experienced persons work within a care home, adding that a member of staff should have the skills and experience necessary to undertake their work. However, they do not actually state what they mean by 'suitably qualified' and there is no direct reference to specialist skills such as mental health.

Training staff about mental health problems in the intellectual disabilities population has been identified as a way of improving staff skills and knowledge (Costello, 2005; Mohr *et al,* 2002). However, improving staff skills, knowledge or even attitudes towards mental health problems does not necessarily translate into improved outcomes for the people they support.

From this it can be seen that staff often require additional training in mental health and that mental health training can be effective. Unfortunately, opportunities to attend training on mental health may be limited due to training budgets being diverted elsewhere. It is helpful to know what methods of training are not only best suited to improve the lives of people with intellectual disabilities who have additional mental health problems, but also which are the most cost-effective for services.

van Oorsouw *et al* (2009) carried out a study of various methods of training to identify the most effective way to train staff. They found that using a combination of in-service 'classroom' based training, with a combination of coaching on-the-job was the most effective way. They also found that trainers need to use a number of training techniques and that giving corrective verbal feedback with praise is preferential.

Much of the staff training in mental health looked at increasing staff knowledge of mental health problems. As discussed earlier, there is no guarantee that this will translate into directly affecting the people they support. Another option might be to look at training that changes people with intellectual disabilities' lifestyles or staff attitudes.

A study into staff attitudes towards challenging behaviour (Campbell & Hogg, 2008) found that the beliefs staff had about why a behaviour was happening could be changed following training and this could then lead to improvements in staff performance. The same principles could be applied to mental health, where work around changing staff attitudes to mental health problems and support may improve service user outcomes.

Another idea for training might be to improve staff skills in supporting people in their lifestyles so that they are less vulnerable to developing mental health problems. For example, active support has been found to improve levels of staff assistance and levels of engagement in activities, community participation and increasing levels of choice (Jones *et al,* 1999; Jones *et al,* 2001a). Another study looking at active support (Stancliffe *et al,* 2007) found that active support may reduce symptoms of depression, suggesting that activity and engagement might be protective factors.

Active support is another method of training which includes classroom-based training with interactive on-the-job training within the care setting. It was also found that when managers were involved in the training it was more effective and improvements were more likely to be maintained over time (Jones *et al,* 2001b).

Another cost-effective method of training could be peer-to-peer staff training. Finn and Sturmey (2009) found that, once trained, staff could train their co-workers in how to interact positively with people with intellectual disabilities who have mental health problems.

Incorporating some of these ideas into training may have a positive effect on skill development and competence of staff:

▶ combining classroom training with on-the-job training is more effective than doing them in isolation

▶ using a combination of training techniques is more effective than just a single method

▶ on-the-job training is enhanced by providing corrective verbal feedback and including praise

▶ peer-to-peer training can be a successful and cost-effective method of training staff

▶ including managers within training may mean that improvements are more likely to be maintained over time

▶ training that tries to change staff attitudes towards mental health problems may improve work performance

▶ training staff to assist people with intellectual disabilities to increase engagement in activities may be a protective factor to developing mental health problems

▶ these methods should improve maintenance of improved behaviours in staff.

Summary

▶ Too much stress can have a detrimental affect on staff, their performance and health, and is likely to reduce the quality of care within the service.

▶ Services have a responsibility to develop a range of effective reactive and proactive strategies to combat stress and improve work performance.

▶ Ensuring that people with intellectual disabilities who have mental health needs are supported by a competent workforce is essential.

▶ There should be a range of blended learning opportunities for staff to develop their skills and improve the quality of support they deliver.

References

Campbell M & Hogg J (2008) Impact of training on cognitive representation of challenging behaviour in staff working with adults with intellectual disabilities. *Journal of Applied Research in Intellectual Disabilities* **21** 561–574.

Costello H (2005) Evaluation of mental health training for carer staff supporting people with learning disabilities In: G Holt, S Hardy & N Bouras (Eds) *Mental Health in Learning Disabilities: A reader.* Brighton: Pavilion Publishing.

Department of Health (2001) *Valuing People: A new strategy for learning disability for the 21st century.* London: TSO.

Finn L & Sturmey P (2009) The effect of peer-to-peer training on staff interactions with adults with dual diagnosis. *Research in Developmental Disabilities* **30** 96–106.

Hatton C, Brown R, Caine A & Emerson E (1995) Stressors, coping strategies and stress-related outcomes among direct care staff in staffed houses for people with intellectual disabilities. *Mental Handicap Research* **8** 252–271.

Hatton C, Emerson E, Rivers H, Mason H, Mason L, Swarbrick R, Kiernan C, Reeves D & Alborz A (1999) Factors associated with staff stress and work satisfaction in services for people with intellectual disability. *Journal of Intellectual Disability Research* **43** 253–267.

Jones E, Perry J, Lowe K, Felce D, Toogood S, Dunstan F, Allen D & Pagler J (1999) Opportunity and the promotion of activity among adults with severe intellectual disability living in community residences: the impact of training staff in active support. *Journal of Intellectual Disability Research* **43** 164–178.

Jones E, Felce D, Lowe K, Bowley C, Pragler J, Strong J, Gallagher B, Roper A & Kurasowka K (2001a) Evaluation of the dissemination of active support training and training trainers. *Journal of Applied Research in Intellectual Disability* **14** 79–99.

Jones E, Felce D, Lowe K, Bowley C, Pragler J, Gallagher B & Roper A (2001b) Evaluation of the dissemination of active support training in staffed community residences. *American Journal on Mental Retardation* **106** 344–358.

Menaghan EG & Merves ES (1984) Coping with occupational problems: the limits of individual efforts. *Journal of Health and Social Behaviour* **25** 406–423.

Mohr C, Phillips A & Rymill A (2002) Interagency training in dual disability. *Australasian Psychiatry* **10** (4) 356–364.

Rose J, Rose D & Hodgkins C (2005) Staff Stress and Coping Strategies. In: G Holt, S Hardy & N Bouras (Eds) *Mental Health in Learning Disabilities: A reader.* Brighton: Pavilion Publishing.

Rose J (1999) Demands, supports and residential staff: a factor analytic study. *Journal of Intellectual Disability Research* **43** 268–278.

Stancliffe R, Harman A, Toogood S & McVilly K (2007) Australian implementation and evaluation of active support. *Journal of Applied Research in Intellectual Disabilities* **20** 211–227.

van Oorsouw W, Embregts P, Bosman A & Jahoda A (2009) Training staff serving clients with intellectual disabilities: a meta-analysis of aspects determining effectiveness. *Research in Developmental Disabilities* **30** 503–511.

Woodward P & Halls S (2009) Staff training in the mental health needs of people with learning disabilities in the UK. *Advances in Mental Health and Learning Disabilities* **3** (2) 15–19.

Chapter 11

Consent to treatment

Steve Hardy

Introduction

Making your own decisions is a fundamental right for all individuals, including adults with intellectual disabilities, and this is reflected in UK law. This chapter will explore how capacity to make decisions in relation to treatment is assessed and how decisions are made on behalf of individuals who lack capacity to make specific decisions. This chapter focuses on English and Welsh government legislation in the Mental Capacity Act (MCA). Scotland has its own legislation in regard to capacity – the Adults with Incapacity (Scotland) Act – and at the time of publication Northern Ireland was in the process of developing legislation. Although this chapter focuses on English and Welsh law, the general principles of capacity and consent are similar throughout the UK.

The expert opinion

'Things can't be forced on you. They need to get your permission first. People need to have choices. They need information about the choices – what's good and what's bad about it.'

The Mental Capacity Act

Mental capacity is an individual's ability to make a decision. It can be about small day-to-day decisions such as deciding what to wear or what to eat, through to more significant decisions such as where to live or whether to have medical treatment. The Mental Capacity Act (MCA) (2005) is applicable to anyone who cares for a person who may lack capacity. This includes both family carers and professionals. The MCA is underpinned by five guiding principles.

The principles of the Mental Capacity Act (2005)

1. We must assume a person has the capacity to make a decision unless proved otherwise.

Just like anyone else, people with intellectual disabilities have the right to make decisions for themselves and should not be denied this right. Having intellectual disabilities does not mean that a person cannot make a decision for themself. Each decision that is to be made should be seen as 'stand-alone' and viewed separately from decisions that were previously made.

2. All practical steps must be made to support an individual to make a decision.

Family carers, services and professionals should make every effort to support the person in making a decision. This includes providing them with all the relevant information in a format that the person understands and over a suitable period of time.

3. A person is not to be treated as unable to make a decision merely because he or she makes a decision that is deemed unwise by others.

The decision a person makes may appear unwise or irrational to others, but this does not mean they cannot make that decision. For example, have you ever made a decision that your parents or family disproved of? Did they have the right to stop you making that decision (if you were over the age of 16)?

4. Anything done for or on behalf of a person who lacks capacity must be done so in their best interests.

When an individual is assessed as lacking capacity to make a specific decision, the decision should be made in their best interests.

5. Any decision made in the best interests of an individual should be the least restrictive option of their basic rights and freedoms.

Before the decision is made we must consider the possible ways of achieving the desired outcome and of these outcomes, which would be the least restrictive for the person.

Assessing capacity to give consent

The vast majority of people are able to make the complete range of decisions that affect their life and their capacity is unlikely to be questioned. The MCA indicates that when a person has a 'mental disorder' (definition includes intellectual disabilities) that capacity may be assessed. This does not mean that the person lacks capacity – the assessment will establish this.

The judgment of whether or not an individual has capacity is based on their ability to understand the nature and effects of the decision to be taken at the time it needs to be taken. Each decision is assessed independently as the information pertaining to each decision will be unique and some individuals may be able to make some decisions but not other more complex decisions. A person's capacity to give consent is not static – it can change. For example, someone who is intoxicated at a party may not be able to make a decision, but 24 hours later when they are sober they would be able to make a decision.

Previous methods of establishing capacity

Prior to the MCA, several methods had been used to establish if individuals had capacity. Among these was the 'status approach'; being what you are determines your ability to make a decision. People with intellectual disabilities were often thought to be incapable of making decisions for themselves and little, if any, attempt was made to discover whether or not they could make decisions. Another example is the 'outcome approach', where judgement is based on the values of the assessor. The individual may have been allowed to make a decision, but if the assessor does not agree with their choice, they are more likely to question the person's capacity (Hardy & Joyce, 2009).

The functional approach

The MCA has adopted a 'functional approach' to assessing capacity and this has been developed through several key court cases. In the case of Re C (a patient detained under the MHA being treated for schizophrenia in a high security hospital), the patient developed a gangrenous foot and refused to give consent to the recommended amputation of his foot. The court ruled in favour of C as they found that after receiving the relevant information C:

▶ understood and retained the information relating to the decision in question

▶ believed the information

▶ weighed that information in the balance to arrive at a choice.

(British Medical Association & The Law Society, 2009)

In the case of Re MB (a pregnant woman who was recommended that a caesarean section was required) the woman agreed to the procedure. With the procedure about to be implemented the woman refused the treatment upon seeing the required venepuncture. It transpired that the woman had a phobia of needles. The court ruled that MB lacked capacity to make this decision as her phobia clouded her judgement to such an extent that she was:

▶ unable to comprehend and retain information which was material to the decision, especially as to the consequences of having or not having the treatment in question

▶ unable to use the information and weigh it in the balance as part of the process of arriving at a decision.

(British Medical Association & The Law Society, 2009)

The functional approach to assessing capacity is a four-stage test and all stages should be passed.

1. Understand the information relating to the decision

The person should be given all the relevant information relating to the decision that needs to be made. They need to understand the information and believe it to be true.

2. Retain the information

The person should be able to remember the information long enough to reach a decision. The MCA sets out no time frame for information to be retained; this would be a matter of professional judgement.

3. Weigh, balance and use the information

The person should be able to weigh the information, looking at both the possible positive and negative outcomes of making the decision, and the same for any alternative options. They should be able to balance these and use this information to come to a decision.

4. Be able to communicate the choice

The person needs to be able to communicate their decision. Communication does not just mean verbally, it could be any form of communication that the person uses (sign language, pictorial symbols etc.).

In regards to capacity to consent to the treatment, the individual responsible for completing the assessment is the professional who would implement the treatment (eg. dental treatment; dentist). But the responsible professional might not have met the person before or know how they communicate, so it would be good practice for them to seek the help of those who know the person well (eg. family or support workers) or have expertise in working with people with intellectual disabilities (eg. psychologist or speech and language therapist).

Once an individual has been given sufficient information about the decision and enough time and support to absorb the information, the assessor will interview the person to ascertain if they pass the functional test. Etchells *et al* (1999) developed a tool called The Aid to Capacity Evaluation, which offers guidance on the type of questions that should be asked in an assessment. See Box 11.1.

Box 11.1: Assessment questions

▶ Ability to understand the medical problem
  ▸ What problem are you having right now?
  ▸ Why are in you hospital?

▶ Ability to understand the proposed treatment
  ▸ What is the treatment for?
  ▸ What can we do to help you?

▶ Ability to understand the alternatives to the proposed treatment (if any)
  ▸ Are there any other treatments?
  ▸ What other options do you have?

▶ Ability to understand the option of refusing treatment (including withdrawing treatment)
  ▸ Can you refuse?
  ▸ Could we stop the treatment?

Box 11.1: Assessment questions (continued)

▶ Ability to appreciate the reasonably foreseeable consequences of accepting the treatment

  ▶ What could happen if you have the treatment?

  ▶ How could the treatment help you?

  ▶ Could the treatment cause problems or side effects?

▶ Ability to appreciate the reasonably foreseeable consequences of refusing the treatment

  ▶ What could happen to you if you don't have the treatment?

  ▶ Could you get sicker/die without the treatment?

▶ The decision is not substantially based because of hallucinations, delusions or cognitive signs of depression

  ▶ Why have you decided to accept/refuse the treatment?

  ▶ Do you think we are trying to harm you?

  ▶ Do you deserve to be treated?

  ▶ Do you feel you are being punished?

  ▶ Do you feel that you are a bad person?

These questions were developed by Etchells *et al* (1999) and may need to be simplified when interviewing people with intellectual disabilities.

Prior to the assessment, the assessor should have a clear understanding of where to set the bar as to passing or failing the functional test. This would include what pertinent information the person should know and understand about the decision. The 'bar' for people with intellectual disabilities would be the same as any other person. It is the way in which we deliver the information and ask the questions that might differ. Whatever the outcome of the assessment, it should be clearly recorded in the person's records and have clear reasoning supporting the conclusion. This should also be communicated to the person.

Supporting the person who cannot give consent to treatment

If a person is assessed as lacking capacity the decision can be made in their 'best interests'. The person who makes the best interests decision will generally be the professional that will implement the decision (ie.

a medical procedure). The MCA provide a 'best interests' checklist that decision makers should follow. It states that the decision maker should consult with those who care for the person; this includes family, friends and professionals. If none of these people are available and it is a serious medical decision or a proposed change in accommodation (provided/commissioned by the NHS or Social Services), an independent mental capacity advocate (IMCA) should be sought. The IMCA's role is to represent the person and not to make the decision.

The best interests process should consider the individual's own past and present wishes, beliefs and values, and should check the person has not made any advanced decisions (when they had capacity) that would affect this 'best interests' decision. Any individual over the age of 16 years who has capacity can make a decision about their future health. Advanced decisions can only be made to refuse treatment, not choose it. An individual may make a preference as to future treatment, but if they lack capacity the clinician will make a best interests decision. When making a best interests decision the majority of time should be spent considering how the decision will affect the person's life in the following aspects; medically, emotionally and their social welfare. A list of possible advantages and disadvantages should be drawn up that will strongly influence the decision. Examples of issues that may be considered are listed in Table 11.1.

Table 11.1: Examples of issues for consideration

	Possible areas for consideration
Emotional	Short and long-term reaction to event/procedure
Medical	Risks and benefits and likelihood of each option occurring Pain Aftercare
Social welfare	Where the person lives Independence Relationships Occupation/daytime activity

In regard to the proposed treatment the decision maker also needs to consider any alternatives that are available and their associated benefits/risks and the impact on the person's life. The decision maker may not have met the person before and only know them in the context of the treatment decision. It is good practice that in these situations – and where the decision is serious – that a best interests meeting is held. This offers all parties who care for or work with the individual to discuss the decision, ensure the MCA best interests checklist is followed, and weigh up the pros and cons of the decision.

Once the best interests decision has been made the details should be clearly recorded in the person's records and if a best interests meeting was held, minutes should be produced. Both records should detail the outcome of the checklist, the decision and how it was reached.

There are some decisions that are considered to be so personal that the MCA states that only a person with capacity can make them – a best interests decision can never be made. These include sexual relationships, marriage, voting and adoption. There are some decisions that can only be made by the Court of Protection – a court that deals with issues of capacity. These decisions include organ and bone marrow donation and non-therapeutic sterilisation.

Consent to treatment for those detained under the Mental Health Act

Sometimes when a person has a mental disorder (ie. schizophrenia or depression) it may be necessary for them to be detained in hospital for a period of treatment in the interest of their own health or safety, or the safety of others. In England and Wales the Mental Health Act (MHA) (1983; 2007) is the law covering all aspects of mental health and can be used in these situations (see Chapter 12 for further details). An individual's consent to treatment in regard to their mental disorder (ie. antidepressant medication for depression) is governed by the MHA as opposed to the MCA. When detained in hospital under the assessment or treatment sections of the MHA, an individual (with or without capacity) can be given medication for their mental disorder without their consent but only with the approval of a second opinion doctor. Prior to this, good practice stipulates that all efforts should be made to discuss treatment with the individual at all stages. For other, less common types of treatment, such as electroconvulsive treatment, the MHA is very specific when this can be used and what the requirements for consent are. The Code of Practice (DCA, 2008) offers further guidance in this area. Physical illness is not covered by the MHA but is covered by the MCA. Under the MHA an individual can be treated in emergency without their consent, in certain situations (eg. life threatening situations).

Conclusion

Historically, people with intellectual disabilities have had very little choice in their lives. The introduction of statute law in relation to capacity in the UK will improve the quality of life for people with intellectual disabilities. It will ensure that everyone has a responsibility to support choice and decision making whenever individuals have capacity and provides a structured approach to making decisions on behalf of those who lack capacity.

Summary

▶ Health professionals are required to make a capacity assessment before carrying out any care or treatment.

▶ The more serious the decision, the more formal the assessment should be.

▶ Generally, the person who will implement the decision is responsible for assessing capacity, but it would be good practice for them to consult with those who know the individual.

▶ If a person is deemed to lack the capacity to make a decision, it can be made in their best interests.

References

British Medical Association and The Law Society (2009) *Assessment of Mental Capacity*. London: The Law Society.

Department of Constitutional Affairs (2005) *Mental Capacity Act 2005: Code of Practice*. London: TSO.

Etchells E, Darzins P, Silberfeld M, Singer PA, McKenny J, Naglie G, Katz M, Guyatt GH, Molloy DW & Strang D (1999) Assessment of patient capacity to consent to treatment. *Journal of General Internal Medicine* **14** 27–34.

Hardy S & Joyce T (2009) The Mental Capacity Act: Practicalities for health and social care professionals. *Advances in Mental Health and Intellectual Disabilities* **3** (1) 9–14.

Re C (*adult: refusal of medical treatment*) (1994) 1 All ER 819.

Re MB (*medical treatment*) (1997) 2 FLR 426.

Chapter 12

The use of the Mental Health Act 1983 (amended 2007) with people who have intellectual disabilities or autism

Jane Barnes

Introduction

This chapter looks at the use, or lack of use, of the Mental Health Act (1983) in relation to people with intellectual disabilities or autism. It will consider how it can and perhaps should be used for the benefit of this group. The chapter refers to current law in England and Wales. The law is significantly different in Scotland, Northern Ireland, the Isle of Man and the Channel Isles.

Note: The term 'autism' is used throughout this reader. However, the Mental Health Act Code of Practice uses the term 'autistic spectrum disorders' and where directly related to the MHA, this is the term that is used.

> ### The expert opinion
> 'Some people might need to be sectioned. They should be told the reason why. If you're sectioned you need an advocate to help speak up for your rights.'

The use of the Mental Health Act

The Mental Health Act is rarely considered when the needs of people with intellectual disabilities or autism are assessed. There may be a number of reasons for this:

▶ it is not felt appropriate to use the act for people with intellectual disabilities or autism

▶ consultant psychiatrists and approved mental health professionals may have little experience of people with intellectual disabilities or autism

▶ practitioners in intellectual disability teams may not have a good knowledge of the Mental Health Act

▶ there is little joint working

▶ there is a shortage of specialist units

▶ intellectual disability consultant psychiatrists often do not have access to beds

▶ acute units are felt to be inappropriate for people with intellectual disabilities or autism

▶ intellectual disabilities and autism are viewed as untreatable.

We must, however, consider the implications of this situation:

▶ people can be left in unsafe situations at home or in placements which may pose a risk to themselves or others

▶ parents or carers can be left to manage unsafe situations

▶ mental illness which may be present does not get identified or treated

▶ autism is frequently missed or misdiagnosed

▶ people are admitted to hospital informally without any understanding of their rights and without an independent review of their treatment.

Even when a person with intellectual disabilities or autism fulfils the criteria, the act may still not be considered. Many practitioners hold the view that it is not appropriate to use the act for people with intellectual disabilities or autism. This assumes that the act is, by definition, oppressive and ignores the fact that individuals' rights may be better protected. Historically, people with intellectual disabilities and autism have been placed in institutional care for long periods of time without any system of independent review.

Community care is now a reality for most, but if they require treatment in hospital, should this always be on an informal basis? (ie. without the use of the act). If they do not realise that they can leave or refuse treatment; if their experience of life is always doing what they are told; if they are kept in hospital for long periods of time without the right of appeal; if they do not have access to independent review by managers' hearings or mental health review tribunals; if they are not covered by the remit of the Mental Health Act Commission (now part of the Care Quality Commission), where is the protection of their rights?

How should we be using the Mental Health Act?

The Mental Health Act (MHA) is not just about mental illness. It is concerned with the reception, care and treatment of mentally disordered patients. In the act, mental disorder means any disorder or disability of the mind.

Under section 2 of the MHA a person can be detained in hospital for up to 28 days for assessment if it can be shown that:

   a. *he is suffering from mental disorder of a nature or degree which warrants his detention in hospital for assessment (or for assessment followed by treatment) for at least a limited period; and*

   b. *he ought to be so detained in the interests of his own health or safety or with a view to the protection of other persons.*

Under section 3 of the MHA a person can be detained in hospital for up to six months for treatment if it can be shown that:

   a. *he is suffering from mental disorder of a nature or degree which makes it appropriate for him to receive medical treatment in hospital; and*

   b. *it is necessary for the health or safety of the patient or for the protection of other persons that he should receive such treatment and it cannot be provided unless he is detained under this section; and*

   c. *appropriate treatment is available.*

For the purposes of the MHA an intellectual disability is defined as '*a state of arrested or incomplete development of the mind which includes significant impairment of intelligence and social functioning*'. The presence of intellectual disabilities alone would not be sufficient to fulfil the criteria for detention under the MHA unless it can be shown that it is associated with abnormally aggressive or seriously irresponsible conduct.
However, if the person suffers from a mental disorder in addition to having intellectual disabilities, that other disorder would be sufficient for consideration of the MHA and the additional criteria for intellectual disability would not be required. In a review of the evidence concerning

psychosocial interventions for adults with intellectual disabilities and mental health problems, Hatton (2002) concluded that *'people with mild intellectual disabilities appear to show the same range of mental health problems as the general population with prevalence rates of most mental health problems likely to be as high, if not higher'*.

Autistic spectrum disorders are considered to be mental disorders within the meaning of the MHA in their own right and without any additional criteria. This would include autism and Asperger's syndrome. *'The Act's definition of mental disorder includes the full range of autistic spectrum disorders, including those existing alongside an intellectual disability or any other kind of mental disorder'* (DH, 2008). This is in marked contrast to the MHA before it was amended in 2007, which did not make reference to autistic spectrum disorders.

We should also look at what the MHA means by treatment. For the purposes of the act, medical treatment includes nursing, psychological intervention and specialist mental health habilitation, rehabilitation and care as well as medication. The purpose of treatment is to alleviate or prevent a worsening of a mental disorder or one or more of its symptoms or manifestations. It can be seen from this that the definition of treatment in the MHA is very wide. It says nothing about cure, nor does it rely on medication.

When an application is made for someone to be detained under the MHA it must be clearly demonstrated that appropriate treatment is available to them. It must take into account *'the nature and degree of the person's disorder and all their particular circumstances, including cultural, ethnic and religious considerations'* (DH, 2008). This means that young people should not be admitted to adult wards and people with special needs such as those with autism should receive treatment on units with particular expertise in this area. *'If people with autistic spectrum disorders do need to be detained under the Act, it is important that they are treated in a setting that can accommodate their social and communication needs as well as being able to treat their mental disorder'* (DH, 2008).

How do we know if someone fulfils the criteria for the use of the MHA? (Guidance from the Code of Practice)

Chapter 34 of the Mental Health Act (1983) Code of Practice (DH, 2008) covers people with intellectual disabilities or autistic spectrum disorders.

Intellectual disabilities

Arrested or incomplete development of mind: This is characterised by impairment in the process of intellectual and social development that occurs during childhood and adolescence. *'Intellectual disability does not include people whose intellectual disorder derives from accident, injury or illness occurring after they have completed normal maturation'* (although these may be covered by other parts of the act) (DH, 2008)

Significant impairment of intelligence: This should be judged on the basis of reliable and careful assessment. Note that *'it is not defined rigidly by the application of an arbitrary cut-off point such as an IQ of 70'* (DH, 2008).

Significant impairment of social functioning: Social functioning assessment tools can be valuable here but reliable observations from a number of sources will also be very helpful in determining this. Sources could include *'social workers, speech and language and occupational therapists and psychologists'* (DH, 2008).

The Code of Practice points out that it is important to assess the person as a whole. *'It may be appropriate to identify intellectual disability in someone with an IQ somewhat higher than 70 if their social functioning is severely impaired. A person with a low IQ may be correctly diagnosed as having an intellectual disability even if their social functioning is relatively good'* (DH, 2008). This is an important point given that some people with intellectual disabilities have found ways to present as more capable than they are by developing a sort of 'street cred'. It is also important because our community services are largely organised on the basis of IQ.

Abnormally aggressive or seriously irresponsible behaviour: Neither of these terms is defined in the MHA and their presence will depend on observations and professional judgement. Has the person's behaviour resulted in harm or distress to themselves or others or damage to property? How persistent and severe is it? Does the behaviour observed suggest a disregard or an inadequate regard for its serious or dangerous consequences? How likely is it to recur? (DH, 2008).

The Code of Practice also reminds us all to be aware of a number of issues when working with people with intellectual disabilities:

▶ a tendency to be overprotective and assume they cannot make decisions for themselves

▶ over-reliance on family members, both for support and for decision-making

▶ denying them involvement in decision-making processes

▶ their intellectual disabilities being seen as the explanation for all their physical and behavioural attributes when there may, in fact, be an underlying cause relating to a separate issue of physical or mental health (diagnostic overshadowing)

▶ the most appropriate method of communication for each person should be identified

▶ set aside sufficient time for communication and the preparation of meetings

▶ choose an environment which is not intimidating.

Autism spectrum disorders

Chapter 34 of the Code of Practice talks at length about the use of the MHA with people who have autistic spectrum disorders and takes the view that it will usually not be helpful: '*Compulsory treatment in a hospital setting is rarely likely to be helpful for a person with autism who may be very distressed by even minor changes in routine and is likely to find detention in hospital anxiety-provoking*' (DH, 2008).

However, this has not been the author's experience. It is true that coming into hospital is very anxiety-provoking for people with autism, as is any change to their environment, routine or the people around them. However, once they have got used to their new situation they often do very well in hospital because ward life is based on routine, regular activities and familiar staff. They have their own rooms and feel safe. Their anxiety is dramatically reduced and they have the opportunity to learn new skills, access psychological therapies and have a proper review of their difficulties including any additional mental or physical disorder. It is discharge planning which proves to be the challenge because they do not want to leave the safety of the hospital and this must be addressed in a very sensitive manner, ensuring that after-care is properly suited to their needs and the staff who support them have a good understanding of autism.

'*Sensitive person-centred support in a familiar setting will usually be more helpful. Where possible, less restrictive alternative ways of providing the treatment or support a person needs should be found*' (DH, 2008). This reflects *Valuing People* (DH, 2001) – the government's initiative for improving social inclusion, but is the emphasis on less restrictive alternatives at the expense of the right to care, treatment and protection?

The author's experience of working on a national inpatient unit for 12 years showed that people with autism often lack appropriate assessment of their condition. Many have often not been diagnosed at all or have been misdiagnosed with a mental illness. Parents are often struggling to cope with them and they are placed in inappropriate residential care with people who do not understand the nature of their condition and cannot respond appropriately to them. This can result in frustration and dangerous behaviour. They may require specialist assessment and treatment to properly understand the nature of their difficulties, treat any additional mental disorder and develop their skills so they fulfil their potential.

Guardianship

Guardianship under section 7 of the MHA was intended to support people in the community, the criteria being that it is '*necessary in the interests of the welfare of the patient or for the protection of other persons*'. However, the number of guardianship applications has decreased dramatically since 1983. One of the reasons for this is probably because the criteria of abnormally aggressive or seriously irresponsible conduct have to be met for those with intellectual disabilities.

Guardianship '*provides an authoritative framework for working with a patient, with a minimum of constraint, to achieve as independent a life as possible within the community*' (DH, 2008).

A comprehensive care plan is required, which includes arrangements for suitable accommodation, access to activities, education, treatment and personal support. The guardian can be a named person or the local authority but the application must be accepted by the local authority in any event. It is not a requirement that the person has been in hospital or previously detained under the MHA.

Guardianship places certain requirements on the service user:

▶ to reside at a specified place

▶ to attend for treatment, work, training or education at specific times and places

▶ to see a doctor, approved mental health professional (AMHP) or any other relevant person at the place where they live.

The MHA confers on the guardian the power to convey the person to the required residence and to return them there if they leave without permission. So, as well as placing certain requirements on the person, guardianship provides support for carers. It also ensures that services stay involved because they have a monitoring and reviewing role. In my experience it can be a very useful framework for supporting a person's care plan in the community where it applies but, unfortunately, it remains difficult to persuade local authorities of its merit.

Supervised community treatment (also known as community treatment order)

This has been introduced as part of the amendments to the MHA and is designed to support people who have been detained in hospital for the treatment of mental disorder and to prevent their relapse in the community. It is only available to those who are currently detained on section 3 or section 37 of the MHA (hospital order made by the court). It enables the responsible clinician (RC) to make the person subject to certain conditions following discharge from hospital. These conditions are intended to:

▶ ensure the person receives medical treatment for mental disorder

▶ prevent a risk of harm to the person's health or safety

▶ protect other people.

If a person fails to follow these conditions following discharge, the clinician can recall them to hospital. This may just be for a short time, in which case the community treatment order (CTO) will remain in place. However, if the RC subsequently revokes the CTO, the person will then be back on their original detaining order.

Supervised community treatment was subject to a lot of controversy during the period when the changes to the MHA were being discussed. However, it is being used much more than was originally expected. It is also worth noting that the person does not have to have the capacity to understand the conditions in order to be made subject to a CTO.

How is an assessment under the MHA organised?

In order for someone to be detained in hospital under section 2 or 3, or made subject to guardianship, there must be two medical recommendations and an application by an AMHP or the nearest relative (in practice, applications by nearest relatives are rare). One of the medical recommendations must be from a doctor who is registered under section 12 of the MHA. This is usually a consultant psychiatrist. Ideally, one of the doctors should have previous knowledge of the person being assessed and this is often the GP. The two doctors must have seen the person with no more than five days between the two assessments.

The AMHP must be warranted by the local social services authority and is required to look at all the circumstances of the case, not just the medical issues, and to consult with the nearest relative as well as interview the person concerned. The AMHP application must be made within 14 days. If it is not possible to locate the nearest relative, the AMHP can go ahead if it is felt that consultation is not reasonably practicable or would involve unreasonable delay. If there is consultation and the nearest relative objects to the making of a section 3 order or guardianship, the application cannot go ahead without taking the case to court. A section 2 order can, however, go ahead even if the nearest relative is objecting.

If carers or members of the family feel that there should be an assessment under the MHA they can contact the GP in the first instance who would then liaise with social services. There is a duty on social services to arrange for an AMHP to take the person's case into consideration. An AMHP has a responsibility to look at the least restrictive alternative to detention in hospital so the outcome may be support or treatment in a different setting or provided in the home or on an outpatient basis (MHA section 13).

Representation

Anyone who is detained under the MHA is entitled to ask to see an independent mental health advocate (IMHA). The hospital is obliged to arrange for an IMHA to visit any detained patient who asks for this. The advocate can represent the patient's views to the treating team and be involved in meetings to review progress and arrange care planning under the Care Programme Approach.

What happens if the person being assessed lacks the capacity to make a decision?

A person who needs to be admitted to hospital for the treatment of their mental disorder and lacks the capacity to give informed consent to their admission and treatment can be admitted without the use of the MHA, provided they do not object. This is called 'informal admission' and most people with intellectual disabilities or autism are admitted in this way. Patients can be treated in their best interests under the Mental Capacity Act (MCA).

There are, however, a number of concerns about this that were highlighted by a very famous case called the Bournewood case (R v Bournewood community and mental health NHS trust, ex parte L). This case concerned a 48-year-old man with intellectual disabilities, autism, very little speech and challenging behaviour. He was admitted to the Bournewood Trust and kept there for several months without being detained under the MHA and without his carers being able to visit him.

The case eventually went to the European Court of Human Rights (ECHR, HL v UK 2004) but prior to this, in 1998, it was heard in the House of Lords and Lord Steyn was very troubled that apparently compliant incapacitated patients would not have the specific protections provided by the MHA. This came to be known as the Bournewood gap.

These protections are:

▶ a formal assessment which involves two medical recommendations and an application by an approved mental health professional

▶ rules governing the medical treatments patients are given

▶ rights of appeal, with legal representation, to an independent legal hearing

- ▶ the right to care after leaving hospital

- ▶ the Code of Practice which provides guidance about the interpretation of the act and the care of patients

- ▶ the Mental Health Act Commission (now part of the CQC) which has a remit to review the situation of detained patients but not informal patients.

In 2004 the ECHR said that the 48-year-old man's detention in hospital was contrary to the Human Rights Act article 5 because someone should only be deprived of liberty through a process of law and that detention must be subject to independent legal review. It said that the MHA should be used where it applies and the UK government should develop other procedures for people who lack capacity where the MHA does not apply and where that treatment amounts to a deprivation of liberty.

As a consequence, the MCA was amended at the same time as the MHA to include the Deprivation of Liberty Safeguards (DOLS). These came into force in April 2009 and cover those people in care homes or hospitals who lack the capacity to consent to their care and treatment where that care and treatment amounts to deprivation of liberty (Mental Capacity Act 2005, amended 2007). The Mental Capacity Act is covered in more detail in Chapter 11.

Unfortunately, these safeguards are still not well understood by organisations providing care and treatment and the number of referrals for DOLS assessments since its inception has been extremely low. By their very nature the people they apply to are unable to advocate for themselves or ensure that their rights are being protected. They and their families often assume that staff have the right to exercise complete and effective control over their care and movements without having to apply for any lawful authority.

This may be true for short periods of time and would be appropriate to ensure the person's safety. However, if someone is *confined to a particular place for a not negligible length of time*' (JE v Surrey CC 2006) then that deprivation of liberty must be authorised in one of the following ways:

- ▶ detention under an appropriate section of the MHA (1983)

- ▶ a personal welfare order by the Court of Protection under section 16 of the MCA (2005)

▶ authorisation under DOLS

▶ life-sustaining treatment or treatment to prevent a deterioration, while awaiting a decision by the Court of Protection.

Please note that people with intellectual disabilities would be eligible for the DOLS, without having to fulfil the additional criteria of being associated with seriously irresponsible or abnormally aggressive conduct.

Conclusion

When assessing the needs of people with intellectual disabilities or autism, it is the responsibility of us all to be aware of the options available and to use the tools we have effectively. The care and treatment of people with intellectual disabilities and autism is still organised in a very paternalistic way with little emphasis on the protection of their rights. It is important that staff involved in their care are aware of these protections and use them appropriately.

We should not dismiss the MHA as being inappropriate for people with intellectual disabilities or autism without proper consideration. It might actually be very helpful in ensuring that someone obtains the assessment, treatment and protection they require as well as supporting the carers who may be so overwhelmed that they cannot make those decisions.

Summary

▶ The use of the Mental Health Act with people who have intellectual disabilities or autism should be considered in mental health services.

▶ A culture of paternalism among carers and professionals does not take into account the protection of rights.

▶ The Mental Health Act ensures access to assessment and treatment.

▶ The Mental Health Act provides a risk management framework.

References

Department of Health (2001) *Valuing People*. London: TSO.

Department of Health (2008) *Mental Health Act 1983: Code of Practice*. London: TSO.

Hatton C (2002) Psychosocial interventions for adults with intellectual disabilities and mental health problems: A review. *Journal of Mental Health* **11** (4) 357–373.

HL v United Kingdom (2004) 45508/99 ECHR 471.

R v Bournewood Community and Mental Health NHS Trust, ex parte L (1998)

Chapter 13

Challenging behaviour

Michael Hearn

Introduction

This chapter provides a brief overview of challenging behaviour. The
definition 'challenging behaviour' is broad and can encompass many
types of behaviour. A large portion of this chapter will be devoted
to summarising the possible causes of challenging behaviour and
interventions. Understanding the causes can help those working with
people whose behaviour is challenging to develop ways of responding in an
appropriate and ethical manner. By understanding the possible causes of
challenging behaviour readers will be able to see that current approaches
to intervention fall in line with government guidelines (eg. DH, 2009) and
reports (Mansell Report, 2007).

The expert opinion

'Staff need training about challenging behaviour like how to calm the
person down and find out what's wrong. Staff should keep calm themselves
and not jump right in.'

Case study: John

John lives at home with his mother and siblings. He is 17 and is described as
having severe intellectual disabilities. He also has mobility problems. When
he is in the family lounge he sits in a purpose built chair, which has a table
attachment. John uses very few words. On most occasions when his mother
leaves the lounge to go into the kitchen, John will start saying 'Mummy,
mummy'. His behaviour then changes and he starts to slap his head very hard
with both hands and bangs it on the table. This can go on for several minutes.

Definition of challenging behaviour

Over 20 years ago, the terms 'aberrant behaviour' or 'maladaptive behaviour' were frequently used to refer to what is now called 'challenging behaviour'. None of these terms, including challenging behaviour, are diagnostic labels. A recent definition, which is based largely on Emerson's (1995) earlier definition, is outlined in a joint report by the Royal College of Psychiatrists, the British Psychological Society and the Royal College of Speech and Language Therapists (2007). They define it as: *'behaviour can be described as challenging when it is of such an intensity, frequency or duration as to threaten the quality of life and/or the physical safety of the individual and others and is likely to lead to responses that are restrictive, aversive or result in exclusion'* (RCP, BPS & RCSLT, 2007).

This definition re-emphasises the idea that the person is not the problem but it is the behaviour that poses a challenge for services and families. Furthermore, it describes behaviour in the context of what could happen to the person as a consequence. This can include potentially punishing responses such as exclusion, unplanned physical interventions ie. restraint, inappropriate use of medications, or restrictions on activities that are enjoyed by wider society (eg. 'we can't take her to the supermarket, it's too challenging when she lies on the floor').

What kinds of behaviour are challenging?

There is no absolute definition of challenging behaviour as what is challenging for one person might not be for another. This is why the term is known as a social construction – it depends on the context and the people involved (eg. shouting at a football match is acceptable, whereas shouting in a lesson might not be). However, experience and research inform us about the types of behaviours that result in individuals being referred to specialist behaviour support services. These might include aggression (eg. hitting, pinching, kicking and scratching others), self-injury (eg. hitting own head with hand, head-banging onto solid surfaces and eye-poking, property destruction such as breaking or throwing objects), more personal behaviours (such as smearing faeces, masturbation in an inappropriate context and anal poking) and repetitive behaviours, sometimes known as stereotypes (eg. body rocking and hand-flapping). This list is by no means exhaustive. See Emerson (1995) for further information.

Prevalence of challenging behaviour

The data reporting on how many people present with behaviour described as challenging varies according to sample and inclusion criteria. For example, Emerson (1998) noted an estimate that of those people supported by intellectual disability services, between 10–15% present with behaviour that would be described as challenging. Emerson *et al* (1997) found, in their sample of nearly 400 people using services in northwest England, just under 90% of people presented with more than one form of behaviour (eg. self-injury and aggression, or more). What complicates the picture is the presence of factors that seem to be related to the increased likelihood of challenging behaviour and these include severity of intellectual disabilities, physical (especially mobility), and sensory impairments and communication difficulties.

Causes of challenging behaviour

To use the term 'cause' is something of a misnomer in the sense that there is rarely a one-to-one correspondence between the presence of a known risk factor (eg. more severe intellectual disabilities) and the occurrence of challenging behaviour. It is perhaps more sensible to think in terms of the increased likelihood of observing behaviour described as challenging given certain underlying factors being present. The possible exception to this concerns the presence of relatively rare genetic syndromes where it is highly likely that the presence of the syndrome is associated with the occurrence of specific forms of challenging behaviour.

Genetic syndromes and other biological causes

With the exception of Down's syndrome, the number of people with genetic syndromes (that are associated with behaviour described as challenging) presenting at specialist intellectual disability services is relatively low. However, the identification of syndromes that have a genetic basis is very useful because it allows health professionals to consider preventative measures and anticipate health issues for the individual. Of note is Lesch-Nyhan syndrome in which individuals characteristically present with severe self-injury involving lip and/or cheek biting. Prader-Willi syndrome is associated with an inability to satiate after eating and therefore, the behavioural presentation includes compulsive-like eating. See Udwin and

Kucznski (2007) for a review of behavioural presentations associated with several genetic syndromes. What is important to remember is that most syndromes described will be associated with the presence of intellectual disabilities and/or other disabilities, which in themselves are risks for the occurrence of other challenging behaviour.

When working with people whose behaviour is described as challenging it is vitally important to consider more 'everyday' physical problems, for example, period pain, toothache or other physical factors. In such cases, and in particular for people with communication impairments, physical problems can set the occasion for occurrences of challenging behaviour. This is known as a 'setting event' and put simply could increase the likelihood of episodes of challenging behaviour, perhaps in conjunction with other environmental factors. Imagine having a migraine; this might be tolerable when one is sitting quietly, but in a noisy environment the person might become angry or irritated.

Mental health problems

People with intellectual disabilities suffer the same mental health problems (if not more so) as the wider population. The difficulty for mental health professionals is identifying these issues in people with communication impairments. The occurrence of behaviour described as challenging could be associated with psychological problems such as depression (eg. someone withdrawing from social interaction) or anxiety. Furthermore, people with intellectual disabilities are by definition vulnerable adults and the literature has shown that they can be the victims of abusive practice and/or trauma. These events could be associated with increased occurrences of challenging behaviour.

Challenging behaviour as a form of communication

For those individuals with intellectual disabilities who lack methods of communication, instances of challenging behaviour are very often responded to as if they are communicative, or more precisely, as intentional communication. Very often, parents or carers will report a process whereby they go through a sequence of trying to guess or interpret what the person wants (in the sense of what it is that is being communicated). There is a very close relationship between this way of thinking about challenging behaviour and challenging behaviour as a learned response (see below). This is because the intervention approach for both involves ways of working with the person to teach alternative ways of communicating the same message. However, there is an additional feature of responding to behaviour as if it is communicative and that relates to the increased chance of the challenging behaviour being reinforced (see learned behaviour).

Challenging behaviour as learned behaviour

The most widely researched approach to understanding challenging behaviour (where other factors such as physical or mental health problems have been ruled out) has developed from a body of literature collectively known as 'applied behaviour analysis'. This is also known as the behavioural approach and it simply means that challenging behaviour can be thought of as learned because of its consequences. Suppose I were to press a button on my phone (behaviour) and a £10 note magically appeared in my pocket (consequence); there is an increased probability that I will continue pressing the button. This is known as reinforcement of behaviour and is both an operation (the pairing of the button press with money) and a process (the behaviour of pressing the button becoming strengthened in my behavioural repertoire).

Behaviours are said to be reinforced when they are made more likely. The term 'reward' is often used in place of reinforcement but this is not strictly accurate. There are two types of reinforcement: positive and negative. Positive reinforcement refers to consequences to the behaviour that are in some way added to the environment. Suppose a man sitting on his own self-injures and receives soothing attention from his sister in the form of hugs. Hugs have been added following the self-injury so this is called 'positive reinforcement'. The man may learn to discriminate that when he is on his own and self-injures, his sister will come over and give him hugs (or at least, this is more likely to happen). If this starts to happen regularly, the self-injurious behaviour is said to be positively reinforced by the sister's hugging. We would not wish to argue that a sister should not hug her brother though (see intervention section). Suppose the scenario is different. When the sister hugs the man, he starts self-injuring and the sister immediately withdraws. The man may discriminate (learn) that it is more likely that his sister will withdraw the hug contingent on his self-injury. In this situation, although the man's behaviour is reinforced (strengthened) it is called 'negative reinforcement' because something is removed (his sister's attention) when he self-injures. To be clear, both positive and negative reinforcement processes relate to behaviour being strengthened. Things that people find reinforcing will vary from person to person, which is why it is best not to think in terms of rewards (because what is reinforcing for one person might not be for the next).

Reinforcement processes help us to understand what might be going on when someone presents with behaviour described as challenging. If there are consequences to occurrences of challenging behaviour then it can be reinforced (note also that consequences can be 'internal' to the person). This also helps us understand our own behaviour as carers or support workers. Some types of challenging behaviour have particularly aversive properties, especially self-injurious behaviour, and we may do our best to stop it or bring about a reduction. To this extent, the process of reinforcement works the other way whereby carer behaviour can be negatively reinforced. In the first example above, the sister learns that when she hugs her brother his self-injury stops, that is, her hugging behaviour is negatively reinforced.

Reinforcement processes have been identified as maintaining occurrences of challenging behaviour under the following broad categories.

Social (positive reinforcement): A consequence to challenging behaviour that is social in nature eg. conversation (can include negative talk such as criticism) or physical contact.

Social escape (negative reinforcement): A consequence that involves removal of social interaction.

Demand avoidance (negative reinforcement): This is also social but may be preceded by a request or instruction and be followed by removal or withdrawal of request. This is also a socially reinforced behaviour.

Access to items/activities: (positive reinforcement): Following the behaviour, a favoured activity or item is made available.

Sensory (non-social reinforcement): This type of reinforcement does not rely on another party to deliver the reinforcement. For example, pressing one's eye gently can result in pleasant sensory feedback (positive reinforcement) or scratching an itchy arm removes the discomfort (negative reinforcement). As can be seen, the reinforcement is thought to be internal to the person and it can be difficult to identify which process is in effect. For this reason, this process is more accurately referred to as automatic reinforcement. Behaviours associated with this process are sometimes referred to as stereotypies (eg. rhythmic and repetitive rocking).

As can be seen, for reinforcement described as social in nature, there is a clear link with responding to an individual's challenging behaviour as if it were communicative.

Finally, it is hoped that the reader will see that behaviour described this way can be thought of as functional, because it appears to serve some purpose for the person concerned.

Environmental influences on challenging behaviour

The previous section shows a clear relationship between behaviour (B) and consequence (C). Understanding what is going on in the environment provides more information about why challenging behaviours become learned. Suppose there is a day centre where there are limitations on social interactions; as a result, a person may need to escalate their behaviours to meet these basic needs. It is an unfortunate observation that impoverished environments are associated with challenging behaviour occurrences, hence the current emphasis on promoting 'capable environments' (Mansell, 2007) where staff are trained to respond to people whose behaviour is described as challenging.

Assessing challenging behaviour

The Mansell Report (2007) describes a holistic approach to the assessment of challenging behaviour, for example, the importance of identifying mental health (including offering psychological therapy where appropriate) and physical problems. This section will now summarise the main aspects of assessments that are collectively known as functional analysis. Functional analysis is an approach to assessing behaviour described as challenging where the main goal is to identify the function of the behaviour. Therefore, it is very important to arrive at a clear description of the behaviour. In the case of John, the description could include any sudden physical contact between head and solid objects (or something like this). This allows all concerned to have a good idea about the behaviour of concern, so all can agree when it is or isn't happening. If we are to consider behaviour as functional, including having some kind of communicative purpose, then it is also important to think about what other means of communication already exist in the person's repertoire (eg. vocal communication and/or signing). It is important to identify these already existing skills as they may form the basis of an intervention around improving communicative behaviours, that is, behaviours that serve the same purpose but are less dangerous.

In essence, what different approaches to functional assessment have in common relates to the identification of antecedents (A) and consequences, as follows.

1. What are the conditions that are associated with an increased probability of the behaviour of concern occurring? This can include more 'distal' setting events like pain or physical illness. It can also include more immediate (or proximal) events like consideration of the environment (staffing and noise levels, what else is going on) or the kind of interaction with the individual (is there lots of interaction, or very little, are there lots of demands or requests made of the person). That is, what seems to be going on just before the behaviour of concern happens?

2. Identifying the events that seem to come after the behaviour. What seems to happen to the person after the behaviour, or, what is it the person seems to achieve by the behaviour. For example, do people back away, or conversely, do they rush over and offer soothing interaction? Or, is the person offered something like a drink or favoured activity?

People with more severe intellectual disabilities are far more likely to 'have' in their repertoire a range of behaviours that might be considered challenging (eg. aggression and property destruction). It is important to separate out these behaviours, rather than lump them together as 'challenging'. This is because any single behaviour might serve more than one purpose eg. to escape a demanding situation or to indicate support is needed. This is known as 'multi-functional behaviour'.

In addition, it is important to get a good idea about the how often the behaviour happens and whether or not it happens only in particular contexts (eg. at a day service but not at home). This information provides us with extra clues about what might be going on and where to focus the work, if indeed that is appropriate.

Functional assessments can involve a number of methods. They can involve structured interviews such as the Functional Analysis Interview (O'Neill *et al,* 1990) and questionnaires, such as the Motivations Assessment Scale (Durand & Crimmins, 1992). Both these methods are completed with any number of people who know the person well, including across different contexts. This is because i) we might behave differently with different people and ii) we might behave differently across different contexts. Also, support workers and families might be asked to record incidents on ABC (antecedent–behaviour–consequence) charts. This allows an informal analysis of the events prior to and following occurrences of challenging behaviour. In addition, structured observations (such as momentary time sampling) of the person in their environment are very informative ways of identifying naturally occurring antecedents and consequences of behaviour.

The above approaches have the common goal of allowing us to come to hypotheses about when the behaviour is more likely (antecedents) and what it is that is reinforcing behaviour (function). This forms the basis of an intervention.

Non-aversive interventions

The development of functional analysis methods described in this chapter is associated with non-aversive and constructional approaches to intervention (eg. Iwata *et al,* 1982). This is because we have more confidence that challenging behaviour is likely to happen for a reason, because it achieves an outcome, and what we are trying to achieve with a non-aversive intervention is based on an ethical approach for reducing the likelihood of challenging behaviour as well as teaching the person other ways to achieve the same outcomes.

Non-aversive interventions are developed as a result of a thorough functional analysis, and drawn up in the context of person-centred approaches (ie. in person-centred planning, what do we know about the person's wishes and preferences). There are various labels for the different types of non-aversive approaches (sometimes similar approaches are given different names as indicated below). Most approaches come in what is described as a multi-element format, meaning that the intervention package comprises different strands. Interested readers are referred to LaVigna and Willis (1995) who are early exponents of the multi-element approach. In summary, a four element model includes:

1. Changing the environment (or, ecological manipulations).

2. Teaching new behaviours (or, positive programming).

3. Focused support (or, direct treatment).

4. Reactive strategies (or, crisis management).

The above features of intervention fall within a positive behaviour support model. That is, we are concerned not just about reducing challenging behaviour, but also about the person's whole life including social inclusion and independence, so the intervention also needs to take account of these quality of life indicators. The first three approaches described above are sometimes described as proactive strategies (because they are meant to have direct or indirect effects on the occurrence of challenging behaviour). It may also be apparent that there is a degree of overlap between some aspects of ecological manipulations and focused support strategies.

Changing the environment/ecological manipulations

The features of a given environment may contribute to the occurrence of challenging behaviour. For example, if we know the function of a behaviour is to escape from requests, then an environment featuring many demanding interactions (as far as the individual is concerned) provides the antecedent conditions for challenging episodes. McGill and Toogood (1993) have usefully outlined what kind of environments might be associated with increased likelihood of challenging behaviour.

Ecological manipulations, therefore, are aimed at changing the features of an environment in an effort to reduce the likelihood of a given episode of challenging behaviour. In the example above a good strategy in the first instance would be to reduce the level of demanding interactions with the person.

In summary, we may think about physical factors in the environment such as noise, access to preferred activities and choice-making alongside the capability of the environment to meet the needs of the person. Clearly, environmental manipulations require some effort on the part of staff in organised settings like day centres. In addition, individuals may need extra support in understanding what is happening. Any approach that helps the person to understand what is being communicated (eg. visual timetables

Mental Health in Intellectual Disabilities: A reader (fourth edition) © Pavilion Publishing (Brighton) Ltd 2011

or object cues) may be thought of as an ecological manipulation. Note that the approaches described here are simply those changes that reduce the likelihood of a challenging behaviour occurring in the first place.

In our case study, we might like to think about what John understands when his mother leaves the room. Is there a communication strategy (perhaps pictorial) that lets John see what his mother needs to do, and that she will come back to him after she has completed what she is doing?

Teaching new behaviours

If we have a clear hypothesis about the function of challenging behaviour (ie. what need does it serve?) the aim of this intervention is to teach a more 'adaptive' behaviour that serves the same function. This is called functional equivalence. In our case study, John's call to mother and his self-injury might be thought of as co-existing, functionally equivalent responses.

There may well be occasions when the person does not seem to display an equivalent behaviour and in this circumstance it is important to teach a new skill. Here, we would need to consider whether the person is physically able to 'do' the behaviour (eg. making a sign for a request for a 'break' or holding up an object cue). We might also need to think about things that are rewarding for the person, as the provision of preferred stimuli will be helpful in motivating a person in a learning episode.

The most important factor in teaching functionally equivalent responses is that the new behaviour needs to be more effective for the person than the challenging behaviour it is meant to supercede. This is sometimes referred to as response efficiency in the literature (eg. Horner & Day, 1991) and there are various parameters that make a response more or less efficient, the main ones being effort (is the behaviour easy to do) and delay to reinforcement (how long before the person gets what he/she wants) and how reliably the behaviour is responded to (this is known as schedule of reinforcement). In practice then, any newly taught response, or any functionally equivalent response that exists already in the person's repertoire, needs to be responded to reliably by people supporting the person, thus avoiding the need for the person to present with more challenging behaviour. If we ignore the new behaviour, or don't respond reliably, then the previous more challenging form of behaviour may re-emerge, quite simply because it is more efficient. Furthermore, the behaviour that is being taught needs to be readily interpretable by others. In the case study describing John, we have an existing behaviour which is socially appropriate (calling mother) and less damaging than self-injury. In the short term, as part of a wider package of intervention, we would be encouraging John's mother as much as possible to respond as quickly as she can to her son's vocal requests.

The teaching of new skills is the approach most in line with challenging behaviour being viewed as a communicative act. The interested reader is referred to Carr *et al* (1994) who have published a practical and comprehensive text on this matter.

Finally, although we would like to create a set of circumstances where appropriate behaviour is always responded to quickly, there is the issue of the real world experience of everyday frustrations, such as having to wait to get what we want, even if it is only a temporary delay. This can be a real issue for people with intellectual disabilities as it may be this very delay that sets the occasion for challenging behaviour episodes. What can be incorporated into intervention packages is an approach that teaches some ability to cope with delay. This can be achieved by an approach called 'fading', with very small increments of delay that increase across time, starting with virtually no delay to reinforcement.

Focused support

The main aim of focused support strategies is to bring about 'control' as quickly as possible on occurrences of challenging behaviour and associated risks. Focused support usually involves applying 'schedules of reinforcement' in a planned way. This means providing the reinforcement to the behaviour of concern under certain conditions. Baker and Shephard (2010) describe three approaches to focused support, differential and non-contingent reinforcement schedules (reinforcement based) and antecedent manipulations.

Differential reinforcement can involve the provision of reinforcement in the absence of a behaviour (differential reinforcement of other behaviour–DRO), or subject to the behaviour occurring at a low rate (differential reinforcement of low rate behaviour, DRL) and finally reinforcement for responses that are physically incompatible with the behaviour of concern (differential reinforcement of alternative responses, DRA). What these approaches have in common is that reinforcement is still provided to the person, acknowledging that the need of the more challenging behaviour is legitimate. The design of differential reinforcement schedules requires some thinking around practical aspects and support workers would not necessarily be expected to carry this intervention out without the assistance of behaviour support practitioners.

Non-contingent reinforcement involves the provision of the identified re-inforcer at pre-determined intervals independently of the occurrence of challenging behaviour. For example, for those behaviours maintained by a positive reinforcement process such as social interaction, supporters would be asked to provide increased amounts of interaction at regular intervals. Strictly speaking, the approach operates on motivational factors. For example, if I self-injure because I'm thirsty and want a drink, providing me with regular drinks reduces my motivation to self-injure.

Antecedent manipulations require careful consideration of events that seem to trigger the occurrence of a challenging behaviour. For example, if large social groups are aversive for a person, going into a busy restaurant would be worth avoiding, at least in the short term, until this scenario can be made less threatening. Here, then, is the overlap with ecological manipulations described previously.

Reactive strategies

Interventions may take time to put in place and/or to demonstrate positive effects. Therefore, it is important to have in place a strategy for responding to occurrences of challenging behaviour as and when it happens. This is called a reactive strategy. The function of a reactive strategy is to let people know how to respond to a person's challenging behaviour in a safe and planned way. The main aim is to minimise any danger or risk to the person or others and bring about the quickest possible resolution. Nevertheless, it is important to stress that reactive strategies should not be used in isolation but as part of a multi-element package.

A reactive strategy documents how to avoid the onset of a behaviour, reduce the chance that the behaviour will escalate, respond to the behaviour when it occurs and to address the consequences of challenging behaviour (Russell, in press). An additional guiding principle is that least intrusive and least restrictive approaches are used before more restrictive approaches.
To avoid the onset of a challenging episode it is important to have a good hypothesis about the antecedent conditions such as triggers and cues.

For example, long hair not tied back could be the signal for hair-pulling. Levels of engagement (activity) and the immediate environment (noise and number of people) might be important factors. Knowing that a possible trigger is in force (eg. noise) will allow people to plan to take immediate action to avoid this trigger.

Sometimes, the function of a behaviour (ie. the person's need) may be quite clear and responding to that need can be the best way to minimise a challenging episode. This is often cited as a counter-intuitive strategy as it means reinforcing the very behaviour described as challenging. This approach is described by LaVigna & Willis (1995) as 'strategic capitulation'. We need to bear in mind that the purpose of the reactive strategy is to make the situation safe, even if in the short-term the behaviour appears to elicit reinforcement. Similarly, there may be early signs in a person's behaviour that an episode is about to escalate. Recognising these early signs and intervening may avoid a more severe outcome. For example, if verbal aggression is likely to precede physical aggression, responding to the verbal aggression may be more likely to avoid an incident of physical aggression.

Stimulus change refers to providing a very novel stimulus into the scenario as a form of distraction; this could create the space that diffuses the situation. Preferably, it would be something that is known to be liked by the person (eg. singing etc.). Finally, instructional control and redirection again relates to the interruption of a sequence, this time by asking the person to do something, such as a preferred activity (which could be incompatible with the behaviour concerned).

All of the above techniques can be applied in the context of low arousal approaches and the interested reader is referred to McDonnell (2010). This author describes verbal de-escalation techniques such as staying calm (even if on the 'inside' we aren't calm), avoiding raised voices, minimising demands and being aware of personal space.

There are those occasions where physical interventions (such as breakaway or restraint) are used. These should only be used in a planned way, as a last resort and in conjunction with Department of Health guidelines. An in-depth text on this matter can be found in Allen (2009). Similarly the use of PRN (medication 'as and when') should only be implemented under appropriate medical supervision.

Conclusion

As should be apparent, there is no unified cause for challenging behaviour, but rather a collection of risk factors that make the occurrence of challenging behaviour more likely. It is important to rule out or address some potential factors, such as mental health problems and medical conditions, and so on. Thinking about challenging behaviour as being potentially communicative or having function has offered a very useful basis for assessment and ethically derived intervention strategies.

Summary

▶ Challenging behaviour has been defined with an emphasis on social construction.

▶ It is important to assess the function of challenging behaviour.

▶ Once hypotheses about function have been developed, a multi-element approach to intervention has been recommended.

References

Allen D (2009) *Ethical Approaches to Physical Interventions Vol II.* Kidderminster: BILD.

Baker P & Shephard J (2010) Focused support strategies. In: S Hardy & T Joyce (Eds) *Challenging Behaviour: A training pack to develop good practice in working with people with learning disabilities whose behaviour is described as challenging.* Brighton: Pavilion.

Carr EG, Levin L, McConnachie G, Carlson JI, Kemp DC & Smith CE (1994) *Communication-based Intervention for Problem Behaviour: A user's guide for producing positive change.* Baltimore: Paul H Brookes Publishing Co.

Department of Health (2009) *Valuing People Now: A new three-year strategy for people with intellectual disabilities.* London: TSO.

Durand VM & Crimmins DB (1992) *The Motivation Assessment Scale.* Topeka, KS: Monaco & Associates.

Emerson E (1995) *Challenging Behaviour: Analysis and intervention in people with learning difficulties.* Cambridge: Cambridge University Press.

Emerson E (1998) Working with people with challenging behaviour. In: E Emerson, C Hatton, J Bromley & A Caine (Eds) *Clinical Psychology and People with Intellectual Disabilities.* Chichester: John Wiley & Sons.

Emerson E, Alborz A, Kiernan C, Mason H, Reeves D, Swarbrick R & Mason L (1997) *The HARC Challenging Behaviour Project Report 2: The prevalence of challenging behaviour.* Manchester: Hester Adrian Research Centre, University of Manchester.

Horner R & Day HM (1991) The effects of response efficiency on functionally equivalent competing behaviors. *Journal of Applied Behaviour Analysis* **24** (4) 719–732.

Iwata B, Dorsey M, Slifer K, Bauman K & Richman G (1982) Towards a functional analysis of self-injury. *Analysis and Intervention in Developmental Disabilities* **2** 3–20.

LaVigna G & Willis T (1995) Challenging behaviour: a model for breaking the barriers to social and community integration. *Positive Practices* **1** 8–15.

Mansell J (2007) *Services for People with Learning Disabilities and Challenging Behaviour or Mental Health Needs.* London: DH.

McDonnell A (2010) *Managing Aggressive Behaviour in Care Settings: Understanding and applying low arousal approaches.* Chichester: John Wiley & Sons Ltd.

McGill P & Toogood A (1993) Providing helpful environments. In: E Emerson, P McGill & J Mansell (Eds) *Severe Learning Disabilities and Challenging Behaviours: Designing high quality services.* London: Chapman and Hall.

O'Neill RE, Horner RH, Albin RW, Storey K & Sprague JR (1990) *Functional Analysis of Problem Behaviour: A practical assessment guide.* Sycamore, IL: Sycamore.

Royal College of Psychiatrists, British Psychological Society & Royal College of Speech and Language Therapists (2007) *Challenging Behaviour: A unified approach.* London: Royal College of Psychiatrists.

Russell L (in press) Reactive strategies. In: S Hardy & S Joyce (Eds) *Challenging Behaviour: A handbook.* Brighton: Pavilion.

Udwin O & Kuczynski A (2007) Behavioural phenotypes in genetic syndromes associated with intellectual disabilities. In: A Carr, G O'Reilly, P Walsh & J McEvoy (Eds) *The Handbook of Intellectual Disability and Clinical Psychology Practice.* Hove: Routledge.

Chapter 14

Autism and mental health

Muthukumar Kannabiran and Jane McCarthy

Introduction

Autism is a group of conditions that arise in the early period of development ie. following birth and during early childhood. The conditions are often referred to as 'developmental disorders' and include intellectual disability. In 1943 Kanner first described the features of early infantile autism in a group of children with social aloofness and repetitive routines (Wing, 1996).

The expert opinion

'Doctors and nurses should have training about people with autism.'

Sub-types of autism

Autism includes the following conditions: childhood or classical autism, Asperger's syndrome and atypical autism.

Childhood autism

According to the *International Classification of Disorders* (ICD-10) (WHO, 1992)– which refers to autism as a 'pervasive developmental disorder' – before a diagnosis of childhood autism can be made evidence of impaired and/or abnormal development before the age of three needs to be established.

This is characterised by:
1. abnormality in social interaction
2. abnormality in communication
3. restrictive, repetitive behaviour.

Asperger's syndrome

Asperger's syndrome is characterised by no delay in language or cognitive development, but with repetitive, stereotyped behaviour and impaired social functioning. People with high functioning autism meet the criteria for autism but do not have intellectual disability. There is often confusion regarding Asperger's syndrome and high functioning autism. Individuals with high functioning autism have a history of delayed and/or impaired communication before the age of three, in contrast to people with Asperger's syndrome who do not.

Atypical autism

Individuals whose symptoms do not meet all the above criteria (ie. impaired communication, impaired social interaction and restrictive repertoire of behaviour), but have some of the above features, are diagnosed as having atypical autism.

Prevalence of autism

The prevalence of autism ranges from 116 people per 10,000 for all types (Baird *et al*, 2006) ie. 1% of the population to a more conservative estimate between 60–65 people per 10,000 (Fombonne, 2005).

Mental health and autism

The mental health needs of individuals with intellectual disabilities and autism are being increasingly recognised. It used to be suggested that this group of individuals had higher rates of mental health problems, compared to individuals with intellectual disabilities alone (without autism). Recent studies have been challenging this view but the quality of the evidence makes it difficult to arrive at firm conclusions (Underwood *et al*, 2010).

Epidemiological studies of mental health problems in people with autism are fraught with difficulties such as referral bias (eg. studies involving clinic populations may have higher levels of psychiatric morbidity compared to studies involving people from the general population), small sample sizes (for example, due to difficulty in recruiting patients who may lack capacity to consent), difficulty in differentiating the features of autism from a co-morbid psychiatric disorder (such as differentiating between repetitive behaviour seen in people with autism from that seen in individual with obsessive compulsive disorder) and difficulty in making psychiatric diagnoses due to impaired communication (Hutton *et al*, 2008).

Bradley *et al* (2004) reported that the prevalence of psychiatric disorders is increased in adolescents with autism and severe intellectual disabilities, who, in the study, had five episodes compared to one episode in those without autism. This is in contrast to a clinic-based study of adults in which a similar prevalence of mental health problems was observed in individuals with intellectual disabilities and autism, compared to those without autism who were referred to services (Tsakanikos *et al*, 2006). A study of 112 children with autism in the UK found that 71% had at least one psychiatric disorder, 29% had social anxiety disorder, 28% had attention deficit hyperactivity disorder and 28% had oppositional defiant disorder (Simonoff *et al*, 2008). Interestingly, a study of adults with autism who . used psychiatric hospitals in Canada found that adults with intellectual disabilities and autism were less likely to have a psychotic disorder when compared to individuals without autism (Lunsky *et al*, 2009). However, the usual limitations ie. small sample size and unmatched samples confound the findings of this study. Skokauskas & Gallagher (2010) reviewed studies of mental health problems in people with autism and reported a wide variation in rates. Similar to findings by other studies in this area, methodological issues were also reported by the authors of this review.

Risk factors for mental health problems

The following factors have been found to increase the risk of mental health problems in individuals with autism – communication problems, life events (including loss), loneliness (associated with rejection by peers) and low self-esteem (related to teasing or bullying).

Assessment of people with autism

When assessing a person with autism, the process of assessment needs to be individually tailored to the needs and abilities of that individual. An individual with autism may have a reduced ability to describe emotions and symptoms of mental illness. They may not have acquired the appropriate language skills needed to engage in a complex assessment of their mental health. It is well recognised that people with autism may have a tendency to interpret questions literally. Hence, when assessing a person with autism for mental health problems it is important to recognise these potential issues and to try to obtain collateral information (with the individual's consent) from another person, such as a family member or a friend. Recent policy also highlights the need for increasing awareness and the understanding of autism by professionals working across health and social services (DH, 2010).

Mental health problems in people with autism

The full range of mental health problems can be seen in individuals with autism, similar to someone without autism, ranging from severe mental illness such as psychotic or bipolar disorder to common mental health problems such as milder forms of depressive disorder and anxiety disorders.

Psychotic disorder

A recent review of studies involving people with autism provided a range of 0–6% for the presence of schizophrenia (Skokauskas & Gallagher, 2010). Autism and psychotic disorders have a long history, with autism being originally considered to be an early manifestation of schizophrenia. The distinction between the two conditions was made in the early 1970s.

A recent study has found that autism can precede as well as occur in 30–50% of children with childhood-onset schizophrenia (Rapoport *et al*, 2009). Individuals with autism may hold rigid beliefs, which may be difficult to distinguish from delusional beliefs. Similarly, it may be difficult to elicit problems such as hallucinations in a person with impaired language ability, as it may be difficult to 'tease out' the finer aspects of the symptoms. Psychotic disorders are, as a rule, associated with an impaired level of functioning. In individuals with autism, a psychotic disorder may be more likely if the above symptoms are associated with impairment of functioning and/or deterioration in behaviour. In individuals with Asperger's syndrome, it has been suggested that delusions with grandiose or persecutory themes are linked to problems in attention, which occurs in the context of low self-esteem and anxiety.

Mood disorders

Both depressive and bipolar disorders have been reported in people with autism. Even individuals with autism and no significant impairment of communication or language may have difficulty describing their emotional state and providing details of their thought processes. They may not be able to identify or 'label' their emotions. Individuals with autism and higher levels of cognitive and social functioning are more likely to report depressive symptoms (Sterling *et al,* 2008). Stewart *et al* (2006) report, in their review of depression in people with autism, that low mood is the most common presentation of depression in people with autism. Presence of symptoms such as loss of interest in pleasurable activities, reduced functioning, disturbed sleep and appetite, and psychomotor retardation assists the diagnosis of depression. Recent onset of or increase in maladaptive behaviour such as self-injury or aggression, and/or a decrease in adaptive behaviour, such as reduced self-care or worsening of stereotyped or ritualistic behavior, such as echolalia, may indicate the presence of a depressive disorder.

Bipolar affective disorder is characterised by episodes of mania or hypomania, alternating with episodes of depression, or with both depressive and manic/hypomanic symptoms occurring within the same episode. As in individuals without autism, episodes of hypomania or mania may present with irritability, increased energy levels, disruptive and aggressive behaviours, reduced and/or decreased need for sleep, increased speech output and activity. The true prevalence of bipolar affective disorder is unknown in people with autism, with the recent review by Skokauskas & Gallagher (2010) reporting a range of 0–50% for affective disorders (which includes both depressive and bipolar disorders). One clinic-based study of 44 patients with high functioning autism reports that, of the 36% of patients diagnosed with a mood disorder, 75% had bipolar affective disorder (Munesue *et al,* 2008).

Anxiety disorders

The review by Skokauskas & Gallagher (2010) found that anxiety disorders were most common in individuals with autism, with rates of 5–35% for generalised anxiety disorder, 10–64% for phobias and 1–37% for obsessive compulsive disorder. Of the anxiety disorders, clinicians find it difficult to distinguish symptoms of obsessive compulsive disorder (OCD) from the repetitive, stereotyped rituals or behaviours in people with autism. McDougle *et al* (1995) reported that individuals with autism were more likely to report or experience repeating, hoarding, touching and tapping behaviour, compared to obsessive thoughts and cleaning, checking or counting compulsions seen in obsessive compulsive disorder. Russell *et al* (2005) undertook a study of obsessions and compulsions in individuals with Asperger's syndrome and high functioning autism. They found that somatic obsessions and repeating rituals were more common and the severity of obsessive compulsive symptoms were higher in individuals with obsessive compulsive disorder.

Other disorders

The other mental health problems reported in individuals with autism include catatonia (a complex disorder of posture, movement, speech and behaviour), attention deficit hyperactivity disorder and Tourette's syndrome. In people with autism, prevalence rates of catatonia range from 12–17% (Kakooza-Mwesige *et al*, 2008). All symptoms of attention deficit hyperactivity disorder are seen in individuals with autism, who are four times more likely to show symptoms of inattention (Bradley & Isaacs, 2006). Interestingly, males and females with autism have an equal risk of developing attention deficit hyperactivity disorder (Brereton *et al*, 2006). Tics and Tourette's syndrome occur more frequently than would be expected by chance (Canitano & Vivanti, 2007). It has been suggested that a shared aetiolgy could be the underlying reason for this.

Conclusion

Individuals with autism present with mental health problems, which are similar to those in people without autism. However, it may be more difficult to elicit symptoms of mental health problems in people with autism. The core features of autism may influence how the symptoms present. Clinicians need to be aware of these issues and need to adapt their assessment according to the needs and abilities of the individual.

Summary

▶ Autism is characterised by abnormalities in social interaction, abnormalities in communication and restrictive, repetitive, stereotyped patterns of behaviour.

▶ People with autism experience the full range of mental health problems.

▶ Diagnosis of mental health problems can be difficult and assessment must be modified to the impairments of the individual.

References

Baird G, Simonoff E, Pickles A, Chandler S, Loucas T, Meldrum D & Charman T (2006) Prevalence of disorders of the autism spectrum in a population cohort of children in South Thames: the Special Needs and Autism Project (SNAP). *The Lancet* **368** 210–215.

Bradley EA, Summers JA, Wood HL & Bryson SE (2004) Comparing rates of psychiatric and behavior disorders in adolescents and young adults with severe intellectual disability with and without autism. *Journal of Autism and Developmental Disorders* **34** (2) 151–161.

Bradley EA & Isaacs BJ (2006) Inattention, hyperactivity and impulsivity in teenagers with intellectual disabilities, with and without autism. *Canadian Journal of Psychiatry* **51** 598–606.

Brereton A, Tonge BJ & Eifeld SL (2006) Psychopathology in children and adolescents with autism compared to young people with intellectual disability. *Journal of Autism and Developmental Disorders* **36** 863–870.

Canitano R & Vivanti G (2007) Tics and Tourette syndrome in autism . spectrum disorders. *Autism* **11** (1) 19–28.

Department of Health (2010) *Fulfilling and Rewarding Lives: The strategy for adults with autism in England.* London: TSO.

Fombonne E (2005) Epidemiology of autistic disorder and other pervasive developmental disorders. *Journal of Clinical Psychiatry* **66** (10) 3–8.

Hutton J, Goode S, Murphy M, Couteur AL & Rutter M (2008) New-onset psychiatric disorders in individuals with autism. *Autism* **12** (4) 373–390.

Kakooza-Mwesige A, Wachtel LE & Dhossche DM (2008) Catatonia in autism: implications across the life span. *European Child and Adolescent Psychiatry* **17** 327–335.

Lunsky Y, Gracey C & Bradley E (2009) Adults with autism spectrum disorders using psychiatric hospitals in Ontario: clinical profile and service needs. *Research in Autism and Developmental Disorders* **3** 1006–1013.

McDougle CJ, Kresch LE, Goodman WK, Naylor ST, Volkmar FR, Cohen DJ & Price LH (1995) A case-controlled study of repetitive thoughts and behavior in adults with autistic disorder and obsessive-compulsive disorder. *American Journal of Psychiatry* **152** 772–777.

Munesue T, Ono Y, Mutoh K, Shimoda K, Nakatani H & Kikuch M (2008) High prevalence of bipolar disorder comorbidity in adolescents and young adults with high-functioning autism spectrum disorder: a preliminary study of 44 outpatients. *Journal of Affective Disorders* **111** 170–175.

Rapoport J, Chavez A, Greenstein D, Addington A & Gogtay A (2009) Autism spectrum disorders and childhood-onset schizophrenia: clinical and biological contributions to a relation revisited. *Journal of the American Academy of Child Adolescent Psychiatry* **48** (1) 10–18.

Russell AJ, Mataix-Cols D, Anson M & Murphy DGM (2005) Obsessions and compulsions in Asperger syndrome and high functioning autism. *British Journal of Psychiatry* **186** 525–528.

Simonoff E, Pickles A, Charman T, Chandler S, Loucas T & Baird G (2008) Psychiatric disorders in children with autism spectrum disorders: prevalence, comorbidity and associated factors in a population-derived sample. *Journal of American Academy Child Adolescent Psychiatry* **47** (8) 921–929.

Skokauskas N & Gallagher L (2010) Psychosis, affective disorders and anxiety in autistic spectrum disorder: prevalence and nosoligical considerations. *Psychopathology* **43** 8-16.

Sterling L, Dawson G, Estes A & Greenson J (2008) Characteristics associated with presence of depressive symptoms in adults with autism spectrum disorder. *Journal of Autism and Developmental Disorders* **38** 1011–1018.

Stewart ME, Barnard L, Pearson J, Hasan R & O'Brien G (2006) Presentation of depression in autism and Asperger syndrome: a review. *Autism* **10** 103–116.

Tsakanikos E, Costello H, Holt G, Bouras N, Sturmey P & Newton T (2006) Psychopathology in adults with autism and intellectual disability. *Journal of Autism and Developmental Disorders* **36** (8) 1123–1129.

Underwood L, McCarthy J & Tsakanikos E (2010) Mental health of adults with autism spectrum disorders and intellectual disability. *Current Opinion in Psychiatry* **23** 21–426.

Wing L (1996) No evidence for or against an increase in prevalence. *British Medical Journal* **312** 327–328.

World Health Organization (1992) *The ICD-10 Classification of Mental and Behavioural Disorders.* Geneva: WHO.

Chapter 15

Working with families

Karin Fuchs

Introduction

People with intellectual disabilities often live their lives within complex support networks. Families are a central part of support networks and it is often essential that professionals supporting people with intellectual disabilities work closely with family members. It is estimated that approximately 60% of adults with intellectual disabilities live with their families (DH, 2001a). Even when they do not live together, families tend to be a key part of a person's life. Families may provide the bulk of support for people with intellectual disabilities and they will have encountered numerous professionals from many different services in this role. This chapter will address some of the key issues that currently face individuals with intellectual disabilities and their families. It will offer an understanding of some of the challenges families can face and offer suggestions in terms of what helps in working with families.

> **The expert opinion**
> 'Families should be involved as well, but staff should remember it's about us.'

National context

Historically, support and funding was mainly targeted at people with intellectual disabilities who lived away from home rather than at families. However, there has been a relatively recent shift in government policy and research that recognises the stresses and support needs of family carers. Carers now have the right to an assessment of their own needs under the Carers (Recognition and Services) Act (1995) and the National Strategy for Carers (DH, 1999). *Family Matters: Counting me in* (DH, 2001b) systematically highlights the perspectives of family carers of people with intellectual disabilities, and highlights three key themes: the need for intellectual disability service development; partnership and participation; and supporting family carers. It offers proposals for change and identifies three specific priority groups: older carers; family carers from minority ethnic and black families; and families supporting a young person through the transition from child to adult services. These recent changes in commitment to families at a national and local level offer an important new context in recognising the role of family carers and, hopefully, will increase the support available for the future.

The family life cycle

A family is a natural social system that extends over at least three generations. Each family has its own beliefs, values and cultural practices. Families are multifaceted and dynamic and operate within wider contexts consisting of social, economic, and political structures, which directly or indirectly influence the family (Knox *et al*, 2000).

Carter and McGoldrick (1989) conceptualise the family as a complex and dynamic system over time. They describe the family life cycle based on the concept that as families go through transitions they re-organise. For example, when children are born, leave home, and get married. There will be changes in family roles and relationships. At each stage, families have different developmental tasks to accomplish. When a family member has a disability the sequences of life events are often different (Vetere, 1993). Goldberg *et al* (1995) describe how life cycle transitions can appear 'out of synchrony' in such families. For example, a family member with intellectual disabilities may not leave home like other siblings, and families may have a continuous role in caring for their son or daughter. As well as life cycle stages being 'out of synchrony', families will typically experience heavy involvement from services at the various stages. For example, transition from child to adult or leaving home.

Transition to adulthood

Parents often describe a real shock in the transition from child to adult services (DH, 2001a). Up until this point, parents have been central to all the decisions in their child's life. Parents describe a shift in the way services are organised, the quality and lack of choice available once their child leaves the education system and the shift from being a 'parent' to a 'carer'. The legal framework also changes when their child reaches 16, with the introduction of the Mental Capacity Act (2005). Whereas families will have been central to decisions for their child before that age, the law shifts firmly towards the person with intellectual disabilities as the decision maker, and if there is sufficient evidence that they do not have capacity, then 'best interests' decisions are made. In relation to treatment, the 'best interests' decision is made by the professional who will implement the decision, but they must consult with family members, advocates and other involved professionals. This can be quite an adjustment for family members, which can be eased by explanation and preparation from professionals.

Older carers

Many older carers worry about what will happen to their son or daughter when they are no longer able to care for them. Families can find it hard to think about the future as this can be very anxiety-provoking. Qualitative studies have found that for many family carers, time perspectives are short-term and focus more about 'getting through' the present than thinking about the future (Todd & Shearn, 1996; Grant, 1986). Todd and Shearn (1996) propose that it was this short-term view, together with a dominant parental identity/role and a lack of alternative service provision that helped form a sense of 'perpetual parenthood'. Often families continue support until there is a crisis, when services may need to respond quickly and where there may be very little choice about placement in the short-term. There is increasing recognition of older carers within services now, where early conversations and planning with individuals with intellectual disabilities and their families about the future can pre-empt some of these potential problems and improve shared planning for the future.

Stress and coping

Families with a disabled child are more likely to experience higher levels of stress; financial hardship from loss of earnings and higher costs of caring; social isolation; health problems of carers; problems finding suitable housing; and an increased risk of marital breakdown (DH, 2001a; Beresford, 1995). Mir *et al* (2001) report that for families from black and ethnic minority communities, the situation is often worse, with increased difficulties including poverty, lack of information, social isolation and culturally inappropriate services. It is estimated that eight out of 10 parents and carers have reached 'breaking point' as a result of not getting the help and support they needed (Mencap, 2003).

Protection and loss

Themes around protection, grief and loss have featured heavily in literature about the experiences of families with a disabled member. Historically, within some services there has been a culture of viewing families as 'overprotective' and construing this as unhelpful to the individual with intellectual disabilities. This view has understandably been seen as critical and unhelpful by some family members. However, issues around grief, loss and protection often do feature prominently in families' experiences. It has been proposed that often families have to face a process of loss and bereavement as they grieve the loss of 'what could have been' with a normal child or 'perfect child' (eg. Bicknell, 1983). Goldberg *et al* (1995) highlight how at each life cycle stage, family members are faced with the loss of previously held expectations and that memories of previous loss and grief are invoked for family members. They argue that to progress through transition, family members may have to grieve their current losses, which will inevitably evoke a series of previous losses. They also propose that family members work hard to protect each other from the perceived consequences of disability and further losses, and this can make any life cycle transitions, such as leaving home, challenging for families. Strong feelings can therefore arise for family members when the person with intellectual disabilities reaches clear life cycle markers such as reaching 18 or leaving school, and when there are other family events such as siblings leaving home, going to university, marrying or having children. These can be difficult reminders of unattained hopes and it is important that professionals/ services are sensitive to such issues and anticipate them in advance. It is at these times that roles and relationships may need re-negotiation and some families struggling with this may benefit from external help to assist them through this process, for example family therapy.

Relationship to help

Reder and Fredman (1996) have considered how people's experiences can shape the relationship that they form with the concept of 'help'.

They suggest that in 'helping' relationships, both family members and professionals/services bring with them pre-existing beliefs about the helping process and that these do not always represent a 'good fit'. Where families with a member with intellectual disabilities may have had early negative experiences from services, this relationship is likely to influence the interaction and dynamic set up with adult services. Shearn and Todd (1997) found from qualitative interviews with parents that they often felt judged by professionals as inappropriately controlling by wanting to protect their child with intellectual disabilities, and that involvement with services often involved greater demands on them and was not based on an adequate understanding of their lives. It is important that professionals are able to hold in mind and be sensitive to the longer-term history families may have had with services and how this influences current interactions.

Additional mental health problems

Families may have been through many struggles and challenges associated with living with and supporting a family member with intellectual disabilities. When that member has additional mental health problems, families may feel confused, distressed, overwhelmed and often unsure of how to manage the situation. Young people with intellectual disabilities appear to be particularly at risk of emotional difficulties, such as anxiety and depression, and of showing challenging behaviour or severe conduct disorders (FPWLD, 2002). More specifically, Emerson and Hatton (1997) in a comprehensive study of the mental health needs of children and young people with intellectual disabilities found that over one in three children and adolescents with an intellectual disability in Britain (36%) has a diagnosable psychiatric disorder. Children and adolescents with intellectual disabilities are over six times more likely to have a diagnosable psychiatric disorder than their peers without intellectual disabilities and are 33 times more likely to have an autism spectrum condition.

Families often have a key role in the prevention of mental health problems and supporting family members with intellectual disabilities who have mental health problems; positive, stable and strong family attachments are key protective factors (Emerson & Hatton, 1997). However, families can struggle with getting problems recognised (diagnosis) and with accessing help, and services are often inadequately equipped to offer good mental health services for this group (Emerson & Hatton, 1997; McCarthy & Boyd, 2002). It is essential, therefore, that professionals work closely and collaboratively with families to provide proactive, preventative support, and to provide information and assist in the recognition of possible mental health problems and access to relevant services.

What helps?

What families have told us

According to the *Family Matters* report (DH, 2001b), what families say is primarily important to them is: having good quality services and more varied housing and day opportunities options for people with intellectual disabilities; having time off/respite; receiving emotional support; receiving training and support to care; financial security; having a voice, being heard and working in partnership; provision of full information; and recognition of their own health and well-being (through carers' assessments).

General ways of supporting families should include:

▶ respect: it is essential that the role family members play in the lives of individuals with intellectual disabilities is recognised, valued and responded to

▶ good listening, keeping families involved and building relationships

▶ being open and honest with family members

▶ accepting and valuing differences; acknowledging and respecting different contexts central to the person with intellectual disabilities and their families, such as race, culture, gender, class, poverty, sexuality; ensuring that services are culturally appropriate and information is accessible (for example, in a range of languages; the use of interpreters)

▶ working pro-actively at some points in the family life cycle, namely transition into adulthood and with older carers in offering information and pre-empting potential difficulties; families often need preparation and good information around the changes in service planning, rights, responsibilities and decision making when the child with intellectual disabilities turns 18

▶ a long-term view: working with families should involve a life span view – what families may have been through/experienced already in relation to services, as well as planning for the future and clarifying what they can expect from services in the future; providing timely, adequate and accessible information to families

▶ inclusion of families in person-centred planning for the person with intellectual disabilities, where possible.

Systemic approaches/family therapy

The application of family therapy/systemic ways of working to people with intellectual disabilities and their families has gained increasing recognition in recent years (Baum & Lynngaard, 2006). As mentioned, adults with intellectual disabilities often live with or have continued close support from their families, and sometimes difficulties can occur in the context of these relationships. There can be difficulties around life cycle issues; in family relationships such as conflict or different views; in relationships between families and services; difficulties managing a person with intellectual . disabilities who may have mental health problems and/or challenging behaviour. A systemic approach can be broadly defined as viewing *'problems within the system of relationships within which they occur, and aims to bring about change in the broader system rather than in the individual alone'* (Burnham, 1986). It enables family members to express and explore difficult thoughts and feelings in a safe way, to understand each other's experiences and views, and appreciate each other's needs. Systemic approaches build on family strengths and help families find solutions that make a difference. This approach can be particularly powerful as the person with intellectual disabilities is central to the conversation and is empowered to have a clear voice within the family/network around them. Central to a systemic approach is context, and a family's particular situation can be thought about and talked about in the broadest way, which can include thinking about issues connected with discrimination, social problems, race, religion, culture and ability/disability, and how these influence families we work with. Families' knowledge and experience is respected and solutions are found through collaboration and exploration of multiple ideas and solutions.

Conclusion

Families play a key part in the lives of people with intellectual disabilities and this is now increasingly recognised through national policy. Research shows that there are some key themes and issues that feature for families who have a member with intellectual disabilities, in particular transitions from childhood to adulthood and older carers. Where a person with intellectual disabilities has mental health problems and/or challenging behaviour, the challenges for families are even greater. While as professionals we need to maintain the rights and confidentiality of adults with intellectual disabilities, we need to have a good appreciation of some of the issues family members can face, and we must work collaboratively and supportively with families to enable better and more consistent support for the person with intellectual disabilities.

Summary

▶ Families are often central to the lives of people with intellectual disabilities.

▶ Professionals and support workers need to be aware of some of the issues and key themes that often feature prominently for families.

▶ A collaborative, respectful approach to working with families is essential.

▶ Sometimes, a person with intellectual disabilities and their family will benefit from specialist support such as family therapy to help discuss and find solutions to difficulties that affect the whole family.

References

Baum S & Lynngaard H (2006) *Intellectual Disabilities: A systemic approach.* London: Karnac Books.

Beresford B (1995) *Expert Opinions: A national survey of parents caring for a severely disabled child.* Bristol: The Policy Press.

Bicknell J (1983) The psychotherapy of handicap. *British Journal of Medical Psychology* **56** 167–168.

Burnham J (1986) *Family Therapy.* (Tavistock Library of Social Work Practice). London: Routledge.

Carter B & McGoldrick M (1989) *The Changing Family Life Cycle: A framework for family therapy* (2nd edition). Boston: Alleyn & Bacon.

Department of Health (1999) *Caring about Carers: A national strategy for carers.* London: Department of Health.

Department of Health (2001a) *Valuing People: A new strategy for learning disability in the 21st century.* London: TSO.

Department of Health (2001b) *Family Matters: Counting me in.* London, TSO.

Emerson E & Hatton (1997) Mental health of children and adolescents with intellectual disabilities in Britain. *British Journal of Psychiatry* **191** 493–499.

Foundation for People with Learning Disabilities (2002) *Count Us In report.* London: Foundation for People with Learning Disabilities.

Goldberg D, Magrill L, Hale J, Damskinidou K, Paul J & Tham S (1995) Protection and loss: working with learning disabled adults and their families. *Journal of Family Therapy* **17** 263–280.

Grant G (1986) Older carers, interdependence and the care of mentally handicapped adults. *Ageing and Society* **6** 33–51.

Knox M (2000) Family control: the views of families who have a child with an intellectual disability. *Journal of Applied Research in Intellectual Disabilities* **13** 17–18.

McCarthy J & Boyd J (2002) Mental health services and young people with intellectual disability: is it time to do better? *Journal of Intellectual Disability Research* **46** (3) 250–256.

Mencap (2003) *Breaking Point: A report on caring without a break for children and adults with severe or profound intellectual disabilities.* London: Mencap.

Mir G, Nocon A, Ahmad W & Jones L (2001) *Learning Difficulties and Ethnicity.* London: Department of Health.

Reder P & Fredman G (1996) The relationship to help: interacting beliefs about the treatment process. *Clinical Child Psychology and Psychiatry* **1** (3) 457–467.

Shearn J & Todd S (1997) Parental work: an account of the day-to-day activities of parents of adults with intellectual disabilities. *Journal of Intellectual Disability Research* **41** (4) 285–301.

Todd S & Shearn J (1996) Struggles with time: the careers of parents with adult sons and daughters with intellectual disabilities. *Disability and Society* **11** (3) 379–402.

Vetere AL (1993) Using family therapy in services for people with learning disabilities. In: J Carpenter & A Treacher (Eds) *Using Family Therapy in the '90s.* Oxford: Blackwell.

Chapter 16

The mental health needs of children with intellectual disabilities

Sarah H Bernard

Introduction

Children with intellectual disabilities are known to have an increased risk of mental health and behavioural problems compared to those of a similar chronological age without a developmental disability. In addition, they are at risk of having a range of physical disabilities, sensory difficulties, and psycho-social problems. These factors affect the quality of life of children and their families. Service provision, while clearly a need, is not yet able to offer the same level of mental health provision as to those without developmental disabilities (Allington-Smith, 2006).

The expert opinion

'Children with intellectual disabilities can have mental health problems too. There should be special teams who can help them get better.'

Epidemiology

There is an expanding evidence base confirming that children with developmental disabilities are at risk of mental health problems. This includes the landmark study of Rutter *et al* (1970), which demonstrated that children aged 10–12 years exhibited an increased level of emotional and behavioural disorders if they had intellectual disabilities. Other studies have confirmed this, for example:

▶ Corbett (1979) showed that almost 50% of 0–15 year olds with severe intellectual disabilities had a psychiatric disorder

▶ Gillberg *et al* (1986) demonstrated an increased rate of autism, language and social impairment and psychosis in 13–17 year olds with an IQ of less than 50

▶ Emerson and Hatton (2007) found higher rates of all psychiatric disorders in a study of 641 children with intellectual disabilities.

Diagnostic overshadowing complicates the picture as it is believed that children with intellectual disabilities are likely to exhibit behavioural problems that are not attributed to an underlying psychiatric or mental health symptomatology (Reiss & Szyszko, 1983).

In a single London borough of 250,000 people, of which 20% are children, approximately 2–3% will have intellectual disabilities and 250 of these children will have an IQ of below 50. It is likely that a third of children with mild/moderate intellectual disabilities are likely to have behavioural and mental health problems, with a further half of those with severe or profound intellectual disabilities having such problems. This equates to approximately 550 children who require child and adolescent (CAMHS) mental health services (Bernard & Turk, 2009).

A range of factors contribute to the risk of developing mental health and behavioural problems, including the child's level of cognitive functioning, the underlying cause of intellectual disabilities, abuse and neglect including poverty, poor parenting, and inappropriate educational demands (Emerson & Hatton, 2007).

The assessment of possible mental or behavioural problems in children with intellectual disabilities demands a multidisciplinary/multiagency approach. The team composition is likely to vary depending on local service provision but generally includes psychiatry, clinical psychology, speech and language therapy, mental health nursing, and social work provision.

Aetiology

The aetiology of the child's intellectual disabilities can be considered as occurring:

▶ before conception – usually a genetic cause and includes chromosomal abnormalities (trisomy 21, deletions, inversions) and inborn errors of metabolism

▶ prenatally – such as fetal malformations (neural tube defect), trauma (irradiation) and infection (rubella, cytomegalic inclusion virus, toxoplasmosis)

▶ peri-natally – such as birth injury and infection (herpes simplex, beta-haemolytic streptococcal infection)

▶ post-natally – such as trauma (road traffic accident, non-accidental injury) and infection (meningitis, encephalitis)

Knowledge of the underlying cause of the disability contributes to the understanding of the child's mental health or behavioural problem as certain disorders increase the risk of specific behavioural disturbance (Turk, 2007). These include:

▶ overeating and skin picking in Prader Willi syndrome

▶ self-injury in Lesch Nyhan syndrome

▶ social anxiety in fragile X syndrome.

The reader should refer to paediatric/genetic texts for more details about the aetiology of intellectual disabilities.

Assessment

Any assessment will look at the following issues:

▶ psychopathology

▶ functional analysis of behavioural disorders looking at the function and meaning of the behaviour

▶ psychometric/cognitive assessment to clarify the child's level of cognitive functioning

▶ communication

▶ exclusion of organic disorder – often done in conjunction with community paediatrics

▶ family functioning and social issues

▶ understanding of educational input

▶ assessment of risk/safeguarding.

The assessment must take into account a child's level of functioning as this will help inform about the appropriateness of specific behaviours. Information should be gained from parents, carers, teachers, social workers and any other people involved with the young person. Direct observations carried out in an environment that is familiar to the child are also important.

The assessment should conclude with the formulation of the case. The ICD-10 multi axis diagnostic approach is a useful framework as it allows consideration of the following areas (WHO, 1992).

1. Axis 1: Psychiatric diagnosis, for example, autism, attention deficit hyperactivity disorder, depression, psychosis

2. Axis 2: Specific developmental disability, for example communication delay

3. Axis 3: Global developmental disability ranging from mild to profound intellectual disability as defined by intellectual quotient (intellectual disability/mental retardation)

4. Axis 4: Physical/medical disorders including syndromes

5. Axis 5 : Psycho-social stressors such as anomalous parenting, parental ill heath, abuse/trauma

6. Axis 6: Overall level of social disability

Challenging behaviour is a descriptive term which is used for any behaviour posing a challenge for the individual's carers or society. Challenging behaviour has been defined as *'behaviour of such an intensity, frequency or duration that the physical safety of the person or others is likely to be placed in serious jeopardy, or behaviour which is likely to seriously limit or delay access to and use of ordinary community facilities'* (Emerson, 2001). Challenging behaviour includes a range of behaviours such as aggression, self-injury, persistent masturbation, and damage to property. Whether or not a child is labelled as having challenging behaviour should not detract from the need for a detailed assessment of the underlying aetiology of the behaviour and exclusion of a diagnosis of psychiatric disorder or physical or/organic disorder.

Specific psychiatric disorders

The range of psychiatric disorders encountered by children with intellectual disabilities is similar to their non-learning disabled peers. The following provides a brief overview of the more common disorders and how their presentation differs in children with intellectual disabilities.

Autism

Autism is pervasive and in general is evident before the age of three. In those with severe intellectual disabilities, autism may account for severe behavioural disturbance, which includes aggression and self-injury (Wing & Gould, 1979). Behaviours exhibited by children with severe/profound intellectual disabilities can mimic autism but are, on assessment, often appropriate for the cognitive level at which the child functions. Additionally, autistic-type behaviours can be mistaken for early onset psychosis with overlap seen when assessing abnormal perceptions and cognitions (Dossetor, 2007).

Attention deficit hyperactivity disorder

Attention-deficit hyperactivity disorder (ADHD) is under-diagnosed in children with intellectual disabilities but it is also overrepresented . (Emerson, 2003), with the child's lack of attention being interpreted as due to their intellectual disabilities rather than a psychiatric disorder. This is an example of diagnostic overshadowing (Reiss & Szyszko, 1983).

Depression

Depression can be displayed as 'challenging behaviour' with lack of recognition of an underlying mood disorder. Symptoms are not dissimilar to those seen in children without intellectual disabilities including low mood, loss of interest in activities and poor concentration. In order to make a diagnosis in non-verbal children, reliance is placed on biological features such as poor or disturbed sleep, reduced appetite and diurnal variation of mood (Bernard, 2009). Suicidal behaviours can occur, although the ability to plan self-harm and suicide and to act on these plans is compromised by the child's level of intellectual functioning.

Psychosis

The diagnosis of psychosis, including schizophrenia and bipolar affective disorder, has major implications for the child, their carers and their service providers. Clinical features include thought disorder, hallucinations and delusions – as in the general population. The assessment of these children may be complicated by the child being unable to report their own thoughts and experiences. Catatonic features are believed to be more common than in children without intellectual disabilities as are negative features or non-specific behavioural changes.

Management

The expectations of what should be provided by a specialist service for children with intellectual disabilities, includes:

▶ collaborative prevention work

▶ diagnosis and assessment

▶ adjustment counselling

▶ family work

▶ specialised psychological interventions including behavioural therapy and CBT

▶ pharmacological therapies

▶ assistance with educational placement

▶ safeguarding

▶ liaison with other agencies (Royal College of Psychiatrists, 2004).

In general, generic CAMHS, services are not able to offer this level of expertise. Treatment is most likely to be successful if specialist, highly trained staff are providing it.

There are a number of interventions that might be offered to children with intellectual disabilities and behavioural or mental health problems. Unfortunately, there remains a lack of evidence-based studies to inform clinicians about the risks and benefits of these. Despite this, interventions may be appropriately offered and are likely to include:

▶ behaviour psychotherapy

▶ family therapy

▶ speech and language therapy

▶ pharmacological therapies

▶ support and psycho-education.

Co-ordination and liaison is crucial as it is highly likely that there will be a range of professionals and agencies working with the young person and their family.

The family

Children with intellectual disabilities, as with all children, cannot be considered in isolation from their family. They are also part of their school community and their wider local community. Family functioning is diverse and cultural variation must be understood when assessing and managing the child.

The majority of young people with intellectual disabilities live at home and families, in general, are the first line of 'therapist' when considering intervention (Bernard & Turk, 2009). Families are frequently under pressure when having to address the needs of their child with a complex disability in addition to meeting the needs of all other members of the family. Families should be offered appropriate support and respite care in order to reduce the risk of family breakdown.

Prognosis

Prognostic factors include the child's level of intellectual disability as children with a high level of cognitive functioning tend to have a better outcome. Social awareness also improves prognosis and the presence of autism can have a negative impact. Good verbal skills are an advantage, as is a supportive family and appropriate education. Poverty, abuse, neglect and deprivation all impact negatively on children with intellectual disabilities and increase the risk of developing health problems (Emerson & Hatton, 2007; Bernard & Turk, 2009).

Summary

▶ Children with intellectual disabilities are at risk of developing a range of behavioural and mental health problems.

▶ These children require specialist provision but mental health services are underdeveloped and, at times, difficult to access.

▶ A comprehensive assessment is important prior to considering intervention.

▶ Intervention, while lacking a comprehensive evidence base, can be successful.

References

Allington-Smith P (2006) Mental Health of children with learning disabilities. *Advances in Psychiatric Treatment* **12** 130–138.

Bernard SH (2009) Mental health and behavioural problems in children and adolescents with learning disabilities. *Psychiatry* **8** (10) 387–390.

Bernard S & Turk J (2009) *Developing Mental Health Services for Children and Adolescents with Intellectual disabilities: A toolkit for clinicians.* London: The Royal College of Psychiatrists.

Corbett JA (1979) Psychiatric morbidity and mental retardation. In: FE James & RP Snaith (Eds) *Psychiatric Illness and Mental Handicap.* London:Gaskell.

Dossetor DR (2007) All that glitters is not gold. Misdiagnosis of psychosis in pervasive developmental disorders – a case series. *Clinical Child Psychology and Psychiatry* **12** (4) 537–548.

Emerson E (2001) *Challenging Behaviour: Analysis and intervention in people with severe intellectual disabilities.* Cambridge: Cambridge University Press.

Emerson E (2003) Prevalence of psychiatric disorders in children and adolescents with and without intellectual disabilities. *Journal of Intellectual Disabilities Research* **17** 51–58.

Emerson E & Hatton C (2007) Contribution of socio economic position to health inequalities of British children and adolescents with intellectual disabilities *American Journal of Mental Retardation* **112** 140–150.

Gillberg C, Persson U, Grufman M & Themner U (1986) Psychiatric disorders in mildly and severely mentally retarded urban children and adolescents. Epidemiological perspectives. *British Journal of Psychiatry* **149** 69–74.

Reiss S & Szyszko J (1983) Diagnostic overshadowing and professional experience with mentally retarded persons. *American Journal of Mental Deficiency* **87** 396–417.

Royal College of Psychiatrists (2004) *Psychiatry Services for Children and Adolescents with Intellectual disabilities. Council Report CR123.* London: RCPsych.

Rutter M, Graham P & Yule WA (1970) *Neuropsychiatric Study in Childhood. Clinical in development Medicine Nos 35/36.* London: Heinemann.

Turk J (2007) Behavioural phenotypes: their applicability to children and young people who have learning disabilities. *Advances in Mental Health and Intellectual Disabilities* **1** (3) 4–13.

Wing L & Gould G (1979) Severe impairments of social interaction and associated abnormalities in children: epidemiology and classifications. . *Journal of Autism and Development Disorders* **9** 11–30.

World Health Organization (1992) *International Classification of Diseases (ICD-10).* Geneva: WHO.

Chapter 17

Mental health needs of older people with intellectual disabilities

Karen Dodd

Introduction

This chapter looks at the specific mental health needs of older people with intellectual disabilities and focuses primarily on the needs of those who develop dementia.

The expert patient

'People with dementia can still do things, but they need more time and support.'

What is old age?

Getting older is a normal stage of the life cycle. However, there is not a clear understanding of what is 'old' for people with intellectual disabilities as there is a lack of agreement about what constitutes old age in this population. Within the intellectual disability literature studies vary in their definition. Some studies consider people to be old at 40 (O'Rourke, 2004) while others use the ages of 50, 55, 60 and 65 (Cooper, 1997; Van Puyenbroeck & Maes 2005; Strydom *et al*, 2005). This means that care needs to be taken when learning from studies according to the ages used.

In the general population people are living longer and staying in better health. People with intellectual disabilities are also living longer, although they still have a significantly lower overall life expectancy. This seems to be due to multiple factors, including:

▶ those who have organic conditions/syndromes/physical and neurological conditions, which are associated with reduced life expectancy

▶ people in the above groups having increased vulnerability to early onset dementia; this is particularly the case for adults with Down's syndrome and particularly related to Alzheimer's disease (discussed later)

▶ those with profound and multiple disabilities having a substantially reduced life expectancy

▶ as people live longer they increasingly suffer from diseases such as cancer, heart, circulatory and respiratory problems; these conditions may be detected later in adults with intellectual disabilities and thus lead to a worse prognosis.

When thinking about older people with intellectual disabilities, it is important to consider the potential for very significant cohort effects (Holland, 2000). Mortality rates and educational opportunities were very different 60 years ago and many children with intellectual disabilities would have been put in an institutional setting. This means that care needs to be taken when extrapolating from current studies of older people with intellectual disabilities, as future cohorts may have very different characteristics and life experiences. Younger people with intellectual disabilities will have had significantly different life experiences, expectations and services, and may need different considerations as they age.

Older people with intellectual disabilities have the same rights to services as older people in the general population. However, services may need to be provided at an earlier age (for those aged 50 years and above). While there have been many positive changes for people with intellectual disabilities, a number of studies (Bigby *et al*, 2001, Thompson & Wright, 2001) still find that older people with intellectual disabilities are more likely to be discriminated against and disadvantaged compared to younger people with intellectual disabilities. Planning should follow the guidance in *Valuing People* (DH, 2001) and ensure that the person has a person-centred plan and health action plan. In addition, if the person has got or develops a diagnosed mental health problem, they should be part of the CPA process (see Chapter 8) and have an individualised relapse prevention plan.
It is important to remember that older age does not exclude the needs of people with intellectual disabilities being addressed through the full range of intellectual disability and generic policies, procedures and guidelines eg.

safeguarding adults, capacity and consent, confidentiality, advocacy and carers' assessments.

What are the particular risks associated with getting older for adults with intellectual disabilities?

Many people with intellectual disabilities do not have a detailed understanding of the normal life cycle. Often, they are in services for their whole lives, which do not differentiate between the needs of younger and older people. The transition to becoming older is still rarely considered within intellectual disabilities services (Dodd, 2008). Services need to . develop strategies in response to the growing numbers of older people with intellectual disabilities who may require a different style of service.

As with the general population, there are health and social changes that are more likely to occur for older people. In health terms, as people get older they often become more frail and their immune systems become less efficient. Hence, diseases can develop more easily and the person may take longer to recover. Existing sensory difficulties, such as hearing and sight problems, often deteriorate and new sensory problems may develop. Reduced exercise and mobility can increase the risk of falls and bone fractures, cardiovascular disease, skin problems, arthritis and constipation. Although the incidence of deaths from cancer in the UK for people with intellectual disabilities is lower than for the general population, people with intellectual disabilities have higher rates of gastrointestinal cancer than the general population (Duff *et al*, 2001). Respiratory disease is considered to be the leading cause of death for people with intellectual disabilities, with much higher rates than in the general population. Medical interventions need to be sensitive to these factors and the increased risks of toxicity with drugs and other medication.

In social terms, ageing is a time when there is a greater risk of major life events. These can include the death of parents, spouse, siblings or close friends. Family networks often change with adult children moving away. Some people retire from their existing day services and have nothing to replace it. This means that older people with intellectual disabilities often have smaller and diminishing social networks and are more at risk of becoming isolated.

The assessment of an older person with intellectual disabilities is a lengthy and often complex process. Each person has different cognitive and functional abilities and different past and current social circumstances. An assessment involves obtaining a detailed history from the person (where possible) and those who know them best, assessments of health, behaviour and cognitive abilities, and medical/psychiatric investigations

The mental health problems of older people with intellectual disabilities

Other sections of this handbook deal in detail with the presentation and treatment of the major mental health problems in people with intellectual disabilities. People can develop the full range of mental health problems in old age, either for the first time or as re-occurrences from earlier in their life. As with all adults with intellectual disabilities, if the person is non-verbal it is often very difficult to ascertain the underlying problem(s) and therapeutic interventions may need to be tried to see if they help to alleviate the symptoms.

The risk of becoming depressed increases as people with intellectual disabilities get older. People with depression are typically seen to slow down, both physically and mentally, and can become withdrawn. Their appetite and sleep patterns are also usually adversely affected. Life events are a significant risk factor for the development of depression and may also mask the early signs of dementia. The symptoms of depression are similar to the early signs of dementia, and in some people depression and dementia may occur simultaneously.

The main differences to look for include:

▶ people with depression are more aware of their problems and are anxious about their cause

▶ people with depression have not lost skills/abilities, but often are not able to use them because of their mental state

▶ patterns of night-time disturbance differ; in depression people are more likely to have problems getting to sleep and they tend to wake up early, while people with dementia often get upset in the evening and 'wander' in the night.

Older people with intellectual disabilities benefit from the full range of pharmacological and psychological interventions for depression, including the use of both talking (eg. cognitive behavioural therapy) and art therapies. Where the differential diagnosis between depression and dementia is not clear, a brief trial of antidepressants may ease symptoms and/or help to clarify the primary diagnosis.

What is dementia and why is it such a key issue?

Dementia is a general term used to describe a collection of illnesses with a similar pattern of symptoms that manifest in a deterioration of functioning and lead to a premature death.

Alzheimer's disease is the most common form of dementia and is a slowly progressive, non-reversible condition characterised by the deterioration of cognitive and functional ability, affecting mood, personality and behaviour. It is characterised by changes in the brain consisting of plaques, tangles and neuronal degeneration. Vascular dementia is the second most common dementia, which is characterised by damage to a number of localised parts of the brain due to damaged blood vessels. Lewy body dementia in people with intellectual disabilities has also begun to be recognised; it is characterised by fluctuations in cognitive ability, visual hallucinations and Parkinsonian features.

The major risk factors for the development of dementia in people with intellectual disabilities are Down's syndrome and having sustained a head injury. The incidence of dementia in people with intellectual disabilities without genetic or neurological cause is thought to be about 15% at the age of 65 and over, which is higher than in the general population (BPS, 2009). However, the incidence for people with Down's syndrome is much greater. Prasher (1995) found age-specific prevalence rates of 9.4% at age 40–49, 36.1% at age 50–59, and 54.5% at age 60–69. The average age of onset was 54 years, and the average duration from diagnosis of dementia to death was 4.6 years.

Characteristics of Alzheimer's disease in people with Down's syndrome

A three-stage model is often used to describe the clinical progress of the disease, with the stages occurring over different time periods in different individuals. Some symptoms may be expressed differently and not all the signs may be observed in all people.

Early stage signs

▶ Subtle changes in behaviour and mood

▶ Performance at day placements deteriorates

▶ Problems with memory, particularly for recent events

▶ Ability to learn new information is affected

▶ Language and word-finding problems

▶ Decline in social, community and daily living skills

▶ Disorientation

▶ Difficulties with steps, stairs and kerbs due to depth perception problems

Middle stage signs

▶ Memory loss becomes more pronounced and the individual may forget personal information or the names of familiar people

▶ Language problems become more evident – they might have trouble maintaining a logical conversation, understanding instructions or naming familiar objects

▶ Confusion and disorientation about time, place and problems finding their way around familiar environments

▶ Difficulty with self-care and then loss of self-care skills

▶ More severe changes in personality and social behaviour eg. mood changes, inactivity or apathy, behavioural disturbances such as wandering, sleep problems, agitation, hallucinations and delusions

▶ Physical problems including the onset of seizures, decreased mobility and incontinence

Late stage signs

▶ Loss of eating/drinking skills

▶ Problems with walking and balance, individuals become chair/bed bound

▶ Problems with recognising people

▶ Increase in stereotyped behaviour

▶ Often require 24-hour care

▶ Can become bedridden and inactive

▶ Greater risk of infections, particularly pneumonia

For adults with severe and profound disabilities, symptoms primarily appear to be social withdrawal, apathy and impaired attention. Many of the early signs of dementia can be due to a range of other treatable conditions. These include depression, thyroid problems, sensory difficulties, other physical, psychological and psychiatric problems, and environmental changes. It is vital that, as part of the assessment process, these are considered and suitable interventions put into place as appropriate.

A diagnosis of dementia can only be made once all other possibilities have been excluded, and where the person's level of functioning is known to have declined in comparison to how they were at a previous time. Best practice now recommends that baseline assessments of all adults with Down's syndrome should be carried out at about the age of 30 (BPS, 2009). These should include assessments of cognitive functioning and adaptive living skills and be carried out in both residential and day settings to give a detailed picture of how the service user is functioning.

Reliable diagnosis can only occur when the following assessments have been completed.

1. Background history eg. medication, medical history, health status, past abilities, risk factors eg. head injury, family history of Alzheimer's disease

2. Medical assessment eg. hearing, sight, blood tests, CAT/MRI scans (as required)

3. Psychosocial/psychiatric assessment eg. mental health problems, recent life events, bereavement, social and physical environment

4. Cognitive assessment eg. orientation, memory, learning, language, visuo-spatial skills

5. Adaptive assessment eg. daily living skills, social and communication skills

6. Behavioural assessment eg. changes in behaviour, personality, unusual or challenging behaviours

Interventions

Pharmacological

The use of drug treatments for people with intellectual disabilities and dementia is now accepted. There is evidence from a double-blind, placebo-controlled pilot study and a further follow-up study that donepezil hydrochloride (Aricept) shows some efficacy in the treatment of symptoms of mild to moderate Alzheimer's disease in adults with Down's syndrome (Prasher *et al*, 2002; Prasher *et al*, 2003).

Non-pharmacological

Currently, there is still little research on what non-pharmacological treatments or supports are effective with people with intellectual disabilities and dementia. However, there are a growing number of books and resources that describe elements of good practice in the psychological and social support of people with intellectual disabilities and dementia, drawing on evidence from research with older people and dementia, from expert opinion and from clinical experience (Dodd *et al*, 2009; Dodd *et al*, 2006; Kerr, 2007).

Key interventions

1. Developing understanding of dementia in people with intellectual disabilities

To provide excellent dementia care, staff and family carers need to understand and know the person, understand dementia and its consequences for the person, and consequently to be able to think ahead and predict 'stressors'. Dodd *et al* (2006) described how staff and family carers need to adapt their approach to ensure that the person with dementia has stress-free, failure-free, individualised care that is consistent but without time pressures. This needs to be incorporated into the person's person-centred plan and care plan, with the focus changing from setting targets to ensuring a good quality of life.

2. Anxiety and stress reduction

As people develop dementia, one of the first symptoms experienced by the person is anxiety. People with intellectual disabilities and dementia can become stressed and anxious about many aspects of their daily life during the early stages of dementia. The person may become very anxious about going out as they may not remember where they are going or why. They may forget where they put one of their possessions and search endlessly for a forgotten object. They may agree to certain demands because they are the last words that someone said to them rather than because it is what they want to do.

In the early stages of dementia, interventions include helping staff to think carefully about the amount of language that they use, checking with the person using visual aids or objects of reference about choices to make life as easy and stress-free for the person, giving reassurance and verbal reminders and the use of familiar relaxation techniques.

Consistency of approach between staff is also vital, as the person begins to lose the ability to complete self-care tasks eg. knowing how to dress themself. Staff and carers should observe and record routines in the early stages of dementia so that these can be used as the basis for appropriate intervention as self-care skills begin to deteriorate (Dodd *et al,* 2006).

Changing the environment to make it dementia-friendly is another key area that can help people and reduce feelings of stress and anxiety (Dodd *et al,* 2006; Kerr, 2007; Mahendiran & Dodd, 2009).

3. Life story work

A key issue in caring for people with intellectual disabilities and dementia is understanding their past. Life story work (Gibson, 1994) is an important intervention and can help to maintain people's sense of self-esteem and identity by focusing on the things that the person did, what they were good at and what they enjoyed (Kerr, 2007). It is the process of talking to people about their memories and collecting objects and pictures, which are the important aspects, rather than the end product. Developing life stories is a useful way of involving family members and friends in remembering and producing memories, anecdotes, photos and possessions for the life story. Using the person's life story regularly helps to reduce anxiety and give the person and staff a sense of the person and who they are rather than focusing on the dementia. For the person with intellectual disabilities, a life story book would remind any new carers there is a person, although they now have dementia, who enjoyed certain things in life.

4. Reminiscence, reality orientation and validation techniques

Staff and carers need to remember that people compensate for their deterioration in functioning by making greater use of remaining abilities (eg. earlier memories). This may mean that the person finds comfort in activities and objects from their childhood. Reminiscence work can help the person with intellectual disabilities and dementia to find anchors with their past and to help steady and engage the person (Kerr, 2007). In early stage dementia, reality orientation is important. The use of cues, gentle reminders, photos and pictures can help the person to engage with the world around them, but this must be achieved in a meaningful and stress-free manner (Kerr, 2007). This should include the use of pictorial timetables, photographs/pictures on bedroom doors, and arranging clothes in the correct order for dressing. Reality orientation should help people to retain control where possible and to make sense of their current world. However, as the dementia progresses the person will not remember more recent events, but will remember things that have happened further back in their past as their memory 'rolls back' to an earlier time. This frequently results in the person asking for people who are no longer alive or part of their lives. This is a very difficult situation to get right. However, clinical experience shows that constantly correcting, challenging or reminding the person of the truth can be very damaging and traumatising for them. For most situations it is important to recognise where the person is in their 'roll back' memory and engage with the person that they were at that time. For example, a person with dementia may ask 'when is David working?' David may have been a favourite member of staff from many years previously. If you say that David has left, it is likely to cause the person great distress, whereas either initiating a conversation about how nice David is, or saying he'll be back later, may be enough to reassure them.

5. Other therapeutic approaches

A range of other therapeutic approaches can be effective with people with intellectual disabilities and dementia. Giving people meaningful but failure-free activities can reduce stress and encourage a sense of well-being, accomplishment and improve their mood. Failure-free activities need to be appropriate to the individual and their stage of dementia, but could include looking at magazines, carers sitting with the person and describing what is happening outside, polishing a favourite object or having a foot spa. Other techniques that have been used include music therapy, aromatherapy, sensory stimulation (including Snoezelen) and touch.

6. Working with behaviours

By implementing the philosophy of care and intervention outlined in earlier sections, many of the difficulties that can occur in dementia can be prevented or minimised (Dodd, 2010). However, there will often be times when people present with behaviours that staff or carers find difficult to understand and respond to. Behaviours in people with intellectual disabilities and dementia may be:

▶ transitory to the current stage of the person's dementia and not need an intervention

▶ caused by the person believing that they are in the past; the situation should be viewed through the eyes of the person with dementia; continual challenge by staff/carers of a false reality (eg. person with dementia asking when a dead parent will visit) will not reduce their immediate confusion and distress

▶ due to the person trying to communicate or to make sense of a bewildering environment (eg. GP practice waiting room is confused with an airport lounge)

▶ an exacerbation or return of previous behaviours; if the person had difficult behaviours/personality traits previously, these may return/reoccur with roll-back memory

▶ caused by a return to a long-term memory that is now inappropriate eg. childhood urinating outdoors in the countryside while on long walks

▶ an underlying neurological change eg. taste bud changes leading to food fads and a liking for stronger flavours, refusing baths resulting from problems with depth perception and/or stepping into the bath.

In most cases, simple and practical solutions may work eg. a net to catch items thrown out of the window, as will simple environmental alterations such as covering a mirror. There are good descriptions of many of the most common problem behaviours seen in dementia in Dodd *et al's* (2009) *Down's Syndrome and Dementia Resource Pack*.

Care management of people with dementia

Good care management is central to the care of people with intellectual disabilities and dementia. Care managers need to have knowledge of the main issues in relation to dementia to ensure that services are co-ordinated without unnecessary delays or duplication. Cases should not be closed once a diagnosis of dementia has been confirmed. Good care management will ensure improved planning and liaison between specialist intellectual disability services, primary health care services, social services, secondary health care services and the private and voluntary sector in order to meet the needs of the person.

The person's needs have to be reviewed regularly. Risks also need regular re-assessment and monitoring (eg. tri-monthly). Care managers need to plan ahead by anticipating the person's needs at the next stage of the dementia and identifying possible solutions.

The person with dementia should be cared for within their familiar environment if both the environment and the care offered can meet their changing needs. In many instances, this can be achieved through a combination of environmental adaptations and an increase in the level of support provided to staff or family carers. In some situations a move is needed, particularly if the environment is unsuitable and cannot be adapted; the level of care is not available; or family carers can no longer cope. This decision is particularly difficult to make if the person with dementia is living with an elderly carer and they have been (or are) mutually dependant on each other. There is increasing evidence that placing people with intellectual disabilities and dementia in nursing homes is detrimental to their health and well-being. If a move is needed it is important to try to find a new home where the person can live for the rest of their life without further upheaval.

Conclusion

Support staff perform a vital role in providing care to older people with intellectual disabilities who have mental health problems. Flexibility in approach and knowledge of the issues will assist staff in being able to continue to care for people within their existing environments as they age. Familiarity and continuity are key to positive psychological well-being in older age.

Summary

▶ Getting older is rarely discussed in intellectual disability services either with the person or with staff and services.

▶ Dementia is becoming more prevalent in older people with intellectual disabilities as their life expectancy increases.

▶ Depression and other mental health needs can be experienced by older people with intellectual disabilities.

▶ Psychological and pharmacological interventions can be used effectively with older people with intellectual disabilities.

References

Bigby C, Fyffe C, Balandin S, Gordon M & McCubbery J (2001) *Day Support Services Options for Older Adults with a Disability.* Melbourne: National Disability Administrators Group.

British Psychological Society (2009) *Learning Disabilities and Dementia: Guidance on the assessment, diagnosis, treatment and support of people with learning disabilities who develop dementia.* Leicester: British Psychological Society.

Cooper S-A (1997) Epidemiology of psychiatric disorders in elderly compared with younger adults with learning disabilities. *British Journal of Psychiatry* **170** 375–380.

Department of Health (2001) *Valuing People: A new strategy for learning disability for the 21st century.* London: The Stationery Office.

Dodd K (2008) Transition to old age – what can we do to aid the process? *Advances in Mental Health and Learning Disabilities* **2** 7–12.

Dodd K (2010) Psychological and other non-pharmacological interventions in services for people with intellectual disabilities and dementia. *Advances in Mental Health and Intellectual Disabilities* **4** 28–36.

Dodd K, Kerr D & Fern S (2006) *Down's Syndrome and Dementia Workbook for Staff.* Teddington: Down's Syndrome Association.

Dodd K, Turk V & Christmas M (2009) *Down's Syndrome and Dementia Resource Pack.* Kidderminster: British Institute of Intellectual disabilities.

Duff M, Hoghton M, Scheepers M, Cooper M & Baddeley P (2001) Helicobacter pylori: has the killer escaped from the institution? A possible cause of increased stomach cancer in a population with intellectual disability. *Journal of Intellectual Disability Research* **45** 219–225.

Gibson F (1994) *Reminiscence and Recall: A guide to good practice.* London: Age Concern.

Holland AJ (2000) Ageing and intellectual disability. *British Journal of Psychiatry* **176** 26–31.

Kerr D (2007) *Understanding Learning Disability and Dementia: Developing effective interventions.* London: Jessica Kingsley Publishers.

Mahendiran S & Dodd K (2009) Dementia-friendly care homes. *Learning Disability Practice* **12** 14–17.

O'Rourke A, Grey I, Fuller R & McLean B (2004) Satisfaction with living arrangements of older adults with intellectual disability: service users' and carers' views. *Journal of Intellectual Disabilities* **8** (1) 12–29.

Prasher VP (1995) Prevalence of psychiatric disorders in adults with Down syndrome. *European Journal of Psychiatry* **9** 77–82.

Prasher VP, Adams C, Holder R & the Down Syndrome Research Group (2003) Long-term safety and efficacy of donepezil in the treatment of dementia in Alzheimer's disease in adults with Down syndrome: open label study. *International Journal of Geriatric Psychiatry* **18** 549–551.

Prasher VP, Huxley A & Haque MS (2002) A 24-week double blind, placebo-controlled trial of donepezil in patients with Down syndrome and Alzheimer's disease – pilot study. *International Journal of Geriatric Psychiatry* **17** 270–278.

Strydom A, Hassiotis A & Livingston G (2005) Mental health and social care needs of older people with intellectual disabilities. *Journal of Applied Research in Intellectual Disabilities* **18** 229–235.

Thomspon D & Wright S (2001) *Misplaced and Forgotten: People with learning disabilities in residential services for older people.* London: Foundation for People with Learning Disabilities.

Van Puyenbroeck J & Maes B (2005) Reminiscence in ageing people with learning disabilities: an exploratory study. *The British Journal of Learning Disabilities* **51** (1) 3–16.

Chapter 18

Mental disorder and offending behaviour

Eddie Chaplin and Jayne Henry

Introduction

Historically, people with intellectual disabilities have been considered to have an increased likelihood of committing offences. Although there is a robust link between intelligence and crime, it remains unclear whether this applies directly to people with intellectual disabilities. This chapter explores the evidence regarding intellectual disabilities, mental disorder and offending, and briefly reports on the treatments currently available.

The closure of institutions and the advent of community care led many to anticipate a rise in offences committed by those who were previously hidden in institutions. The evidence for whether, and to what extent, this may have occurred is unclear. In the UK, Day (1993) reported small increases in offending rates in people with intellectual disabilities compared to the general population. In contrast, a study carried out in Sweden, a country without a history of institutionalising this population, found that those with 'special needs' were up to three-to-four times more likely to have committed a crime than those without 'special needs' (Hodgins, 1996).

Despite conflicting opinions presented by research regarding the exact relationship between intellectual disabilities and offending, there has been a growth in secure services – both within the NHS and the independent sector – to meet the needs of mentally disordered offenders with and without intellectual disabilities. In addition to this, the *No One Knows* report (Talbot, 2007) reported prevalence rates in prisons of around 7% for those with an IQ below 70 and 25% for those with an IQ below 80. Prior to *No One Knows*, it was considered that the population was around 2%. For young offenders under 18, 23% had an IQ below 70.

Issues within the Criminal Justice System

Although criminal behaviour carried out by an individual with intellectual disabilities should be dealt with by the Criminal Justice System (CJS), just as with anyone accused of committing a criminal offence, there are a number of issues relating to this process which have to be addressed in order to protect the rights of the offender. These include issues of capacity, cognitive functioning and fitness to plead, and require medico-legal assessment. In addition, there are a number of safeguards to support adults with intellectual disabilities, such as the use of an appropriate adult during police interviews and the availability of witness schemes. Finally, where appropriate and based on psychiatric assessment, a range of disposal options are available to divert individuals towards a health setting.

Despite these developments within the CJS there remains an inconsistent approach to the reporting of crimes by adults with intellectual disabilities (Lyall *et al*, 1995). This is reported to be due to a range of factors, including the mixed attitudes of carers, professionals and services to people with intellectual disabilities. For example, some may feel it is wrong to report criminal behaviour due to a fear of consequences for carers, services or the individual. Misplaced perceptions such as 'this is what people with intellectual disabilities do' or where the victim has intellectual disabilities express beliefs such as 'it did not really affect them like it would others' also exist. There is also the perception that the police may be reluctant to become involved in these cases.

Once an individual with intellectual disabilities enters the CJS, professionals within the system may feel unprepared to carry out an investigation involving adults with intellectual disabilities, leading to cases being closed after only limited investigation, or cautions administered without the individual being aware of the consequences of what they have agreed to ie. a caution being an admission of guilt to the charges. Finally, it is not uncommon for proceedings to be dropped if the witness has intellectual disabilities and the person is felt to be unreliable as a witness. In those cases where the police decide an offence has taken place, it is referred to the CPS to decide whether to proceed based on two criteria:

1. there is likelihood of a conviction

2. it is in the public interest.

By dropping cases without good cause, the CPS is prevented from completing an independent assessment as to whether to proceed. Furthermore, this might result in individuals not gaining access to specialist treatment, risk assessment and support.

The relationship between intellectual disabilities, mental illness and offending

We know that people with intellectual disabilities are more likely to experience mental health problems. Although there is no agreement on exact rates, it is estimated that between 20–74% of adults with intellectual disabilities have a co-morbid mental illness (Cooper *et al*, 2007).

It has long been believed that people with mental disorder are at increased risk of offending (Hodgins *et al*, 1996; Robertson *et al*, 2009); here we explore mental disorders explained earlier in the book along with other common co-morbid issues and their associations with offending. The most common way of exploring the relationship between intellectual disabilities, mental illness and offending is to ask if there are greater rates of mental illness in offenders with intellectual disabilities.

The literature which examines the relationship between mental illness and offending has examined specific disorders as well as exploring the presence and impact of certain symptoms. Below is a list of those covered in this chapter.

▶ Mental disorder

  ▶ Psychotic disorders

  ▶ Depressive disorders

  ▶ Personality disorders

▶ Autism

▶ Attention deficit hyperactivity disorder (ADHD)

▶ Brain damage during childhood

▶ Substance abuse

Psychotic disorders

There have been reports of an association between positive psychotic symptoms, such as hallucinations and delusions, and offending behaviour, albeit in offenders without intellectual disabilities. The most common example of this is the role of delusional beliefs with an individual acting upon a false belief eg. believing that someone is trying to kill them and to prevent this they take action against the person. Whereas it may be true in a small number of cases, the vast majority of people with delusional ideas do not act on them (Robertson *et al,* 2009). Similarly, it is commonly believed that command auditory hallucinations (ie. those that contain instructions to behave in a particular way) are an indicator of risk, though consistent evidence for a simple relationship is lacking. Zisook *et al* (1995) found that people with command hallucinations were no more violent than matched controls. One of the few studies involving offenders with intellectual disabilities specifically, (Smith *et al,* 2008) reported that offenders with intellectual disabilities who had a diagnosis of schizophrenia were more likely than offenders with intellectual disabilities and mood disorders to commit a violent offence. Once treated, those with a diagnosis of schizophrenia had a lower re-offending rate compared to those without.

Mood disorders

Depression
Depression is often associated with irritability in both those with and without intellectual disabilities. This may lead to aggressive behaviour, although there is no evidence that depressive disorder leads to an increased risk of violent offending in people with intellectual disabilities.

Bipolar disorder
People with mania may behave in a grandiose, irritable or disinhibited way, and this may lead to public order offences and violent offending. It has been reported that people with intellectual disabilities and hypomania who committed assault were less likely to re-offend than offenders with intellectual disabilities and no co-morbid mental illness (Smith *et al,* 2008). One interpretation is that the illness confers risk for the offence, and that treatment of the illness decreases risk of offending. While violent offences obviously occur in the context of mania/hypomania, more commonly people fail to pay their bills, spend money they do not have, thus committing fraud, and incur considerable debt.

People with intellectual disabilities are reported to suffer from increased rates of more minor degrees of mood abnormality (especially increased depressive symptoms), although there is no established relationship between persistent mood disorders and offending behaviour in people with intellectual disabilities.

Personality disorder

The issue of personality disorder and intellectual disabilities is one that has been of increasing interest for clinicians. However, there are still lingering disagreements as to whether this is a valid diagnosis. Alexander and Cooray (2003) found a huge variation in the prevalence of personality disorders in an intellectual disabilities population ranging from 1– 91% in the community and 22–92% in hospital settings. Recent studies suggest that there are significant numbers of offenders with intellectual disabilities with a diagnosis of personality disorder in high secure settings (56%) but no significant difference between medium/low secure (26.2%) and community (33.3%) settings (Lindsay *et al,* 2006) with dissocial personality disorder being the most common. Alexander *et al* (2006) found that within a 12-year follow-up period, people with personality disorder were nine times more likely to re-offend. This has significant implications for assessment and treatment in order to meet the needs of this complex group.

Autism

People with Asperger's syndrome are overrepresented within forensic settings. Although the reason for this remains unclear, there are some key features of autism which are likely to be particularly relevant, such as a lack of empathy, specific rituals and routines, circumscribed interests, difficulty in communication, and misinterpretation of social cues. The absence of these factors and behaviours act has a control against offending or anti-social behaviour in most people.

Attention deficit hyperactivity disorder (ADHD)

Significant characteristics of ADHD are behavioural problems; poor concentration and poor impulse control, which are important risk factors for offending behaviour. Children with the disorder are more likely to develop a personality disorder and have a greater likelihood of offending. There is also a strong link between childhood ADHD and childhood conduct disorder, which can often lead to adult personality disorder and criminality (Connor *et al,* 2007).

Brain damage

This may result in behavioural and personality disturbance, which can include emotional changes, disinhibition leading to sexualised behaviours, increased irritability, poor impulse control, increased frustration and reduced tolerance.

Substance misuse

It is widely believed that people with intellectual disabilities have a lower prevalence of substance misuse and given that this is an under-researched area, many believe that the figures available may be an underestimate. People using substances are more likely to suffer with mental illness and those with intellectual disabilities may be more at risk of adverse side effects or later problems given developmental delays. It is estimated that 90% of the cost of drugs to society is linked to offending (UKDPC, 2008). Substance misuse is often associated with personality disorder and ADHD, and as such is often found in offenders with complex needs.

Assessment and treatment

Drug treatment

There are no drugs that cure offending. For those with co-morbid mental disorder often the most appropriate drug treatments are those designed to decrease symptoms of any underlying mental disorder, which may in turn reduce the risk of further offending. For example, treating depression with antidepressants for an individual who sets fire or sexually offends often occurs within the context of low mood. However, many offenders with intellectual disabilities and mental illness present with complex needs as highlighted above and therefore it is uncommon to achieve such a straightforward and simple outcome.

There is a long-history in the field of intellectual disabilities of antipsychotic medication prescribed to address aggressive challenging behaviour and this has continued in relation to violent offending behaviour. However, a recent study found that in trialing haloperidol vs risperidone vs placebo, those given the placebo improved most, bringing into question the routine management of aggression through medication (Tyrer *et al*, 2008).

In terms of sex offenders, another approach has been to use antilibidinal drugs to reduce sex drive.

Psychological treatment

There has been a significant shift over the past 15 years within mainstream forensic services to develop the use of individual and group psychological treatment programmes to address the needs of mentally disordered offenders. This includes therapy aimed specifically at co-morbid mental illness such as depression, anxiety and psychosis, in addition to offence-specific treatment programmes for sex offenders, arsonists and violent offenders and more recently generic offender programmes. These developments now also apply to services for offenders with intellectual disabilities where, although the evidence is still small, there have been some promising results. This is a reflection of the more general changes in the field of intellectual disabilities over the past 10 years where clinicians and researchers have been able to challenge the idea that adults with intellectual disabilities are not able to benefit from individual or group psychological treatments.

There is now a growing evidence base for the use of individual cognitive behavioural therapy (CBT) for the treatment of co-morbid mental illness of adults with intellectual disabilities. However, the most robust evidence base currently relates to the use of individual CBT for anger treatment designed specifically for offenders with intellectual disabilities (Taylor, 2002). Group CBT for sex offenders with intellectual disabilities has also been an area of interest with some recent developments in a multi-site research study examining the effectiveness of this programme.

Conclusion

Although the link between crime and low intelligence is robust, there is still doubt how this applies to people with intellectual disabilities. Although there is a greater prevalence of mental illness in people with intellectual disabilities, the reported association between mental disorder and offending varies greatly between studies. Offenders with intellectual disabilities as a clinical population present with significant co-morbidity of mental health and neurodevelopmental problems, cognitive and social impairment, lower social economic status, poorer housing and issues such as substance abuse, which together highlight the difficulty in determining the link between intellectual disabilities and offending, and the role each individual factor plays in increasing the likelihood of offending.

Summary

▶ Historically, people with intellectual disabilities have been linked to crime. Although there is robust evidence linking intelligence to crime, it is unclear whether this applies directly to people with intellectual disabilities.

▶ Latest prison estimates from *No One Knows* suggest as much as seven percent of people in prison have intellectual disabilities.

▶ We know that people with intellectual disabilities are more likely to experience mental health problems. It has long been believed that people with mental disorders are at increased risk of offending. However, the figures for people with intellectual disabilities vary greatly, making it difficult to reach any valid conclusion.

▶ Any link between intellectual disabilities and crime is made harder to establish due to other co-morbidity eg. mental health, cognitive and social impairment, lower social economic status, which all increase the likelihood of offending.

References

Alexander R & Cooray S (2003) Diagnosis of personality disorders in learning disability. *British Journal of Psychiatry* **182** (44) 28–31.

Alexander RT, Crouch K, Halstead S & Pichaud J (2006) Long-term outcome from a medium secure service for people with intellectual disability. *Journal of Intellectual Disability Research* **50** (4) 305–315.

Connor DF, Ford JD, Albert DB & Doerfler LA (2007) Conduct disorder subtype and comorbidity. *Annals of Clinical Psychiatry* **19** 161–168.

Cooper SA, Smiley E, Morrison J, Williamson A & Allan L (2007) Mental ill-health in adults with intellectual disabilities: prevalence and associated factors. *British Journal of Psychiatry* **109** 27–35.

Day D (1993) Crime and mental retardation: a review. In: K Howells & CR Holland (Eds) *Clinical Approaches to the Mentally Disordered Offender.* Chichester: John Wiley & Sons.

Hodgins S, Menick SA, Brennan PA, Schlusinger F & Engberg M (1996) Mental disorder and crime: evidence from a Danish birth cohort. *Archives General Psychiatry* **53** 489–496.

Lindsay WR, Hogue T, Taylor JL, Mooney P, Steptoe L, Johnston S & O'Brien G, Smith A (2006) Two studies of the prevalence and validity of personality disorder in three forensic intellectual disability samples. *Journal of Forensic Psychiatry and Psychology* **17** 485–506.

Lyall I, Holland AJ, Collins S & Styles P (1995) Incidence of persons with a intellectual disability detained in police custody. A needs assessment for service development. *Medicine, Science and the Law* **35** 61–71.

Robertson D, Henry J, Yacoub E & Chaplin E (2009) Mental illness, psychopathology and offending, Section 3 Psychopathology and offending. In: E Chaplin, J Henry & S Hardy (Eds) *Working with People with Learning Disabilities and Offending Behaviour.* Brighton: Pavilion.

Smith H, White T & Walker P (2008) Offending in the learning disabled population: a retrospective audit of Tayside learning disability service court reports. *Medicine, Science and the Law* **48** (1) 31–36.

Talbot J (2007) *No One Knows: Identifying and supporting prisoners with learning difficulties and learning disabilities: the views of prison staff.* London: Prison Reform Trust.

Taylor JL (2002) A review of the assessment and treatment of anger and aggression in offenders with intellectual disability. *Journal of Intellectual Disability Research* **46** (1) 57–73.

Tyrer P, Oliver-Africano PC, Ahmed Z, Bouras N, Cooray S, Deb S, Murphy D, Hare M, Meade M, Reece B, Kramo K, Bhaumik S, Harley D, Regan A, Thomas D, Rao B, North B, Eliahoo J, Karatela S, Soni A & Crawford M (2008) Risperidone, haloperidol, and placebo in the treatment of aggressive challenging behaviour in patients with intellectual disability: a randomized controlled trial. *Lancet* **371** 57–63.

UK Drug Policy Commission (2008) *Reducing Drug Use, Reducing Reoffending.* London: UKDPC.

Zisook S, Byrd D, Kuck J & Jeste DV (1995) Command hallucinations in outpatients with schizophrenia. *Journal of Clinical Psychiatry* **56** 462–465.

Chapter 19

Diversity and mental health

Saadia Arshad and Jean O'Hara

Introduction

Individuals with intellectual disabilities from black and minority ethnic communities face challenges in accessing and receiving services, and often, those they do receive are not sensitive to their ethnic and cultural needs. They face the double discrimination of having intellectual disabilities and being from a minority ethnic group (Azmi *et al*, 1997). Appreciation of diversity requires heightened awareness of our own attitudes and sensitivity to issues of stereotyping, prejudice, misunderstanding cultural practices and communication. Insensitivity or 'cultural incompetence' may seriously interfere with provision or delivery of care and may result in poorer outcomes.

The expert opinion

'Everyone's culture and religion should be respected. You shouldn't run anyone's religion down just because it's different from yours.'

Definitions

Culture and ethnicity are two different concepts, yet they are often used interchangeably or mistaken for each other. Culture is about the way people choose to live their lives; it is not static but changes over time. It encompasses all human phenomena that are not purely the result of genetics. An individual's culture will be determined and influenced by a number of factors, such as experiences, imagination and creativity. Culture may be hard to identify because it is based on many aspects of our identity. Often, the best way to find out about a person's culture is to ask them about it. Understanding an individual's culture can enable a more positive relationship to develop. Ethnicity, on the other hand, is a complex concept, which incorporates a common heritage whether real or assumed; it is based on common language, religious and cultural backgrounds, shared histories and common descent; it is an individual's psychological sense of belonging (O'Hara, 2010). The UK government is keen to 'monitor' ethnicity but this may often be reduced to a tick box exercise rather than being a true reflection of the individual's own perceived ethnic identity.

Cultural/ethnicity perspectives

In UK the size of the minority ethnic population was estimated to be 7.9% of the total population (ie. 4.6 million) in 2001 (Office of the National Statistics, 2001) rising to 21% by 2051 (Wohland *et al*, 2010). While little is known about prevalence rates of intellectual disabilities among many ethnic communities, it has been reported that the prevalence of severe intellectual disabilities in South Asian children and young adults in the UK is up to three times higher than in other ethnic groups (4.9 or 8.8/1000 compared with 1.6 or 3.2/1000). Of these families, 19% have more than one member with intellectual disabilities (Emerson & Hatton, 2004).

Reconciling different cultural needs and religious perspectives while at the same time supporting, promoting and helping to maintain the mental well-being of an individual with intellectual disabilities from a minority ethnic community can be a demanding task and may require training.

Below are some of the factors that may interfere with service delivery or the uptake of services by people with intellectual disabilities from minority ethnic communities:

▶ perceptions or beliefs regarding intellectual disability and mental ill-health (whether from the carer, individual with intellectual disabilities or service provider)

▶ communication barriers, including where English is not the first language; accessible information

▶ tendency towards self-reliance vs accepting support offered by the family and/or others

▶ individual's or carer's spritual and/or religious beliefs

▶ limited understanding/awareness of cultural needs and differences

▶ difficulties navigating or accessing health services and/or mental health services.

Intellectual disabilities and/or mental ill-health is often associated with discrimination and stigma, particularly among people from ethnic minority communities (Mir *et al,* 2001). Evidence from mental health research shows that the pathway to care is significantly different for people from black and minority ethnic (BME) communities compared to non-BME communities. People from BME communities have higher rates of compulsory admission, longer average lengths of stay and are more likely to be prescribed drugs or ECT rather than psychotherapy or counselling (O'Hara & Bouras, 2007). Among professionals, it is often wrongly assumed that people from BME communities prefer help and support from their extended families. This may result in wrongly denying them a right to choose what is on offer.

Language is an issue which may hinder access to services or the delivery of care (Bhui *et al,* 2003). This can apply to both written and verbal communication; and what is chosen to be communicated may be perceived as discriminatory (O'Hara, 2010). It is always important to try to communicate with the individual in their first language, particularly when assessing difficult emotions or thoughts (Shah, 1992). Services often rely on interpreters but fail to consider or negotiate beforehand how to use this resource most effectively. Working through an interpreter may give rise to conflicts and tensions for the individual, their families, the interpreter and staff who may feel disempowered, de-skilled or resentful (O'Hara, 2010)

Although widely discouraged, it is not uncommon for services to rely upon a family member with the most fluent language skills to act as an informal interpreter. While this may be acceptable for simple tasks such as making an appointment, it should be avoided because of the possible biases and power relationships within the family. Figure 19.1 gives an example of some initial considerations when a health service is asked to assess or treat someone from a BME community.

Figure 19.1: Initial considerations for health services

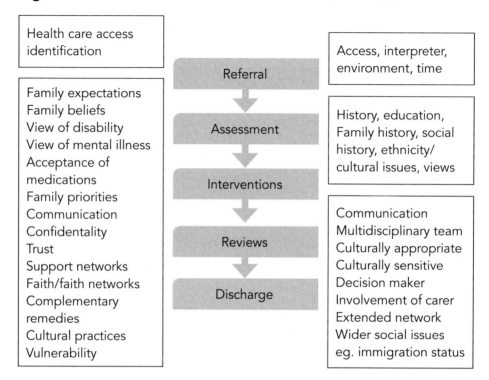

Some people from ethnic minority communities may find it hard to accept a medical explanation for intellectual disability or may incorrectly believe it to be a curable condition. This may delay referrals and access to appropriate services. At the same time, families often seek alternative help and reassurance from other sources such as complementary medicine and/or faith healers. At times, this makes them particularly vulnerable, especially to financial exploitation. It is important to be non-judgemental and to enquire about all sources of help and support during consultations/discussions (Bhugra, 2002).

It is worth clarifying that emphasis is often paid to the allocation of same-sex support staff when it comes to certain ethnic minorities or religions, when in fact it is not unusual to find the same wish across other cultures and religions (O'Hara, 2010).

Issues of sexuality

Sexuality, both in terms of practice and preference, is a taboo subject in various parts of the world, and more so in certain communities and cultures than others. Certain sexual practices are either looked down upon or not accepted in particular communities or religions. Unfortunately, this is an under-researched subject in intellectual disabilities. People with intellectual disabilities and their families (and interpreters) may find it difficult to talk about sexuality or may not want to talk about it at all. Asking about sexual preferences is a sensitive area and carers may not feel confident about raising the issue. Similarly, if service users or families feel uneasy and find it hard to relate to carers, they might not want to raise the issue at all. Hall and Yacoub (2008) reported that the expression of sexual preferences is often limited in people with intellectual disabilities, possibly because of the supervised environment, lack of knowledge or awareness of societal norms, or concerns and fears of consequences of disclosure (Raghavan & Waseem, 2007). However, undisclosed conflicts around sexuality may predispose an individual to emotional difficulty, anger, frustration and therefore mental ill-health. There may be similar conflicts and tensions around marriage and arranged marriages in certain minority ethnic communities (O'Hara, 2010).

Faith and spirituality

Faith and religious beliefs may offer vital support to families, enabling a positive attitude and supporting them to deal with negative aspects and uncertainties for the future (RCPsych, 2011). It is crucially important for professionals to have knowledge about religious beliefs, cultural practices and spiritual needs when working with people from ethnic minority communities. Failure to acknowledge these influences may seriously interfere with rapport building and therefore the uptake of services. For example, Raghavan and Waseem (2007) reported a reluctance to make use of overnight respite care and the uptake of day services was low as parents felt these services were not appropriate to their cultural or religious needs (McCarthy *et al,* 2008). (See Box 19.1 for a brief case example).

Box 19.1: Case example – issues and considerations for service response

Omar is a 26-year-old man of British Pakistani origin and Muslim faith.

▶ What immediate issues spring to mind?

▶ How might you try to make your service more accessible to Omar and his family?

Omar suffers from moderate intellectual disabilities, autism and depression.

▶ How might you approach identifying his particular needs?

▶ What communication issues might there be?

▶ How would you arrange to see him?

Omar recently moved to an out of area supported house where most of the staff members were female. At the new house Omar began withdrawing and isolating himself. He started spending most of the time in his room, refusing help with personal care and preferring foods like biscuits or bread instead of cooked meals. An interpreter was called and Omar was assessed because it was suspected that his depression was worsening. Omar said that he felt lonely and unhappy.

▶ Consider what cultural/ethnicity issues might be contributing to how he is feeling.

▶ How might you negotiate to work with the interpreter?

Omar said that he wished someone had introduced him to the local mosque and had taken him shopping for halal food.

▶ What might you be able to do to facilitate this?

A meeting was arranged for Omar with his home staff members, the health team and his family. During the meeting, Omar and his family were encouraged to inform his staff team about his cultural, religious and spiritual needs through an interpreter.

▶ What particular information might help you to help Omar?

Following the discussions, arrangements were made for Omar to be escorted to the local mosque until he familiarised himself with the directions. He was also invited to participate in shopping and cooking to assure his dietary requirements were met. With the introduction of these changes, Omar's motivation gradually improved and so did his interaction with staff and other residents.

▶ What lessons can be learnt from Omar's case?

Spirituality is considered an essential and integral part of who we are as individuals. Aldridge and Ferguson (2007) described the spiritual self as 'the core of the individual and encompasses how they see themselves, what they think about themselves and how they feel about themselves'.

It has recently been acknowledged that spiritual well-being is an integral part of overall mental health. Spirituality and religious beliefs are not uncommonly mistaken for each other and are sadly often overlooked. A caring and thoughtful relationship is vital to explore one's spiritual needs. Many resources are now becoming available to the general population to help acknowledge, identify and meet these needs. Adopting a similar approach in intellectual disability services would be a positive step.

Conclusion

Diversity and cultural sensitivity should be seen as integral to service development and delivery. Diversity helps us value differences and learn more about and respect the perspectives of others. This is at the heart of any person-centred approach, and without it, supportive, co-operative, effective and efficient working relationships are not possible.

Summary

▶ Beliefs and attitudes about intellectual disabilities and/or mental illness as a concept may differ between or even within cultures.

▶ Medical explanation for physical and/or mental ill-health is not always or most widely accepted in various diverse groups.

▶ Don't make assumptions about someone's needs based on myths, stereotypes or generalisations.

▶ It is important to reflect on your own practice and work towards a culturally sensitive workforce eg. specific and sensitive practical knowledge about certain issues like illness, health, death, pregnancy, etc. should be made readily available.

References

Aldridge J & Ferguson D (2007) The ecology of mental health framework. In: M Jukes & J Aldridge (Eds) *Person-Centred Practices: A holistic and integral approach.* London: Quay Books.

Azmi S, Hatton C, Emerson E & Caine A (1997) Listening to adolescents and adults with intellectual disability in South Asian communities. *Journal of Applied Research in Intellectual Disability* **10** 250–263.

Bhugra D (2002) Assessing psychiatric problems in ethnic minority patients. *Practitioner* **246** 147–163.

Bhui K, Stanfeld S, Hull S, Priebie S, Mole F & Feder G (2003) Ethnic variations in pathways to and use of specialist mental health services in the UK: systematic review. *The British Journal of Psychiatry* **182** 105–116.

Emerson E & Hatton C (2004) The prevalence of intellectual disability among South Asian communities in the UK. *Journal of Intellectual Disability Research* **48** 201–202.

Hall I & Yacoub E (2008) Sex, relationships and the law for people with intellectual disability. *Advances in Mental Health and Learning Disabilities* **2** 19–24.

McCarthy J, Mir G & Wright S (2008) People with learning disabilities and mental health problems: the impact of ethnicity. *Advances in Mental Health and Learning Disabilities* **2** 31–36.

Mir G, Nocon A & Ahmad W (2001) *Learning Difficulties and Ethnicity.* London: Department of Health.

Office of the National Statistics (2001) Minority ethnic groups in the UK [online]. Available at: www.statistics.gov.uk/statbase/Product.asp?vlnk=9763 (accessed 22 May 2011)

O'Hara J (2010) Intellectual disability and ethnicity: achieving cultural competence. In: R Bhattacharya, S Cross & D Bhugra (Eds) *Clinical Topics in Cultural Psychiatry.* London: Royal College of Psychiatrists Publications.

O'Hara J & Bouras N (2007) Intellectual disabilities across cultures. In: D Bhugra & K Bhui (Eds) *Textbook of Cultural Psychiatry*. Cambridge: Cambridge University Press.

Raghavan R & Waseem F (2007) Services for young people with learning disabilities and mental health needs from South Asian communities. *Advances in Mental Health and Learning disabilities* **1** 27–31.

Royal College of Psychiatrists (2011) *Minority Ethnic Community and Specialist Learning Disability Service: A position statement and recommendations for improving the service provisions*. London: RCPsych.

Shah R (1992) *The Silent Minority: Children with disabilities in Asian families*. London: National Children's Bureau.

Wohland P, Rees P, Norman P, Boden P & Jasinska M (2010) *Ethnic Population Projections for the UK and Local Areas, 2001–2051. Version 1.03*. Leeds: University of Leeds.

Glossary of mental health terminology

Compiled by Robert Winterhalder and Peter Woodward

Acute	Of sudden onset and often short in duration
Adaptive behaviour	Implies that an advantageous change has taken place regarding behaviour
Aetiology	The study of the causes of disease
Alzheimer's disease	A progressive irreversible dementia of unknown origin (although research has shown a strong genetic component)
Anxiety disorder	A group of disorders such as panic disorder, generalised anxiety disorder and phobias. Characterised by unpleasant physiological (increased heart rate, rapid breathing, sweating, restlessness) and psychological (feelings of apprehension, worry, dread, fear, alertness) symptoms. This may be in response to an imagined danger
Autism	A condition which usually manifests itself before the age of three, characterised by delay and deviation in the development of social relationships, verbal and non-verbal communication and imaginative activity, and a very restricted range of activities and interests

Bipolar affective disorder (manic depression)	A disorder of mood, which involves episodes of depression and mania: **depression:** the prevailing mood is one of sadness, varying from mild despondency to despair **manic:** the prevailing mood is one of elation, with high spirits, excitement and over-confidence, some individuals can become very irritable In both depression and mania, there are associated changes in thinking, behaviour, efficiency and physiological functioning. In very severe cases, the person may lose touch with reality ie. develop hallucinations or delusions
Chronic	Usually refers to disorders of long duration; for example, in chronic schizophrenia it means an episode that has been continuous for two years or more
Clouding of consciousness	A reduced awareness or misinterpretation of the surrounding environment; the individual may display poor attention and disjointed thinking
Cognitive impairment	A decline in the level of intellectual functioning – memory, concentration, communication, orientation, general intelligence and so on
Delirium	A condition of extreme mental and usually motor excitement caused by a variety of physical illnesses. Delirium is marked by impaired consciousness, confusion and memory impairment, and is often accompanied by abnormal perceptions such as hallucinations

Delusion	A false belief not amenable to persuasion or argument and out of keeping with the person's cultural and educational background
Dementia	An acquired global impairment of intelligence, memory and personality without any impairment of consciousness; most cases are progressive and irreversible
Depersonalisation	A change of self-awareness, such that the person feels unreal. It is an unpleasant experience
Depression	A mental disorder characterised by a persistent lowering of mood and accompanied by various associated symptoms such as alteration in sleep pattern, low self-esteem, diminished drive and so on
Derealisation	An unpleasant feeling that the surrounding environment has changed and become 'unreal' or artificial. The individual feels detached and apart from their surroundings
Environmental causes	Causes that are external ie. in the environment
Epidemiology	The study of the prevalence and spread of disease in a community
Flight of ideas	The person's thoughts and speech jumps from one topic to another, often related but separate, topics. This may be displayed as an almost continuous flow of speech
Genetic causes	Causes which are a result of the influence of genes. A gene contains information which codes an individual's make-up and is passed on from generation to generation

Hallucinations	This is a perception in the absence of a stimulus; for example, hearing a voice when there is no sound
	Hearing a voice: perception
	No sound: absent stimulus
	Hallucinations can occur in different forms; for example, visual, auditory, or to do with taste or smell or touch
Hyperactivity	General restless and excessive movement
Hypochondria	Over-concern and preoccupation about how the body functions with an exaggeration of the symptoms of physical illnesses. The individual may fear or believe that they are unwell even when there is no evidence to suggest that they are
Hypomania	A less severe form of mania. There is mild elevation in mood with increased energy and activity, without the hallucinations and delusions that might be seen in mania. The behaviours displayed due to hypomania are unlikely to disrupt the individual's work and social life to the extent that is seen in mania
Hypothyroid	Diminished production of thyroid hormones from the thyroid gland in the neck. This leads to an intolerance of cold, increased weight, constipation, slow pulse, a general slowing down in all physical and mental processes, and various psychiatric manifestations, such as, delirium, dementia, depression or psychosis

Illusions	A false perception to a stimuli. For example: seeing something that is there but misinterpreting it as something else. This may be more likely to happen when an individual is tired or in a room that is badly lit
Incidence	The number of new cases of a disease in a population over a period of time
Maladaptive	Often refers to types of behaviour that have been learned and which are inappropriate responses to the situation in question. Usually, someone suffers as a result
Mania	Elevated or euphoric mood with increased motor activity. An individual may appear as restless or agitated and might have grandiose ideas. Other symptoms such as increased appetite, reduced sleep, or flight of ideas are common. In severe cases the individual may display psychotic features with delusions reflecting the individual's grandiose mood
Mental health problems	See **psychiatric disorders**
Mental health	The absence of a mental or behavioural disorder; mental health is a state of psychological well-being in which the individual has been able to integrate his or her more primitive drives with the norms expected by society
Mentalisation	Ability to understand your own state of mind and that of others. It helps an individual to perceive and interpret human behaviour eg. beliefs, feelings etc.

Obsessive compulsive	Obsessions refer to words, ideas, images and the like, recognised by the person as his or her own, that intrude forcibly into the mind. Obsessions are unpleasant and often the person will try to resist them. Compulsions refer to repetitive, purposeful intentional behaviours performed in response to an obsession such as hand washing or checking
Organic	Physical or structural ie. not psychological or social
Paranoid	A morbid and distorted view of the relationships between oneself and other people. Consequently, people who are paranoid are often suspicious
Personality disorder	Disorders arising in childhood or adolescence that continue through adult life. Characterised by inflexible personalities that make it difficult for them to conform to what society considers normal due to their maladaptive behaviour. Their behaviour often brings them into conflict with others. They are insensitive to the feelings of others and have difficulty understanding that their behaviour has an impact on others. They do not learn from their experiences even if their previous experiences were unpleasant or harmful to themselves or others. They may appear irresponsible or demanding. Their own behaviour causes them distress
Phobia	An irrational abnormal fear in relation to a thing, situation or stimulus which normally would not evoke such fear. The individual realises that the fear is irrational; however, the phobia often leads to avoidance of the feared stimulus or situation

Mental Health in Intellectual Disabilities: A reader (fourth edition) © Pavilion Publishing (Brighton) Ltd 2011

Pressure of speech/ thought	The rapid appearance of varied and plentiful thoughts in an individual's mind. The individual may feel that these thoughts have been inserted into their mind by others
Prevalence	The number of existing cases of a disease in a given population at a specific time
Psychomotor	Refers to a combination of mental and behavioural events. For example: **psychomotor retardation:** this is often seen in depression where both mental processes and the body movements are slowed down **psychomotor epilepsy:** this is an old term which describes a type of epilepsy with both behavioural and mental features
Psychopathic disorder	A type of personality disorder in which there is a deeply ingrained, maladaptive pattern of behaviour, recognisable by adolescence and continuing throughout most of adult life. The individual or society suffers. Psychopathic disorder is not a result of intellectual disabilities, psychosis, neurosis or any other form of psychiatric illness. The characteristics of this disorder are: self-centredness with little or no regard for the rights of others – immediate satisfaction of desire is imperative, the individual acting violently if frustrated – and associated with lack of conscience or guilt; and inability to learn from previous experience

Psychiatric disorder	A significant behavioural or psychological pattern occurring in a person that is associated with distress, disability (an impairment in one or more areas of functioning) or with a significant risk of suffering death, pain, disability or important loss of freedom. It does not encompass an expected response to a particular event - such as the loss of a loved one – nor does it include religious, sexual or political deviant behaviours
Psychoses	A group of mental disorders characterised by an inability to recognise reality and to distinguish it from subjective experience. It is often accompanied by lack of insight (an awareness of one's own mental condition). As a result hallucinations, delusions and so on may occur
Schizophrenia	A group of psychiatric disorders characterised by disordered thought processes, hallucinations, delusions (false beliefs not amenable to persuasion or argument and out of keeping with the client's cultural and educational background), bizarre behaviour and social withdrawal. Not all of these characteristics have to be present to make the diagnosis
Social	Pertaining to society; often refers to the influence of society
Stereotypies	Repetitive primitive and self-stimulatory movements such as body-rocking and head-shaking

Mental Health in Intellectual Disabilities: A reader (fourth edition) © Pavilion Publishing (Brighton) Ltd 2011